THE PROMISE OF HERMENEUTICS

The Promise of Hermeneutics

ROGER LUNDIN

CLARENCE WALHOUT

ANTHONY C. THISELTON

WILLIAM B. EERDMANS PUBLISHING COMPANY
GRAND RAPIDS, MICHIGAN / CAMBRIDGE, U.K.

paternoster press

© 1999 Wm. B. Eerdmans Publishing Co.

Published jointly 1999 in the United States of America by
Wm. B. Eerdmans Publishing Co.
255 Jefferson Ave. S.E., Grand Rapids, Michigan 49503 /
P.O. Box 163, Cambridge CB3 9PU U.K.
and in the UK by
Paternoster Press
an imprint of Paternoster Publishing
PO Box 300, Kingstown Broadway
Carlisle, Cumbria CA3 0QS, United Kingdom

Printed in the United States of America

04 03 02 01 00 99   7 6 5 4 3 2 1

Library of Congress Cataloging-in-Publication Data

Lundin, Roger.
The promise of hermeneutics /
Roger Lundin, Anthony C. Thiselton, Clarence Walhout.
p.   cm.
Includes bibliographical references.
Eerdmans ISBN 0-8028-4635-1 (pbk.: alk. paper)
1. Hermeneutics.   2. Bible — Hermeneutics.
I. Thiselton, Anthony C.   II. Walhout, Clarence, 1934-   .   III. Title.
BD241.L857   1999
121′.686 — dc21   99-12924
                                               CIP

British Library Cataloguing in Publication Data

A catalogue record for this book is available from the British Library

Paternoster ISBN 0-85364-900-6

Contents

v

CONTENTS

Contents

Acknowledgments

We could not have written this book without the generous support of the Center for Christian Scholarship at Calvin College. The predecessor to this volume, *The Responsibility of Hermeneutics,* grew out of the year we spent as Fellows at the Center in 1982-83. This present book, which represents a complete revision and expansion of that earlier work, came about as a result of the vision and support of the current director of the Center, Ronald Wells. It was Ron who had the idea for a completely new version of the earlier book. Under his leadership, the Center provided the funding that enabled us to meet twice — once in Nottingham, England, and once in Grand Rapids, Michigan — at the start of the project. At each step of the process, Ron has provided the encouragement and financial support needed for us to complete the task.

Mary Elmer and Donna Romanowski deserve thanks for their help in coordinating our collaborative visits at the University of Nottingham and Calvin College. At Wheaton, Sung-Sup Kim did superb work in proof-reading the entire manuscript, verifying our quotations, and providing a uniform format for all citations.

Beyond our immediate debts, we owe a special thanks to the faculty and administrative leadership of Calvin College. In the past several decades, there has been a renaissance of Christian scholarship, whose fruits can be seen in works produced with the support of the Pew Evangelical Scholarship Initiative, the Erasmus Institute at the University of Notre Dame, and any number of other projects, many of which have been funded by the Lilly Foundation and the Pew Charitable Trusts. But before

ACKNOWLEDGMENTS

them all came the Center for Christian Scholarship at Calvin College. For their remarkable support of Christian scholarship at and beyond the boundaries of Calvin, we are grateful to those who had the pioneering vision for the Calvin Center.

ROGER LUNDIN
CLARENCE WALHOUT
ANTHONY C. THISELTON

Preface

When we published our first volume on the theory of interpretation, we entitled it *The Responsibility of Hermeneutics*. We did so because we emphasized that interpretation was merely one of many forms of human action. As such, it has an unmistakably ethical character. To read a text of any kind — be it a novel, a musical score, or the action of another human being — is to respond to a given reality which makes a claim upon our lives. Learning how to respond to such texts with integrity, creativity, and care is one of the most important of all human skills.

When we wrote the earlier volume, we were concerned to counter certain assumptions about interpretation both within the Christian church and in the larger culture and academic community. Within the Christian church, the quest for validity and certainty has at times obscured the nuanced complexity of the interpretive act. If there were fixed procedures available for determining the precise meaning of an ancient or modern text, then all that one needed to do, it might appear, was to apply a method to procure a meaning. Knowing that an emphasis upon procedure may lead to a neglect of the role that wisdom and responsible action play in interpreting texts, we argued that a Christian understanding of hermeneutics must embrace questions of ethics as well as those of method.

At the same time that we were responding to dynamics within the Christian church, we were also engaging trends in the larger culture. There, the emphasis was not so much on method and certainty as on their opposites, liberty and indeterminacy. If the Christian community erred so dramatically on the side of procedure that it ignored responsibility, then academic criticism frequently so emphasized the groundless freedom of reading that interpretation became an action without context or constraint. Once again, we stressed the situated, responsible nature of interpretation.

The Promise of Hermeneutics develops key themes of our earlier book but does so with an eye to the particular needs of the present situation in the Church and the academy. Where the earlier volume stressed the responsibility of human agents, this book shifts the emphasis to the promise that hermeneutics holds for us.

In speaking of promise, we are thinking, first, of what we might call the secular promise of hermeneutics. The work of continental philosophers, theologians, and speech-act theorists offers extraordinary resources for thinking constructively about the complex problems of human understanding. Such thinkers as Hans-Georg Gadamer, Paul Ricoeur, and John Searle offer compelling accounts of the act of interpretation in its many dimensions.

In more specific theological terms, this volume argues that interpretation is an activity that Christians engage in within the context of the promises of God. More important than the question of human certainty is that of divine fidelity. For the sake of human understanding and the future of the Christian church, it is more important for God to be seen as the maker and keeper of promises than it is for us to perfect the procedures we employ as we interpret texts and the world about us.

The Promise of Hermeneutics, in short, offers a sustained literary, philosophical, and theological analysis of contemporary theories of interpretation. In addition to making a critique of a number of those theories and the practices that issue from them, the book proposes models of human understanding that demonstrate the lasting promise of hermeneutics.

Interpreting Orphans: Hermeneutics in the Cartesian Tradition

ROGER LUNDIN

"Do You Play Alone?" asks the ad for the Asolo climbing boot, one of several products promoted in a recent campaign to sell the goods of the Benetton Sportsystem. "When there is nothing but you and the mountain," the ad's copy intones, "don't feel abandoned. You have something strong to believe in. Asolo — Count on it for extreme performance."

What give this ad and others in the Benetton series their highly provocative edge are the visual images that accompany the scant copy. In the Asolo ad, that means a single hiking boot depicted against a background of white on one side of the page and a picture of Christ upon the cross on the other side. As Roman centurions hoist the cross into place, they are cast in shadows, while Christ is bathed, in his agony, in sunlight.

In a press conference called to introduce the latest in a series of controversial campaigns mounted by Benetton, the company's creative director, Oliviero Toscani, marshaled the rhetoric of romantic individualism to defend his exploitation of the crucifixion of Jesus. "Creativity is not based on security," he argued. "Once you're secure, you're doing something that's already been done." According to Toscani, the problem is that modern advertising keeps producing "the same old thing" to sell products. "They spent billions and billions, and in the end there's no difference between Coke and Pepsi, Avis and Hertz, American Express and Visa. We try to go another way."

For Toscani, "going another way" means trading upon famous images of terror and suffering, including such things as pictures of refugees marooned on makeshift boats at sea, of a solitary Chinese student defying the tanks in Tiananmen Square, and of German athletes raising the Nazi salute during the 1936 Summer Olympics. He said that using the crucifixion to sell hiking boots was no more shocking than reading a daily newspaper and finding "in the same pages war, AIDS, love, hate, sport, life, death, product." After all, the goal in advertising is to tap into the values of the age to sell the goods. "Sport is very much linked with life," Toscani observed. "Survival is the name of the game."

In linking the experience of Christ upon the cross to the travails of mountain climbing, the Benetton ad trades shamelessly upon our fears of loneliness and abandonment and upon our need to "have something strong to believe in" in the face of those terrifying realities. And in depicting the anxieties of metaphysical abandonment, the Asolo advertisement confronts one of the most profound spiritual traumas of our postmodern world. At the same time, in offering a hiking boot as healing balm for that deepest of wounds, the ad exposes the spiritual poverty of our age.

Both the crucifixion ad itself and the Benetton creative director's commentary upon it reveal a web of theological and cultural influences stretching back over several centuries. The portrayal of the crucifixion and the discussion of abandonment, belief, and extreme circumstances call to mind the dread of cosmic loneliness that haunts so much of the music, art, poetry, and fiction of the modern West. Are we alone in what Pascal called "the eternal silence of these infinite spaces"? Have we been abandoned by God, as Christ was forsaken by him on the cross? Are we orphans in a world in which "survival is the *only* name of the game"?

The ad and its creator's self-justification also point, however unwittingly, to the complex history underlying contemporary debates about the theory and practice of interpretation. They do so both through their exploitation of the orphan imagery and through their implicit but sharp critique of repetition and imitation, which are irreducible elements of the Christian faith. "Once you're secure, you're doing something that's already been done. . . . The fact they censor us is a big honor," Toscani proudly proclaimed in announcing his ad campaign. "It says we're saying something new."[1]

To understand this drive to "say something new," we can follow a

---

1. "Benetton's Unrepentant Adman Vows to Keep Pushing the Envelope," *The New York Times*, 21 July 1995, D4.

trail of concern for *originality* leading from the postmodern present back through the romantic poets and philosophers to its ultimate origin in the work of René Descartes. With his stress upon "first-person certainty," Descartes in good measure began the drive toward autonomy and originality that has proved to be a distinguishing characteristic of modernity.[2] His fabled *Cogito* is, after all, a parentless, autonomous thinking agent who is dependent upon nothing outside himself for the truth he has uncovered within himself. Perhaps more than any other figure at the dawn of modernity, Descartes launched the tradition of living without tradition; he became the father of all who would seek to live in a parentless world. After Descartes, in the words of Gerald Bruns, "we are always in the post position, primed and impatient to start history over again in an endless recuperation of the Cartesian moment of self-fathering."[3] This was especially to be the case at the end of the eighteenth century and the beginning of the nineteenth century. Poets and revolutionaries happily found in the parentless state an ideal of absolute first-person liberty. To be an orphan was to be free to "start history over again," and while the postmodern order may not share the revolutionaries' faith in human perfectibility and progress, the dream of radical originality lives on in its contemporary permutations.

Throughout this book, and especially in the second section, we will be making the argument that interpretation, like artistic creation, is a form of human action and is thus subject to the same vicissitudes and open to the same possibilities as all human actions. "Because the writing and reading of texts are actions that occur in the context of social and historical life," Clarence Walhout writes at the beginning of section two, "texts and the language that composes them are never autonomous and context-free." As such, the theory and practice of interpretation have much to learn from the central place assigned to the orphan in modernity. In *After Virtue*, Alasdair MacIntyre asserts that "man is in his actions and practice, as well as in his fictions, essentially a story-telling animal." But the key question for us, he argues, is not that of "self-fathering" or "our authorship" of the stories we live. "I can only answer the question 'What am I to do?'" — or "How am I to read?" it might be added —

2. Roger Scruton, *From Descartes to Wittgenstein: A Short History of Modern Philosophy* (New York: Harper & Row, 1981), 284.

3. Gerald Bruns, *Hermeneutics Ancient and Modern* (New Haven: Yale University Press, 1992), 199.

"if I can answer the prior question 'Of what story or stories do I find myself a part?'"[4]

After all, MacIntyre explains, "only in fantasy do we live what story we please. In life, as both Aristotle and Engels noted, we are always under certain constraints." Employing the metaphor of the theater, he notes that "we enter upon a stage which we did not design and we find ourselves part of an action that was not of our making." To know how we are to act in this setting, we listen, observe, reflect, and begin to participate in the drama. We receive, in other words, imputed characters in our social world — "roles into which we have been drafted — and we have to learn what they are in order to be able to understand how others respond to us and how our responses to them are apt to be construed."[5] Or as Paul Ricoeur puts it at the close of one of the landmark books of modern hermeneutical reflection: "The illusion is not in looking for a point of departure, but in looking for it without presuppositions. There is no philosophy without presuppositions."[6]

If MacIntyre and Ricoeur are right about the nature of human understanding — and it will be the burden of this book's argument that they are — then we have good reason to question all theories of creation and interpretation that take the orphan as their ideal. If they are right, it is neither desirable nor possible to read as though we were beginning history anew with each interpretive act. We are always already indebted to the past and implicated in the tangled web of action and reaction that make up the course of human history. We cannot remove ourselves from that history. Nor can we transform any of our actions — including those of interpreting — into timeless activities that neither bear the stamp of history nor share its responsibilities and promise. Christian theology, after all, holds that while history may bear the signs of human bondage, it is also the scene

4. Alasdair MacIntyre, *After Virtue*, 2nd ed. (Notre Dame: University of Notre Dame Press, 1984), 216.

5. MacIntyre, *After Virtue*, 213, 216. MacIntyre's point is similar to the one made by Clarence Walhout in section two: "If the historicity of actions implies that all understanding is based on a relation of resemblance between the new and the familiar, then all understanding is also dynamic or progressive. Every moment introduces new perceptions and contexts in which the new and the familiar are continuously interacting.... We are constantly absorbing, evaluating, and using new experiences. And we do so by relating them, consciously or not, to the patterns of experience that we have previously developed."

6. Paul Ricoeur, *The Symbolism of Evil*, trans. Emerson Buchanan (Boston: Beacon, 1967), 348.

of God's liberating activities. As Anthony Thiselton argues at the close of the third and final section, at the heart of the Christian faith is "the biblical understanding of God as one who chooses in sovereign freedom to constrain that freedom by graciously entering into the constraints imposed upon action by undertaking covenantal promise." A contemporary hermeneutical theory informed by the Christian faith will be more concerned, that is, with questions of trustworthy fidelity than with those of absolute certainty.

In the end, this means that it would be neither necessary nor wise to accept Descartes's desire for "self-fathering" as the necessary precondition for human understanding; instead, *The Promise of Hermeneutics* questions both the Cartesian move to the first person and the modern traditions which take that move as their starting point. To trace the line of influence running from Descartes to his nineteenth-century descendants is to see the delight of autonomy gradually turn into the terror of abandonment. It was in the Romantic era that the confidence in the Cartesian project was first shaken. In the literature of the nineteenth century, we first begin to hear of the orphaned state as a terrifying sign of our cosmic loneliness. Over the course of that century, faith in autonomy gave way to anxiety over the fate of the orphaned individual.

One of the many consequences of the crisis of confidence in the modern self proved a hermeneutical division that has marked interpretive theory since the romantic era. It has surfaced in different forms as an argument between those who believe with Friedrich Schleiermacher that interpretation must recover an author's world or intention, and those who agree with G. W. F. Hegel that the creative spirit must appropriate the dead letter of text or tradition. This division runs through most contemporary hermeneutical debates and helps to explain the evident gap between contemporary evangelical Protestant hermeneutics and postmodern interpretation theory.

The poetry and fiction of the past two centuries have brilliantly taken the measure of orphaning's hermeneutical implications. Long before the slaughter of the First World War and the unspeakable horrors of the Holocaust, the orphans of modern fiction opened up the darkness at the heart of modernity. Through these characters, modern men and women began to sense the starker consequences of Cartesian isolation for the modern self. The world Descartes had envisioned is a parentless one in which autonomous subjects, freed from oppressive tradition and feckless opinion, bring a bold new order into being; but the world inhabited by modern fictional or-

5

phans is much darker than the kingdom illuminated by Cartesian rationalism. In an orphaned world, abandoned children ask the question posed by Herman Melville in *Moby-Dick,* "Where is the foundling's father hidden?" The orphans scan the horizon for any sign of their absent parents and pose dramatic questions about the nature of interpretation. Who authored the text of this world, the orphans ask, and what does it mean? In their struggles to comprehend their own condition, modern fictional orphans bring us to the heart of the hermeneutical tensions of the present day.

Descartes: The Endless Recuperation

We begin with Descartes and with the Lutheran Reformation. Exactly one hundred years separate a founding moment of the Reformation — Luther's dispute with Johannes Eck at Leipzig in 1519 — and Descartes's fireside discovery of certainty in the winter of 1619-20. Over the course of the century separating Luther and Descartes, both contemporary hermeneutics and the literary orphans of the modern world have their origins.

It was at Leipzig that the divisive potential of Luther's critique of the Catholic Church began to become most fully evident. A reluctant reformer at first, Luther had been drawn into the debate with Eck as a result of the latter's vituperative attacks upon him. In the aftermath of their exchange, Luther published an open letter to Pope Leo X, in which he assured the pope that he "never intended to attack the Roman Curia or to raise any controversy concerning it." He claimed to have turned to "the quiet and peaceful study of the Holy Scriptures," when "Satan . . . filled his servant Johann Eck . . . with an insatiable lust for glory and thus aroused him to drag me unawares to a debate. . . ."[7] However reluctant he may have been to enter this contest with Eck, once he was embroiled in it, Luther withheld nothing. He questioned the authority of the papacy, ridiculed the infallibility of church councils, and switched from the constraints of Latin to the freedom of the German tongue in debating Eck.[8] As he hammered

---

7. Martin Luther, "The Freedom of a Christian," in *Martin Luther: Selections from His Writings,* ed. John Dillenberger (New York: Anchor, 1951), 47.

8. Heiko Oberman notes that "Luther's diatribes resemble public exorcisms and are futile as attempts to persuade persons of different opinions of the rightness of his position. Thus it is probably no coincidence, and only seemingly a consequence of rhetoric, that Luther rarely used the commonly employed scholarly qualification 'if I am not mistaken' — *ni fallor* — but made generous use of his favorite expression, 'certainly' —

away at Eck, Luther allowed only the Bible to be used as an authority in their dispute, "refusing even to consider arguments from other sources."[9] Through his arguments in this and later confrontations, Luther unleashed forces that neither he nor anyone else would be able to control. He challenged established authority with his own will, just as some who followed his lead would be quick to pit their authority against Luther's. As disputes and centers of authority proliferated, Luther had to face in his own lifetime the reality that his reforming impulse had taken on a life of its own and led to consequences he had not intended. "As competing authorities multiplied and began to diverge more and more sharply," writes Jeffrey Stout, "conventional means for resolving disputes arising from such competition became less and less effective. . . . This problem, which we may name 'the problem of many authorities,' is the central social and intellectual difficulty of the Reformation."[10]

The century after Luther proved to be a divisive one. National and sectarian differences ran deep in the wake of reform, and dramatic upheavals in philosophy and cosmology went hand in hand with the tumultuous political changes. "Above all, it [the Reformation] dealt a fatal blow to the ideal of a united Christendom," writes a recent historian. "The scandal was so great, and the fragmentation so widespread, that people stopped talking about Christendom, and began to talk instead about 'Europe.'"[11] By the time that Descartes was born in 1596, both *scientia* — the medieval view of certain and demonstrable knowledge — and *opinio* — those disputed beliefs that required the testimony of authority to support them — were under assault.

Scientia had been subjected to the sharp critique of nominalism, which questioned the fundamental principles of medieval theology and philosophy. In rejecting the category of universals, William of Ockham and those who followed him posited a world in which God was all-powerful and

---

immo. Luther's certainty left its mark on German academic linguistic usage. Where Anglo-American scholars qualify their statements with an 'I am inclined to believe,' the Germans say 'it is patently obvious.'" *Luther: Man Between God and the Devil*, trans. Eileen Walliser-Schwarzbart (New Haven: Yale University Press, 1989), 299.

9. Steven Ozment, *The Age of Reform, 1250-1550: An Intellectual and Religious History of Late Medieval and Reformation Europe* (New Haven: Yale University Press, 1980), 327.

10. Jeffrey Stout, *The Flight from Authority: Religion, Morality, and the Quest for Autonomy* (Notre Dame: University of Notre Dame Press, 1981), 41.

11. Norman Davies, *Europe: A History* (Oxford: Oxford University Press, 1996; reprint, New York: HarperCollins, 1998), 494, 496.

arbitrary, while the created order was filled with separate entities called into being by the will of God in a dramatically contingent manner. The nominalist turn in philosophy shaped the Reformers' view of God in myriad ways and was in turn itself shaped, to some degree, by the Reformation's doctrine of Christ. Because of the nuanced complexity of the doctrine of the Trinity, the precursors of the Reformation, as well as the central Reformation theologians themselves, were able to temper the arbitrariness of God the Father with the suffering and sacrifices of God the Son. But while they sought to humanize the nominalist God, they had no desire to salvage the Aristotelian model of science as the study of formal and final causes, which had also come under nominalist attack. "The whole of Aristotle is to theology as shadow is to light," Luther complained in 1517.[12]

By demystifying the world, nominalism opened the way for the modern scientific study of nature and human experience. In rejecting formal and final causes, it left only material and efficient causality as plausible modes of explaining movement and development. According to Michael Allen Gillespie, Ockham and his descendants established the "foundation for a science that is based on experience and hypothesis, which examines the contingent relationships among extended entities to determine the efficient causes that govern their motion, and which attempts to provide a quantitative rather than a qualitative explanation of phenomena."[13] A world of predictable, efficient causes is one that can be readily manipulated for human purposes.

Yet even as it posited a means of studying nature as a predictable mechanism, nominalism also promoted, through its doctrine of God's absolute freedom, the terrifying possibility of divine deception and random intervention. How could men and women study nature with confidence and predict its movements, if they had to consider that God either could be deceiving them entirely about what they saw or could act without warning to alter the state of all they knew? If *scientia* was to proceed, it needed protection of some sort against what Emily Dickinson would call, several centuries later, Heaven's "marauding Hand."[14]

12. As cited in Oberman, *Luther,* 160.

13. Michael Allen Gillespie, *Nihilism Before Nietzsche* (Chicago: University of Chicago Press, 1995), 21.

14. See Ian Hacking, *The Emergence of Probability* (Cambridge: Cambridge University Press, 1975), 18-30, and Stephen Toulmin, "Descartes in His Time," in *Discourse on the Method and Meditations on First Philosophy,* ed. David Weissman (New Haven: Yale University Press, 1996), 121-46.

Descartes wrote of his consternation with this state of affairs, and of his desire to shelter human life from the "marauding Hand," in the *Discourse on Method* (1637). He blamed the state of confusion present in his day on the residual power of antiquated bodies of knowledge and outdated methods of learning. In justifying his own embrace of mathematics and deductive reasoning, Descartes attacked the humanistic training he had received as a young man. "I have been nourished on letters since my childhood," he wrote, "and since I was given to believe that by their means a clear and certain knowledge could be obtained of all that is useful in life, I had an extreme desire to acquire instruction." But instead of gaining useful knowledge, Descartes had found himself "embarrassed with so many doubts and errors that it seemed to me that the effort to instruct myself had no effect other than the increasing discovery of my own ignorance."[15] There was precious little *science* in the literature, philosophy, and theology Descartes had read, and all too many *opinions* swirling about his early seventeenth-century world.

In the *Discourse on Method*, Descartes claimed to have coursed his way through the whole of the liberal arts curriculum and to have found nothing of real worth on the journey. Even though they provide pleasing enough stimulation for the mind, ancient languages and literatures have the power to make the student a "stranger in one's own country" and to seduce their readers into forming "projects beyond their power of performance"; rhetoric teaches skills that have nothing intrinsic to do with the ability to render our thoughts "clear and intelligible"; the truths of theology are "quite above our intelligence" and would require for their proper elaboration "some extraordinary assistance from above," something that Descartes clearly did not expect to receive; and even philosophy offered no useful guidance, for although "it has been cultivated for many centuries by the best minds that have ever lived," there is still nothing "to be found in it which is not subject to dispute, and in consequence which is not dubious." Having surveyed the fruitless discord of contemporary opinion, Descartes could only conclude that "one could have built nothing solid on foundations so far from firm." For that reason, "as soon as age permitted me to emerge from the control of my tutors, I entirely quitted the study of letters" (*Method*, 6, 7, 8).

For Descartes, then, the problem was one of weak foundations.

---

15. Descartes, *Discourse on the Method and Meditations on First Philosophy*, ed. David Weissman, trans. Elizabeth S. Haldane and G. R. T. Ross (New Haven: Yale University Press, 1996), 5. All further references are to this edition and will be cited in parentheses within the body of the essay.

Wherever he looked, he could not find a firm footing of certainty upon which to build the scientific enterprise. He was confident that such a foundation could be unearthed somewhere, but it was buried beneath the rubble of received opinion. So, he formed the "resolution of also making myself an object of study and of employing all the strength of my mind in choosing the road I should follow" in searching for the spot where a solid foundation might be discovered (*Method*, 8).

Descartes's journey began with the realization that "there is very often less perfection in works composed of several portions" and executed by several hands, "than in those on which one individual alone has worked." Cities which were once villages, for example, seem poorly constructed "in comparison with those which are regularly laid out on a plain by a surveyor who is free to follow his own ideas." In the haphazard cities of Europe, he complained, large buildings jostled incongruously against smaller ones, and crooked streets meandered without plan or precision. These unkempt products of tradition made it appear that "chance rather than the will of men guided by reason . . . led to such an arrangement." In a similar fashion, the laws that had evolved haphazardly over the centuries, bridging the gulf between our "half-savage" past and our rational present, needed to be replaced. Such laws could not "succeed in establishing so good a system of government as those" which have been produced by a rational people, "who, from the time they first came together as communities, carried into effect the constitution laid down by some prudent legislator" (*Method*, 9).

Descartes's fruitless studies had disclosed to him the sorry state of what Paul Ricoeur has called "the conflict of interpretations."[16] No matter how carefully he guarded himself against the follies of the "ancients," Descartes feared that he would remain in danger of becoming "infected with their errors" as long as he placed them at the heart of his education. With their improvised theories and irrational prejudices, the "ancients" had hopelessly compromised the foundations of knowledge. Even when they came upon "something certain and evident," the ancient writers could not resist the temptation "to surround it with ambiguities" because they feared the "simplicity of their explanation" would bring ridicule or "because they grudge us an open view of the truth."[17]

16. Paul Ricoeur, *The Conflict of Interpretations: Essays in Hermeneutics,* ed. Don Ihde (Evanston, Ill.: Northwestern University Press, 1974).

17. Descartes, "Rules for the Direction of the Mind," in *The Philosophical Works of Descartes,* trans. Elizabeth S. Haldane and G. R. T. Ross, vol. 1 (n.p.: Dover, 1955), 6.

Hence, as Descartes saw it, confusion reigned in the texts of the ancient world and the practices of Reformation Europe, because of "the problem of many authorities." Yet there was hope: "Supposing now that all were wholly open and candid, and never thrust upon us doubtful opinions as true, . . . yet since scarce anything has been asserted by any one man the contrary of which has not been alleged by another, we should be eternally uncertain which of the two to believe." If we were to try to resolve a dispute between conflicting truth claims, it would not do to "total up the testimonies in favour of each" and call "true" the version with the greatest support; "for if it is a question of difficulty that is in dispute, it is more likely that the truth would have been discovered by few than by many."[18]

Having rejected the conflicting opinions of "the many authorities," Descartes turned to the only two "most certain routes to knowledge," *intuition* and *deduction*.[19] He determined to "reject as absolutely false everything as to which I could imagine the least ground of doubt, in order to see if afterwards there remained anything in my belief that was entirely certain." Left with nothing but the thought "that everything that ever entered into my mind was no more true than the illusions of my dreams," Descartes immediately afterward "noticed that whilst I thus wished to think all things false, it was absolutely essential that the 'I' who thought this should be somewhat, and remarking that this truth '*I think, therefore I am*' was so certain and so assured that all the most extravagant suppositions brought forward by the sceptics were incapable of shaking it" (*Method*, 21).

By unearthing the foundational *ego cogito, ergo sum*, Descartes believed he had provided humanity with the secure foundation needed for the construction of a grand dwelling-place for knowledge. As an implacable foe of Aristotelianism and Scholastic obscurity, Descartes was looking for nothing less than a universal method for discovering truth. He sought to replace the messiness of tradition and authority with the cleanliness of method; in the search for indubitable truth, Descartes took the inner resources of the human mind to be adequate in ways that he believed institutions and traditions could not be.[20]

18. Descartes, "Rules for the Direction of the Mind," 6.
19. See Descartes, "Rules for the Direction of the Mind," 7-8.
20. "In place of a specific plurality of *human* sciences, . . . we have one single knowledge: science, Science with a capital 'S,' Science such as the modern world was to worship it; Science in the pure state, radiating from unique and unparalleled geometric clarity, and that Science is the human mind." Jacques Maritain, *The Dream of Descartes*, trans. Mabelle L. Andison (New York: Philosophical Library, 1944), 168.

Having established the foundational certainty of his own existence, Descartes went on to prove the existence of both God and the external world on the basis of his own self-consciousness. But the price paid for such certainty was high. Assurance about the self, God, and the world became entwined with self-awareness. Only because I think and am conscious of that fact can I be sure of my own existence and of innumerable other truths about the world and my experiences. "Descartes paves the way for making the relevance of the knowing self the center of thought," theologian Helmut Thielicke has observed. "Henceforth every object of thought, understanding, perception, and indeed will and belief, is related to the conditions contained for these acts in the subject that executes them. . . . Man, then, always stands over against when he observes; he is always himself a theme."[21]

In the modern West, Descartes was to become the authority for all who would live without authority, the founder of the tradition of spurning tradition, and the father of all who would live without the aid or imposition of their parents.[22] Paul de Man calls this modern spirit one of "ruthless forgetting." For his understanding of modernity, de Man was in turn indebted to Friedrich Nietzsche, who had radicalized the Cartesian *Cogito* by emptying it of its epistemological certainty and metaphysical pretensions, leaving it a will in the shell of the self. "As he who acts is," according

21. Helmut Thielicke, *Prolegomena: The Relation of Theology to Modern Thought Forms*, vol. 1 of *The Evangelical Faith*, trans. and ed. Geoffrey W. Bromiley (Grand Rapids: William B. Eerdmans, 1974), 34-35.

22. As central as Descartes has proved to be in the formation of modernity, we should not overemphasize his role to the exclusion of other figures and forces. Walter Ong, for example, points out the "utter inadequacy of the view which regards interest in method as stemming from Bacon and Descartes. These late writers on method were great explosive forces indeed, but the reason was less the size of the bombs which they manufactured than the size of the ammunition dumps, stocked by whole centuries of scholasticism, on which the bombs were dropped." *Ramus, Method, and the Decay of Dialogue: From the Art of Discourse to the Art of Reason* (Cambridge: Harvard University Press, 1983), 230. Stephen Toulmin has also recently argued that though Descartes was enormously influential, his work was not an isolated intellectual phenomenon. "The shift within philosophy, away from practical issues to an exclusive concern with the theoretical — by which local, particular, timely, and oral issues surrendered their centrality to issues that were ubiquitous, universal, timeless, and written — was no quirk of Descartes. All the protagonists of modern philosophy promoted theory, devalued practice, and insisted equally on the need to find foundations for knowledge that were clear, distinct, and certain." *Cosmopolis: The Hidden Agenda of Modernity* (New York: Free Press, 1990), 69-70.

to Nietzsche, "always without a conscience, so is he also always without knowledge; he forgets most things so as to do one thing, he is unjust towards what lies behind him, and he recognizes the rights only of that which is now to come into being and no other rights whatever."[23] Or, as de Man explains: "Modernity exists in the form of a desire to wipe out whatever came earlier, in the hope of reaching at last a point that could be called a true present, a point of origin that marks a new departure."[24] In Descartes's practice and de Man's rhetoric, one can detect more than a hint of parricidal desire.

To borrow imagery from our earlier discussion of Luther, Descartes and others in the seventeenth century had witnessed the fragmentation of the Mother Church and the rejection of the papal Father's authority. Power flowed away from the aged parents and toward the warring children. With the "problem of too many authorities," even the Catholic Church became merely one more of the squabbling siblings of modernity. While some children longed to rebuild their parents' home, most were content to rummage in the rubble and start building anew. "The ancient monuments had begun to crumble," explains Jeffrey Stout. "Sacred spaces had become scenes of fragmentation and occasions for conflict. Better to begin again from scratch in circumstances of one's own choosing."[25]

In the face of such fragmentation, Descartes and others began the slow transformation of Western culture from the model of authority (from the Latin *auctor,* meaning "author" or "originator") to that of originality. Before Descartes, originality had meant the creative appropriation of the thought of one's immediate predecessors; after him, it involved the adoption of an unprecedented point of view. Descartes's break with the past had established a compelling pattern for the future; it legitimated the desire at the heart of modernity: the urge to become one's own origin, author, and *father.*

W. H. Auden notes that with the advent of "the Protestant Era" the specific question of fatherhood assumes a centrality it had never possessed

23. Friedrich Nietzsche, "On the Uses and Disadvantages of History for Life," in *Untimely Meditations,* trans. R. J. Hollingdale (Cambridge: Cambridge University Press, 1983), 64.

24. Paul de Man, "Literary History and Literary Modernity," in *Blindness and Insight: Essays in the Rhetoric of Contemporary Criticism,* 2d ed., rev. (Minneapolis: University of Minnesota Press, 1983), 147, 148.

25. Stout, *The Flight from Authority,* 1.

in medieval Catholicism. Protestantism sought to replace the "collective external voice of tradition" with "the internal voice of the individual conscience." It thus shifted the emphasis in faith away from the rational capacities we share with other human beings and away from the human body, which enables us to partake with others in "the same liturgical acts." In place of reason and the body, Protestantism put the human will, which is "unique and private to every individual." Because the "interiorization of the paternal conscience is a process that each person can only do for himself," the "character and behavior of the actual father" became more significant in the development of the Protestant self than it had been in the Catholic era.

Auden suggests that Protestantism implies a rejection of the Mother, not because she is an antagonist, but because she has been rendered irrelevant. With the doctrines of predestination, Luther and Calvin stressed the sovereign arbitrariness of God to such an extent that they rendered the "notion of necessity meaningless" and thereby denied "any spiritual significance to the fact that we are born from the bodies of our mothers through the necessary processes of nature." For medieval Catholics, the self was saved by virtue of its having been born and baptized into the Mother church; for the Reformers, a free and conscious choice, a clear and certain appropriation of one's predestined salvation was required. In this crisis of election, the inwardness of the spirit alone mattered, while the flesh became a spectator of the drama enacted upon the stage of the will.[26]

In the seventeenth century, the impulse behind what Gerald Bruns calls the "Cartesian moment of self-fathering" energized the cosmological and political struggles of that era, as well as the remarkable lyric poetry of the time. At the beginning of the eighteenth century, the same impulse was to play a crucial role in the "quarrel between the ancients and the moderns." In that battle, the moderns successfully promoted "the cult of originality, the notion that original, personal genius was the only value, that, beside it, (mere) imitation was virtually worthless."[27] And, finally, at the end of the eighteenth century, the drive for originality would prove central both to the political revolutions in America and France and to the cultural

26. W. H. Auden, *Forewords and Afterwords,* ed. Edward Mendelson (New York: Random House, 1973; reprint, Vintage, 1989), 83.

27. Joan DeJean, *Ancients and Moderns: Culture Wars and the Making of a Fin de Siècle* (Chicago: University of Chicago Press, 1997), 50.

revolution we call romanticism.[28] These disparate movements share a common longing for sound foundations, new beginnings, and self-originating acts.

Just as the Enlightenment rationalists and romantic intuitionists were in the school of Descartes, so too are we postmodernists the descendants of our Enlightenment and romantic forebears. We have inherited from them the equivalent of a cultural tic, that is, the habit of defining ourselves over against the history from which we have emerged and against which we contend. Nowhere is this contemporary cast of mind made more evident than in our penchant for attaching the prefix "post" to each of our efforts to name our present state. We call ourselves "post-industrial," "post-modern," "post-structuralist," "post-Marxist," "post-Gutenberg," and the like. Historian Eric Hobsbawm observes that "the smell of impending death" rises from these labels. They take recognition of the death of something past, but they do not reveal anything in particular about the future to come.[29] We know what has died but not what is about

---

28. Alexis de Tocqueville perceptively argued that American culture was thoroughly Cartesian, even though few citizens of the American nation had ever read Descartes:

> To escape from imposed systems, the yoke of habit, family maxims, class prejudices, and to a certain extent national prejudices as well; to treat tradition as valuable for information only and to accept existing facts as no more than a useful sketch to show how things could be done differently and better; to seek by themselves and in themselves for the only reason for things, looking to results without getting entangled in the means toward them and looking through forms to the basis of things — such are the principal characteristics of what I would call the American philosophical method.
>
> To carry the argument further and to select the chief among these various features, and the one which includes almost all the others within itself, I should say that in most mental operations each American relies on individual effort and judgment.
>
> So, of all countries in the world, America is the one in which the precepts of Descartes are least studied and best followed. . . .
>
> The American[s] never read Descartes'[s] works because their state of society distracts them from speculative inquiries, and they follow his precepts because this same state of society naturally leads them to adopt them.
>
> *Democracy in America*, ed. J. P. Mayer, trans. George Lawrence
> (Garden City, N.Y.: Anchor Books, 1969), 429.

29. Eric Hobsbawm, *The Age of Extremes: A History of the World, 1914-1991* (New York: Vintage, 1996), 516.

to be born. In a "post" world, that is, we know a great deal about the judgment of history but very little about its promise.

"I must Create a System, or be enslav'd by another Mans," declared William Blake two centuries ago. "I will not Reason & Compare: my business is to Create."[30] From England, Blake watched as France was torn asunder, first by the Reign of Terror and then by the Napoleonic wars. A Cartesian to the core, the English poet was always searching for signs of the dramatic rupture with the past that would secure a glorious future. During a brief peace between England and Napoleon in 1801, he read the signs of the times and anticipated nothing less than the coming of the millennial kingdom: "The Kingdoms of this World are now become the Kingdoms Of God & his Christ, & we shall reign with him for ever & ever. The reign of Literature & the Arts Commences."[31]

The optimism of Blake is but an indicator of the dramatic shifts in views of poetry and selfhood that came into play in romanticism and would have a signal influence on modern theories of interpretation. With the romantics, the mimetic view of poetry — which had held sway in one form or another for more than two thousand years in the West — gave way to an expressive theory of the arts.[32] The mimetic theory stressed imitation, which implies the priority and primacy of the thing imitated. In the many different forms it assumed from the time of Aristotle to the eighteenth century, the mimetic theory held that art was in some fundamental sense a re- presentation of a prior reality; its purpose was to hold "the mirror up to nature," in Hamlet's words. Romantic expressivism, on the other hand, promoted the expansive powers of the creative self and downplayed the need for models to be imitated or inherited; for expressivism, both the creation and the interpretation of art involve making the internal external.

In part, expressivism arose at the end of the eighteenth century as a response to the "disenchanting" of the world that had taken place over the previous two centuries. According to Max Weber, such "disenchanting" was fostered in good measure by the Protestant denigration of the sacraments and the modern scientific attack upon magic. By stressing what he

30. William Blake, *Jerusalem*, Plate 10, ll. 20-21, *The Poetry and Prose of William Blake*, ed. David Erdman (Garden City, N.Y.: Doubleday, 1970), 151.

31. Blake, as quoted in M. H. Abrams, *Natural Supernaturalism: Tradition and Revolution in Romantic Literature* (New York: Norton, 1971), 340.

32. The classic treatment of this subject remains M. H. Abrams, *The Mirror and the Lamp: Romantic Theory and the Critical Tradition* (New York: Oxford University Press, 1953).

calls "the absolute transcendality of God" and "the inner isolation of the individual," Protestantism situated the modern self in an alien environment.[33] Between the transcendent God and inward individual stood a vast array of spiritless forms in nature and society. In many respects, modernity has been keenly marked by what philosopher Charles Taylor has called the loss of the "ontic logos" — the belief, that is, that all of reality is informed by a purposive and personal order. According to Taylor, we have come increasingly to view the world not as a creation of the divine mind, but as "a domain of objects to which we can respond in varying ways." In such a world, the human agent is "no longer to be understood as an element in a larger, meaningful order. His paradigm purposes are to be discovered within." And according to the logic of romantic modernity, once those purposes have been discovered within, they must be expressed.[34]

A self that possesses and expresses a truth which it has intuited on its own has little need of resources that come to it from outside itself. This is the case whether those resources are derived from putatively authoritative sources in the present or from the traditions of the past. Both the Enlightenment and romanticism followed Descartes and "set at naught books and traditions" — Ralph Waldo Emerson's phrase — as a matter of principle.[35] They viewed those books and traditions as sources of disabling prejudice. As Hans-Georg Gadamer notes, "The fundamental prejudice of the Enlightenment is the prejudice against prejudice itself, which denies tradition its power."[36]

In the Enlightenment, the assault upon prejudice was often couched in the language of parent-child relations. In "On Enlightenment," an important document in the German debate over the Enlightenment, Andreas Riem defended the movement and attacked the forces of "prejudice" aligned against it. "The child on its mother's breast feels the impulse toward" enlightenment, he explained. That child follows its instincts, and its "restless spirit tirelessly pursues its efforts toward instruction and truth, until death gives its noble strivings an end." For parents to blunt their chil-

33. Max Weber, *The Protestant Ethic and the Spirit of Capitalism,* trans. Talcott Parsons (New York: Scribner, 1958), 221-22, 104-6.

34. Charles Taylor, *Sources of the Self: The Making of the Modern Identity* (Cambridge: Harvard University Press, 1989), 187, 193.

35. Ralph Waldo Emerson, "Self-Reliance," in *Emerson: Essays and Lectures,* ed. Joel Porte (New York: Library of America, 1983), 259.

36. Hans-Georg Gadamer, *Truth and Method,* 2nd rev. ed., trans. Joel Weinsheimer and Donald Marshall (New York: Crossroad, 1989), 270.

dren's drives toward enlightenment would be for them to condemn those children to be raised "like animals." Riem is clear about the need to be rid of prejudice so that children may grow into truth: "Yes, you say, but one must allow this impulse to develop only to a certain degree, mix in prejudice instead of truth, and block it where wisdom would be harmful. But who of you has ever demonstrated that prejudice, this shameful synonym of falsehood, is more useful than enlightenment, which is the result of truth?"[37]

The attack upon prejudice begun in the Enlightenment was radicalized in romanticism and the French Revolution, and at its height it nourished a spirit of enormous optimism and parricidal power. Indeed, at times the romantics and revolutionaries seemed eager to make themselves orphans through their own acts of murder, whether real or symbolic. In the French Revolution, the parricidal impulse took the specific form of an attack upon the ultimate father figure and representative of prejudicial authority, the king. Saint-Just articulated the logic of regicide in a speech in late 1792. Arguing against a trial for the imprisoned Louis XVI, he explained that there was no question but that the king deserved death as a tyrant, because "one cannot reign innocently." As Simon Schama explains, Saint-Just argued that because the very existence of the Republic was predicated on the destruction of tyranny, Louis had to be eliminated. "All that was needed was a summary proscription, the surgical removal of this excrescence from the body of the Nation," writes Schama. "A king had to die so a republic could live. It was as simple as that."[38]

In a less overt manner, the impulse to usurp or kill the father runs throughout the literature of high romanticism. It is particularly strong in American Romanticism, due in part to the Puritan heritage of the culture. Situated squarely within the Reformation tradition, the New England Calvinists developed the Reformers' insight that faith required strenuous appropriation rather than casual assent; one could not simply inherit one's parents' faith. Jay Fliegelman notes that the Puritans' language of conversion focused upon the fact that in Christ, "the old man was dead." The new Adam, Christ, replaced the old Adam, and "conversion effected a rhetori-

---

37. Andreas Riem, "On Enlightenment," in *What Is Enlightenment? Eighteenth-Century Answers and Twentieth-Century Questions*, ed. James Schmidt (Berkeley and Los Angeles: University of California Press, 1996), 170.

38. Simon Schama, *Citizens: A Chronicle of the French Revolution* (New York: Knopf, 1989), 651.

cal patricide."[39] To be fair, in seventeenth- and eighteenth-century Puritanism, the imagery of the Adamic struggle applied to a battle within the human heart much more than it did to a revolt against the past in its entirety. But in romanticism, that Protestant imagery came to symbolize a primal conflict between warring generations, with Christ clearly on the side of the emerging generation in the struggle. In the opening chapter of *Walden,* for instance, Henry David Thoreau kills off the parents with gusto. "It is never too late to give up our prejudices," he notes in true Cartesian fashion. "No way of thinking or doing, however ancient, can be trusted without proof. . . . Old deeds for old people, and new deeds for new." The past has nothing of worth to say to the present, which may listen for a while and then walk silently away. "You may say the wisest thing you can old man, — you who have lived seventy years, not without honor of a kind, — I hear an irresistible voice which invites me away from all that. One generation abandons the enterprises of another like stranded vessels."[40]

Being parentless, then, was not a bane but a blessing for many who lived in the era of revolution and romance. To be orphaned was to have the freedom to name, define, or generate oneself. "The man prophesied by the Romantics is a central man who is always in the process of becoming his own begetter," explains Harold Bloom. The "full Romantic quest . . . must make all things new, and then marry what it has made."[41] As long as those who worked in the Enlightenment and romantic traditions were able to sustain their faith in the powers of the self and its innocence, then that self's rationality, autonomy, and intuition seemed adequate for its spiritual and ethical needs. "I know that the hand of God is the promise of my own," declared Walt Whitman in *Song of Myself,* "And I know that the spirit of God is the brother of my own, / And that all the men ever born are also my brothers, and the women my sisters and lovers."[42] For Whitman,

39. Jay Fliegelman, *Prodigals and Pilgrims: The American Revolution against Patriarchal Authority, 1750-1800* (Cambridge: Cambridge University Press, 1982), 186.

40. Henry David Thoreau, *Walden,* in *Thoreau: A Week on the Concord and Merrimack Rivers, Walden, The Maine Woods, Cape Cod,* ed. Robert F. Sayre (New York: Library of America, 1985), 329, 331.

41. Harold Bloom, "The Internalization of Quest-Romance," in *Romanticism and Consciousness: Essays in Criticism,* ed. Harold Bloom (New York: Norton, 1970), 24.

42. Walt Whitman, *Leaves of Grass,* sec. 5, in *Whitman: Poetry and Prose,* ed. Justin Kaplan (New York: Library of America, 1982), 192.

Jesus as brother renders God the Father and Son superfluous. In *Song of Myself* Whitman makes explicit his rejection of God as Father:

> Magnifying and applying come I,
> Outbidding at the start the old cautious hucksters,
> Taking myself the exact dimensions of Jehovah,
> Lithographing Kronos, Zeus his son,
>   . . . Brahma, Buddha, . . .
> Taking them all for what they are worth and not a cent more,
> Admitting they were alive and did the work of their days,
> (They bore mites as for unfledg'd birds who have now to rise and fly
> and sing for themselves.)[43]

Here Whitman longs to become an orphan. Like an heir desperate to get his hands on the benefaction he believes to be his due, Whitman's romantic self gladly pulls the plug on the systems maintaining the feeble pulse of the "old cautious huckster."

What was arguably the most important of the romantic efforts to be rid of God the Father can be found in the poetry of William Wordsworth. In some poems, Wordsworth developed the theme with an audacity to match that of Blake and Whitman. Consider, for instance, the "Prospectus" he wrote as a young man for a long poem that he was never to finish:

> All strength — all terror, single or in bands,
> That ever was put forth in personal form;
> Jehovah — with his thunder, and the choir
> Of shouting Angels, and the empyreal thrones,
> I pass them, unalarmed. Not Chaos, not
> The darkest pit of lowest Erebus,
> Nor aught of blinder vacancy — scooped out
> By help of dreams, can breed such fear and awe
> As fall upon us often when we look
> Into our Minds, into the Mind of Man,
> My haunt, and the main region of my Song.[44]

In the main, Wordsworth pursued a less insistent line of argument in several of his most memorable lyrics, as he sought to complete the transfer

---

43. Whitman, *Leaves of Grass*, sec. 41, in *Whitman: Poetry and Prose*, 233.
44. William Wordsworth, "Prospectus," cited in Abrams, *Natural Supernaturalism*, 467.

of authority, begun by Descartes, from parent to child. Where Descartes had shifted authority away from institutions and received opinion to the rational, adult self, the English romantic poet snatched this same authority from the adult and bestowed it upon the child:

> My heart leaps up when I behold
>   A Rainbow in the sky:
> So was it when my life began;
> So is it now I am a Man;
> So be it when I shall grow old,
>   Or let me die!
> The Child is Father of the Man;
> And I could wish my days to be
> Bound each to each by natural piety.[45]

Where Augustinian orthodoxy had seen in the child a welter of confusion and rebellion, Wordsworth discovered in it a divine surplus of "natural piety" that adulthood had the chance to recover and preserve.

If the "Child is Father of the Man," who is father of the child? Wordsworth's "Intimations Ode" would seem to indicate that the child's earthly father is of little importance, in contrast to his heavenly one. The poem treats conception and birth not as the start of life but as the beginning of loss. "There hath passed away a glory from the earth," Wordsworth laments. "Whither is fled the visionary gleam? / Where is it now, the glory and the dream?" The answer follows immediately:

> Our birth is but a sleep and a forgetting:
> The Soul that rises with us, our life's Star,
>   Hath had elsewhere its setting,
>   And cometh from afar:
>   Not in entire forgetfulness
>   And not in utter nakedness,
> But trailing clouds of glory do we come
>   From God, who is our home:
> Heaven lies about us in our infancy!

The "Intimations Ode" pictures the body as a "prison-house" and the earth as a "homely Nurse" who tries to "make her Foster-child, her In-

---

45. Wordsworth, "My Heart Leaps Up," in *William Wordsworth*, ed. Stephen Gill (New York: Oxford University Press, 1984), 246.

mate Man, / Forget the glories he hath known, / And that imperial palace whence he came." That "Inmate" is a "little Actor" who "cons another part" at each stage of growth, arriving at last at the indignity of "palsied Age."

Wordsworth sees these struggles of the soul as conflicts of knowledge and interpretation. The self that "cons" its parts becomes the slave of *mimesis,* "As if his whole vocation / Were endless imitation." Imitating and interpreting from the surface of things, such a self will neglect the "Soul's immensity" that resides beneath the surface of "exterior semblance." The only hope of adulthood is to trace the trail marked by our "obstinate questionings" and "shadowy recollections." If we follow it, we will come upon "what remains" of "the primal sympathy / Which having been must ever be."[46] The best that a "self-fathered" self can do in adulthood, in other words, is to *re-collect* the primal unity of childhood.

In short, in romanticism, the dream of Cartesian self-creation realized its fullest potential. Descartes had believed that through strenuous effort, free rational agents could deduce the foundational truths essential for building the secure structures of modern science. For more than a century after Descartes, his descendants worked methodically to build upon the foundations laid by the rational analysis of the human mind or the empirical study of the natural world. With romanticism, however, the primary mechanism of the Cartesian quest changed, and its scope grew dramatically, as intuition and recollection replaced ratiocination and empirical study as the means to the truth. Romanticism was to continue the work of the Enlightenment, but only on different terms.

Romantic hermeneutics in particular drew upon its resources in rationalism and intuitionism and became, as a result, an odd amalgam of methodical study and creative illumination, as the romantic theorists employed procedural means to suggestive, intuitive ends.[47] According to Gadamer, Friedrich Schleiermacher, the most influential theoretician of romantic hermeneutics, did not seek "the unity of hermeneutics in the *unity of the content of tradition* to which understanding is applied, but . . . in the unity of a procedure." We need procedures and a universal hermeneutic to understand texts, whether they are oral or written, because "the experience of the alien and the possibility of misunderstanding is [*sic*] universal." With Schleiermacher, "in a new and universal sense, alienation is

46. *Wordsworth,* ed. Gill, 297-302.
47. See Gadamer, *Truth and Method,* 173-218.

inextricably given with the individuality of the Thou."[48] Hermeneutics is the "art of avoiding misunderstanding," but it must be practiced with both the rigor of a science and the subtlety of an art. This is so because of the isolation inherent to the condition of the post-Cartesian self. That self is isolated within its own consciousness so dramatically that all communication appears to be a case of translation fraught with peril and difficulty. As a result, in Schleiermacher's words, "misunderstanding occurs as a matter of course, and so understanding must be willed and sought at every point."[49]

For Schleiermacher, the primacy of misunderstanding in the interpretive process meant that the interpreter had to work strenuously to overcome the obstacles to proper comprehension. To understand a text, he argued, "the interpreter must put himself both objectively and subjectively in the position of the author." The interpreter does so objectively through an exhaustive study of the historical and linguistic background of the work. Only when any particular utterance has been set fully within its original context, and considered "in [its] relation to the language as a whole," can a serious misunderstanding of it be avoided. But with the proper blend of "historical and divinatory" techniques, we can not only avoid misconstruing the meaning of another person's utterance; we can potentially understand that person's words better than he or she may comprehend them. The more we learn about an author, the better equipped we are for interpretation, the ultimate goal of which is "to understand the text at first as well as and then even better than its author."[50]

This means that to understand a text we must proceed methodically, employing all the tools of historical research, as we reconstruct the life-world behind the work. The goal of the process was for Schleiermacher, as it had been for Descartes, the obliteration of the mediating traditions separating the interpreter from the immediacy of the text's world. Schleiermacher believed that we come to perfect clarity about the object of our study only when we have bridged the gap of opinions, traditions, and prejudices that separate us from it. He was confident that the final span of that bridge could be built by a creative act of illumination, by what he called the "divinatory" act of knowing and intuiting the

48. Gadamer, *Truth and Method*, 178-79.

49. Friedrich Schleiermacher, *Hermeneutics: The Handwritten Manuscripts*, in *Friedrich Schleiermacher: Pioneer of Modern Theology*, ed. Keith Clements (London: Collins, 1987), 166.

50. Schleiermacher, *Hermeneutics*, 167.

"inner and outer aspects of the author's life." In Schleiermacher's hermeneutics, Gadamer explains, "what corresponds to the production of genius is divination, the immediate solution, which ultimately presupposes a kind of con-geniality." This act of divination "depends on a pre-existing bond between all individuals."[51]

For the Enlightenment and romanticism, that "bond" was made possible through the presence in the self of a God-given capacity for knowledge and understanding; the clockmaker God of the Newtonian universe may have distanced himself dramatically from his creation, but before removing himself, he had planted within the human mind a means to the truth. In the century and a half after Descartes, we can witness what Helmut Thielicke has called "an increasing depersonalizing of God, whether as substance or idea."[52] But the more God became impersonal and distant, the more modern views stressed the compensating properties of the expansive, universal self. In Gadamer's words, according to romanticism, each individual manifests a portion of the "universal life and hence 'everyone carries a tiny bit of everyone else within him, so that divination is stimulated by comparison with oneself.'" As a result, the individuality of an author can "be directly grasped 'by, as it were, transforming oneself into the other.'"[53]

Fueled by confidence in the autonomous self and its innate powers, for two centuries the Cartesian tradition happily embraced the image of the orphan. Free of its prejudicial parents at last, the human spirit could develop its innate potential and emerge into its long-postponed adult maturity. *"Enlightenment is mankind's exit from its self-incurred immaturity,"* wrote Immanuel Kant in 1784. *"Immaturity* is the inability to make use of one's own understanding without the guidance of another."[54] To be enlightened, a person or an age must be under no obligation to appropriate the dead symbols or claims of the past. It "is completely impossible," Kant argued, for the members of a society to bind "one another by oath to a certain unalterable symbol." And in a similar manner, "one age cannot . . . place the succeeding age in a situation in which it becomes impossible for it to broaden its knowledge, particularly such pressing knowledge, to

51. Gadamer, *Truth and Method*, 189.

52. Helmut Thielicke, *Modern Faith and Thought*, trans. Geoffrey W. Bromiley (Grand Rapids: William B. Eerdmans, 1990), 73.

53. Gadamer, *Truth and Method*, 189.

54. Immanuel Kant, "An Answer to the Question: What Is Enlightenment?" in *What Is Enlightenment?*, ed. Schmidt, 58.

cleanse itself of errors, and generally to progress in enlightenment."[55] Whether it be the "opinions of others," the crippling forces of imitation and tradition, or the historical distance that separates us from the object of our understanding, we must slip free of the parental grip that holds us back in our journey to the truth. Only then, when free at last of parents and the past, will we begin to see the truth and understand others as we ought.

"Beautiful Fruit Already Picked from the Tree": Texts in an Orphaned Age

There is more than a little irony in the fact that in the very years that the Cartesian tradition of "self-fathering" reached its self-congratulatory peak in romanticism and the French Revolution, the ideal of autonomy — that ideal which stood behind the dream of living in a parentless world — began to be questioned sharply. At the start of the nineteenth century, the questioning surfaced in isolated incidents or stories but did not resonate in the larger culture. As the century wore on, however, the questioning of autonomy developed quietly but steadily, until, by the second half of the century, it became a central concern of the age.

One of the earliest provocative treatments of the theme of orphaning emerged at the height of romanticism. It was Jean Paul Friedrich Richter's "Speech of Christ, after death, from the universe, that there is no God." In this fable, "a lofty, noble form, having the expression of a never-ending sorrow, now sank down from above upon the altar" in a church adjoining a graveyard. From that graveyard the dead arise each night at midnight to "mimic the religious services of the living in the churches." As they emerge from their graves, they cry out, "'Christ! is there no God?'" The response of Jesus is plaintively chilling: "There is none! . . . I traversed the worlds. I ascended into the suns, and flew with the milky ways through the wildernesses of the heavens; but there is no God! I descended . . . into the abyss, and cried aloud — 'Father, where art thou?' but I heard nothing but the eternal storm which no one rules; . . . and when I looked up to the immea-

---

55. Kant, "What Is Enlightenment?," 61. "In modernity, traditional wisdom becomes irrational 'prejudice,' and the 'grounds' for knowledge are decentered from the shared conventions of a substantive 'we' to the sort of abstract 'I' . . . characteristic of the marketplace." Paul Redding, *Hegel's Hermeneutics* (Ithaca: Cornell University Press, 1996), 198.

surable world for the Divine Eye, it glared upon me from an empty, bottomless socket. . . ." And when the dead children arise and stream into the temple, they throw themselves before Jesus. Desperate for reassurance, they ask him, "Jesus! have we no Father?" And with his eyes filled with tears, he can only answer, "'We are all orphans, I and you; we are without a Father.'"

With the shrieks of the children still sounding, the walls of the temple split apart, and then children, temple, earth, sun, and "the whole immeasurable universe" sink down "as into a mine dug out of the Eternal Night." From "the summit of infinite Nature," Christ looks down and beholds the "grinding concourse of worlds, the torch-dances of the heavenly *ignes fatui,* and the coral-banks of beating hearts." He lifts his eyes "to the Nothing, and the empty Immensity," and cries out, "'How lonely is every one in the wide charnel house of the universe!'" And then he asks what was in the early nineteenth century a prescient and prophetic question: "'If every being is its own father and creator, why cannot it also be its own destroying angel?'"[56]

Though he shared many of the concerns of the romantic poets and philosophers, Jean Paul was deeply skeptical of their individualistic tendencies. He wrote scornfully of "the lawless, capricious spirit of the present age, which would egotistically annihilate the world and the universe in order to clear a space merely for free *play.*" Disregarding history and scornful of authority, the modern age is committed to nothing more than "the arbitrariness of egotism." That egotism is hopelessly disappointed by the "hard, sharp commandments of reality" and retreats to a "desert of fantasy." There, the dreams of delight eventually give way to nightmares of nihilism: "In an age when God has set like the sun, soon afterwards the world too passes into darkness. He who scorns the universe respects nothing more than himself and at night fears only his own creations."[57]

Jean Paul's anxieties proved uncannily prophetic for the nineteenth century. They surfaced in various romantic and Victorian poems, pulsed at the heart of Friedrich Nietzsche's critique of Christianity and Western culture, and dominated the characterization of protagonists in the nineteenth-century novel. The torment of Jean Paul's Christ had focused atten-

---

56. Jean Paul Friedrich Richter, *Flower, Fruit and Thorn Pieces; or, The Married Life, Death, and Wedding of the Advocate of the Poor, Firmian Stanislaus Siebenkäs,* trans. Edward Henry Noel (Boston: James Munroe, 1845), 332-40.

57. Jean Paul, "School for Aesthetics," trans. Margaret R. Hale, in *German Romantic Criticism,* ed. A. Leslie Willson (New York: Continuum, 1982), 32.

tion upon the terrible price to be paid for the "self-fathering" drive of modernity and had raised the hitherto unspeakable subject of the "death of God."[58] Particularly in the second half of the century, there were orphans everywhere in the fiction of the day, and a number of crucial philosophical texts examined the theme of the eclipse of God.

It was to be Hegel who would offer the first extended philosophical meditation on the subject of the "death of God." He did so in a passage from the *Phenomenology of Spirit*, written at the same time as Wordsworth's "Intimations Ode." It is hard to imagine two less similar works than the English poet's hymn to the innate knowledge of God and the German philosopher's steely assessment of our disenchanted belatedness. Where Wordsworth sees the self "trailing clouds of glory," Hegel finds it afflicted by the travails of the "Unhappy Consciousness" that gains *"certainty of itself"* by losing everything else, including "all essential being." The "Unhappy Consciousness" is that self-awareness which stands in the void as the only vibrant agent in an otherwise senseless world of matter in motion. Surrounded by death, "it is the grief which expresses itself in the hard saying that 'God is dead.'" For that Unhappy Consciousness,

> Trust in the eternal laws of the gods has vanished, and the Oracles, which pronounced on particular questions, are dumb. The statues are now only stones from which the living soul has flown, just as the hymns are words from which belief has gone. The tables of the gods provide no spiritual food and drink, and in his games and festivals man no longer recovers the joyful consciousness of his unity with the divine. The works of the Muse now lack the power of the Spirit, for the Spirit has gained its certainty of itself from the crushing of gods and men. They have become what they are for us now — beautiful fruit already picked from the tree,

58. Perhaps the subject was not entirely unspeakable. Eberhard Jüngel notes that a 1641 Lutheran hymn by Johannes Rist contained the lines "'O great distress! / God himself lies dead. / On the cross he died, / and by doing so he has won for us the realm of heaven.'"

"The sentence 'God himself lies dead' was known and debated as a pronounced expression of Lutheran theology; it was so controversial that, for example, the Dortmund hymnbook replaced it with the less objectionable 'The Lord is dead.' At the theological faculties, learned disputations were conducted about the dogmatic correctness of the chorale." *God as the Mystery of the World: On the Foundation of the Theology of the Crucified One in the Dispute between Theism and Atheism,* trans. Darrell L. Guder (Grand Rapids: William B. Eerdmans, 1983), 64.

Jüngel observes that Hegel quoted this passage from the hymn a number of times in the lectures he gave in the final decade of his life.

which a friendly Fate has offered us, as a girl might set the fruit before us. It cannot give us the actual life in which they existed, . . . nor the cycle of the changing seasons that governed the process of their growth. So Fate does not restore their world to us along with the works of antique Art, it gives not the spring and summer of the ethical life in which they blossomed and ripened, but only the veiled recollection of that actual world. Our active enjoyment of them is therefore not an act of divine worship through which our consciousness might come to its perfect truth and fulfilment; it is an external activity — the wiping-off of some drops of rain or specks of dust from these fruits, so to speak — one which erects an intricate scaffolding of the dead elements of their outward existence — the language, the historical circumstances, etc. in place of the inner elements of the ethical life which environed, created, and inspired them. And all this we do, not in order to enter into their very life but only to possess an idea of them in our imagination. But, just as the girl who offers us the plucked fruits is more than the Nature which directly provides them — the Nature diversified into their conditions and elements, the tree, air, light, and so on — because she sums all this up . . . in the gesture with which she offers them, so, too, the Spirit of the Fate that presents us with those works of art is more than the ethical life and the actual world of that nation, for it is the *inwardizing* in us of the Spirit which in them was still [only] *outwardly* manifested; it is the Spirit of the tragic Fate which gathers all those individual gods and attributes of the [divine] substance into one pantheon, into the Spirit that is itself conscious of itself as Spirit.[59]

If the history of philosophy has been a footnote to Plato, then contemporary hermeneutics might be seen as an extended reflection upon this passage from Hegel's *Phenomenology*. At its heart, Hegel's metaphorical treatment of the "Spirit of Fate" speaks of that sense of alienation from the past — from its vital life, its beliefs, and its texts — that is one of the central phenomena of modernity. As potent as they had been in their day, both the antiquities of the classical world and the scriptures of Christian and Jewish eras are now no more than "stones from which the living soul has flown." If they are to speak to us and to have any authority over our lives, how are they to be brought back to life? How are we to bridge the chasm of time that yawns between us and them?

59. G. W. F. Hegel, *Phenomenology of Spirit*, trans. A. V. Miller (Oxford: Oxford University Press, 1977), 455-56.

Hegel's answers to such questions differed dramatically from previous ones. In the period from Descartes to Schleiermacher, the ruling question for human understanding had been, "How might I rid myself of those prejudices and encumbrances that separate me from the truth or from the meaning of what another has written?" The assumption here was that everything which mediates our knowledge of truth or interpretation of texts serves little or no good purpose. This includes, especially, the history between us and the object of our concern. Through critical reflection and historical research, we build a trail all the way back to the ancient past, and we travel on it until we reach the point at which our object of interest originated. Having cleared the obstacles in our way and having traversed the ground, we are at last free to confront that object directly. In Emerson's classic formulation of the argument, we ought "to go alone; to refuse the good models, even those which are sacred in the imagination of men, and dare to love God without mediator or veil."[60]

Although Hegel rejected the Cartesian ideal of an unmediated understanding, he also recognized that Descartes's shift represented an irreversible development in the history of philosophy: it was, he understood, one of the means by which Spirit has become fully conscious of itself. He harbored no illusions about returning to a pre-Cartesian understanding of knowledge, but he also realized that Descartes's move threatened to turn the history of philosophy into a "simple accumulation of local opinions and perspectives."[61] After Descartes, Hegel noted, the *history* of philosophy

---

60. Emerson, "The Divinity School Address," in *Emerson: Essays and Lectures*, 88-89. This disdain for mediating agents has great theological and linguistic significance, of course. Both Keith Thomas and Charles Taylor trace it, in part, to the Reformation's anti-sacramental impulses, which fed into the desacralizing of nature that seventeenth-century science and commerce eagerly promoted. The process accelerated through the eighteenth century and issued in the romantic reaction at the end of that century. Thomas writes of the Reformation's "onslaught on the central Catholic doctrine of the Mass. . . . The Papists, wrote Calvin, 'pretend there is a magical force in the sacraments, independent of efficacious faith'. . . . In place of the miraculous transubstantiation of the consecrated elements was substituted a simple commemorative rite, and the reservation of the sacrament was discontinued. It went without saying that none of the Protestant reformers would countenance any of the old notions concerning the temporal benefits which might spring from communicating or from contemplating the consecrated elements." Keith Thomas, *Religion and the Decline of Magic* (New York: Scribner, 1971), 53.

61. Bruns, *Hermeneutics Ancient and Modern*, 149. For this discussion of Hegel, I am greatly indebted to Bruns.

yielded nothing but a "bare knowledge of opinions, i.e. other people's peculiarities. . . . But the peculiarities of other people are external and foreign to me, purely historical and dead material. In that case the history of philosophy is superfluous, wearisome, devoid of interest except perhaps to scholars. . . . It does not belong to me and I am not in it." In modernity, our relationship to all that we inherit becomes painfully strained. Myths, metaphors, and stories are handed on to us like so many corpses pulled from the morgue of the past; we detect no life in them and do not know how to dispose of them.

To illustrate his point, Hegel offered the example of a teacher of the history of philosophy called upon to remain neutral about the ideas he studies and teaches. "Such a teacher is to act in expounding the philosophies as if he were dead, that he is to treat them as something cut off from his spirit, as something external to him," Hegel explained. Implored to remain neutral, the teacher faces a clearly untenable situation. If he treats ideas from the past as dead opinions without weight or power, "in that event the history of philosophy is a miserable occupation," because the teacher "knows in advance that he must deal solely with unsuccessful enterprises." If "we are to study the history of philosophy in a worthwhile way," wrote Hegel, ". . . we must be partisans of philosophy and must not restrict ourselves to, or content ourselves with, merely knowing the thinking of other people. Truth is only known when we are present in it with our own spirit; mere knowledge of it is not proof that we are really at home in it."[62] Having passed through the alienating stance of Cartesian skepticism, the self had to internalize it and yet move it to a higher unity.

For interpretation, Hegel's solution means that when we have become alienated from history or texts, we can make ourselves at home in them only by appropriating them — that is, by taking them up into our own lives and experiences. In doing so, we raise the past to life through the power of our creative spirit. Hegel terms this process *Aufhebung;* it is what he calls in the *Phenomenology of Spirit* the "inwardizing" of the Spirit that had once breathed in the ancient myths and now discredited beliefs. Through *Aufhebung,* alienation proves to be a blessing and a gain, rather than a curse and a loss, because the "Spirit of Fate" that delivers the works of the past to us is greater than "the ethical life and the actual world" of that past, "just as the girl who offers us the plucked fruits is more than the

---

62. Hegel, *Introduction to the Lectures on the History of Philosophy,* trans. T. M. Knox and A. V. Miller (Oxford: Clarendon Press, 1985), 100.

Nature which directly provides them." That which had been present in an outward form in the ancient beliefs and rituals has now been *"inwardized,"* or gathered "into one pantheon, into the Spirit that is itself conscious of itself as Spirit."[63] And so the lifeless, mechanistic world of Cartesian philosophy and Newtonian science comes to life through the internalizing power of Spirit.

In one form or another, this view of a triumphant consciousness as Spirit had surfaced earlier in the German idealist philosophers and English romantic poets; after Hegel, it became one of the central tenets of the romantic and post-romantic creeds. For Hegel, according to M. H. Abrams, "the spirit recognizes that all the mysteries of religion are intrinsic to itself, as moments in its own educational development: human consciousness becomes aware that it has been its own betrayer, and can be its own redeemer."[64] In the final sentence of the *Phenomenology,* Hegel calls this process "the inwardizing and the Calvary of absolute Spirit."[65]

Hegel's "inwardizing" of texts and the historical represents the radical realization of the anti-sacramental potential of the Reformation. With their attacks upon magic and the Mass, the Protestant Reformers served as a powerful force in the desacralizing of the world. In their view of the Lord's Supper in particular, and the seven sacraments in general, Protestants shifted their focus from the liturgical act to the spiritual state of the recipient. Luther was unambiguous on this matter. In his 1519 treatise entitled "The Blessed Sacrament," he explained that the sacrament of "the holy and true body of Christ" has three parts: "The first is the sacrament, or sign. The second is the significance of this sacrament. The third is the faith required with each of the first two. These three parts must be found in every sacrament." While the

---

63. For Hegel, the appropriation of dead traditions and formulations by consciousness offers a way of recovering, albeit in a different form, something of an earlier immediacy of belief. "The sublation of mediation into immediacy is similar to an entity's sublation of its own conditions. Both processes occur, on Hegel's view, in our knowledge of God. God (Jacobi has argued) is unmediated and unconditioned, while our knowledge of him is mediated and conditioned; thus either our cognition falls short of God or it degrades him to a mediated entity. The solution, Hegel replies, is that while both God and our cognition of him are mediated, they sublate their mediation into immediacy." Michael Inwood, *A Hegel Dictionary* (Oxford: Blackwell, 1992), 185.

A modified Hegelianism informs most hermeneutical enterprises in the modern world. For a succinct and compelling representation of the power of the Hegelian vision for contemporary hermeneutics, see Ricoeur, *The Symbolism of Evil,* 347-57.

64. Abrams, *Natural Supernaturalism,* 233.

65. Hegel, *Phenomenology of Spirit,* 493.

sacrament takes an external, visible form, its significance "must be internal and spiritual, within the spirit of the person. Faith must make both of them together operative and useful."[66] With this definition, Luther was rejecting the Catholic view that the sacraments have the power to confer grace *ex opere operato;* he refused to grant that they could be effective regardless of the disposition of the persons administering or receiving them. Instead, while Luther and most of his fellow Reformers saw an objective property in the sacraments, they also held that the animating presence of the believer's faith was required to make the sacrament efficacious.

Luther remained poised between his trust in the objective power of the sacraments and his understanding of the necessity of faith. But romanticism, of which Hegel's philosophy stood as one of the most complex and powerful representations, was to tilt completely in the direction of inwardness. In the Hegelian understanding of Spirit, the quickening power of self-consciousness raises dead realities to life and enables us to appropriate the lifeless legacy of the past. Emerson again provides the memorable illustration of this romantic doctrine of appropriation: "The scholar . . . received into him the world around; brooded thereon; gave it the new arrangement of his own mind, and uttered it again. It came into him, life; it went out from him, truth. It came to him, short-lived actions; it went out from him, immortal thoughts. It came to him, business; it went out from him, poetry. It was dead fact; now it is quick thought."[67] Or, as he put it in another essay, in an unblushing declaration of the primacy of self-consciousness: "History is an impertinence and an injury, if it be any thing more than a cheerful apologue or parable of my being and becoming."[68] In

---

66. Martin Luther, "The Blessed Sacrament of the Holy and True Body and Blood of Christ, and the Brotherhoods," in *Martin Luther's Basic Theological Writings,* ed. Timothy F. Lull (Minneapolis: Fortress, 1989), 242.

67. Emerson, "The American Scholar," in *Emerson: Essays and Lectures,* 56.

68. Emerson, "Self-Reliance," in *Emerson: Essays and Lectures,* 270. According to Hans Frei, "Religious theory after Kant focused more and more on faith as a distinctive and self-conscious human stance which is reducible to no other. And faith in this sense qualifies whatever 'reality' it is properly in touch with, analogous to the way in which for Kant the structure of reason qualifies the transcendental ego's contact with the objects of the sensible world, turning them from things-in-themselves into phenomena for human consciousness. It became a commonplace in nineteenth-century Protestant theology that we know God only under the qualification of a religious relation to him (be it revelation or some other), and not as he is in himself." Hans Frei, *The Eclipse of Biblical Narrative: A Study in Eighteenth- and Nineteenth-Century Hermeneutics* (New Haven: Yale University Press, 1974), 283-84.

interpreting a text or an event from the past, we cannot transport our-selves back to its world, Hegel held, but must rather bring it forward into ours. "Neither does an individual transcend his time; he is a son of it," he argued, employing an image that makes the present age, rather than an ongoing tradition, its own parent and authority. "No one can escape from the substance of his time any more than he can jump out of his skin."[69]

Hegel's view of interpretation and history accepted the irreversibility of the Cartesian discovery of consciousness, and on this point, at least, he was in agreement with Schleiermacher. For Hegel, Descartes's isolation of the skeptical subject was a necessary stage in the developing self-consciousness of Spirit, and for Schleiermacher it led eventually to a higher consciousness of God. There are, the German theologian wrote, "three grades of self-consciousness," the first of which is "the confused ani-mal grade" seen in "the consciousness of children"; the second, or "middle stage," is that of "sensible self-consciousness" and "antithesis"; and the third and final stage is that in which the self experiences a "feeling of abso-lute dependence" and "unites and identifies itself with everything which, in the middle grade, was set over against it, as the highest."[70] Schleiermacher's view of consciousness resembles Hegel's judgment about the salutary metaphysical loss that has made Spirit at last "conscious of it-self as Spirit." For Schleiermacher, "the highest self-consciousness is in no wise dependent on outwardly given objects which may affect us at one mo-ment and not another." Instead, "it is quite simple, and remains self-identical while all other states are changing."[71]

Whatever similarities they had in their view of Cartesian isolation, however, Hegel and Schleiermacher differed dramatically on the aims and mechanics of interpretation. To the end, Schleiermacher remained confi-dent in the power of methodical interpretation to obliterate the historical distance between readers and their texts. If anything, the distancing of his-tory spurs us to such rigorous efforts of understanding that eventually we may "understand the text at first as well as and then even better than its au-thor." In his confidence about recovering the original intentions of the au-thor, Schleiermacher was one with Descartes in his efforts to recapture perfect epistemological certainty, one with the Revolutionaries in France

---

69. Hegel, *Introduction to the Lectures on the History of Philosophy*, 112.

70. Friedrich Schleiermacher, *The Christian Faith*, ed. H. R. Mackintosh and J. S. Stewart (Edinburgh: T. & T. Clark, n.d.), sec. 5, 18-20.

71. Schleiermacher, *The Christian Faith*, sec. 5, 21.

in their drive to retrieve a state of natural perfection, and one with Words-worth in his passion to recuperate the immortal glory of childhood. Cut off from the past but able to reconstruct it through diligent effort, Schleiermacher's interpreter is an orphan who fabricates a family through methodical interpretive labors and feats of divinatory understanding.

Schleiermacher's goal of "understanding the text at first as well as and then even better than its author" may explain his appeal to conservative American biblical scholars who might otherwise question his orthodoxy. At first glance, Schleiermacher and the heirs of fundamentalism would seem to be unlikely allies. He, after all, is the father of the theological modernism against which the fundamentalists reacted so strongly in the early decades of the twentieth century. There is little in his theology of feeling or his accommodating apologetics that can be squared with the unblinking supernaturalism of fundamentalism or with its animus toward culture.

Nonetheless, Schleiermacher and the evangelicals come together on key questions of interpretation through their common disregard of the constructive hermeneutical significance of history. In Schleiermacher, the bias against history followed from his conviction that in interpretation "misunderstanding occurs as a matter of course." If we interpret in order to understand a text better than its own author understood it, then history can only be a hindrance and not a help. It is the void through which we must travel to reach the text in its original purity, the debris we must clear before we can dig beneath the surface of the text into the very mind of its author. As a repository of prejudices, misconceptions, and illusions, the history of interpretation is almost always more likely to conceal rather than reveal the meaning of a text. With his emphasis upon method and divination, Schleiermacher sought nothing less than to overcome history and its opposition to right understanding.[72]

---

72. Unlike many fundamentalists and evangelicals, however, Schleiermacher did not allow his hermeneutical disdain for tradition to assume the form of a universal denial of the irreversibility of history. For example, he did not dream, as many modern conservative Christians do, of overturning history and re-establishing the church as it was in the time of the New Testament. He wrote, "As a universal rule, what has previously existed never recurs at a later time in quite the same form; and . . . no one particular point of time could be given, all over, to which the Church should have been brought back, . . . partly because we cannot sacrifice the dogmatic precision of our ideas, partly because we can as little re-establish the then relations to Judaism and Heathenism as we can the political passivity." *The Christian Faith*, sec. 24, 104.

American evangelicalism has its own history of looking askance at history. George Marsden observes that at the end of the nineteenth century, "Americans had relatively little history of their own, and their national experience often seemed like a new dispensation, totally discontinuous with the past." (And here we have yet another instance of modernity's desire to be orphaned from the past.) Because dispensationalism had a nondevelopmental view of history, Marsden conjectures, it was ideally suited to thrive in American soil after it was transplanted from England in the closing decades of the nineteenth century.[73] In its fundamentalist flowering, dispensationalism did away with the need to take the history of doctrine and interpretation seriously. The institutional church and its traditions, after all, were more often the scene of error and apostasy than right understanding. Those who could interpret the scriptures correctly belonged to that saving remnant of "Bible-believing" Christians present in every era of history. Members of that remnant could, with the help of the Holy Spirit, leap over almost two thousand years of history and land safely back in the presence of the prophets and apostles themselves.

Although most evangelical biblical scholars have left behind the dispensationalism of their fundamentalist past, they have at the same time still clung to their predecessors' view of history. And in doing so, they have unwittingly appropriated the Enlightenment "prejudice against prejudice." Like politics, hermeneutics makes for strange bedfellows. In a history of early American religion, Nathan Hatch notes that "no less than Tom Paine or Thomas Jefferson, populist Christians of the early republic, sought to start the world over again."[74] In like manner, no less than Schleiermacher, conservative biblical scholars have sought to read the Bible as though it had never been read before. They have, that is, labored to suppress the history of interpretation in their quest for the pristine historical origins of the text.

To be certain, the evangelical desire to go behind history makes a certain kind of sense, in light of the recent history of theories of interpretation and human understanding. Understandably concerned about some of the subjectivist excesses of the Hegelian tradition of inwardizing

---

73. George Marsden, *Fundamentalism and American Culture: The Shaping of Twentieth-Century Evangelicalism, 1870-1925* (New York: Oxford University Press, 1980), 226.

74. Nathan Hatch, *The Democratization of American Christianity* (New Haven: Yale University Press, 1989), 213.

appropriation, evangelical scholars have generally adopted as their alternative Schleiermacher's two-stage approach to interpretation. In the first stage, careful historical and textual analysis is meant to yield the fixed meaning of the text. With that *meaning* secured, the interpreter is then free to articulate the *significance* of the text for the present day. "*Meaning* is that which is represented by a text; it is what the author meant by his use of a particular sign sequence; it is what the signs represent," writes E. D. Hirsch, whose *Validity in Interpretation* has been enormously influential in evangelical biblical studies. "*Significance,* on the other hand, names a relationship between that meaning and a person, or a conception, or a situation, or indeed anything imaginable."[75] Evangelical scholar Gordon Fee clearly states the case for the two-stage approach: "The first step toward valid interpretation of Scripture is a historical investigation known as *exegesis,* which means the determination of the originally intended meaning of a text." Fee speaks of "taking history seriously" but makes it clear that he means by that not the history that stands between us and the text but the "original setting(s) of the biblical texts themselves." The task of the interpreter is "nothing less

---

75. E. D. Hirsch, *Validity in Interpretation* (New Haven: Yale University Press, 1967), 8. For a recent evangelical elaboration of the Hirschian viewpoint, see Walter C. Kaiser and Moisés Silva, *An Introduction to Biblical Hermeneutics: The Search for Meaning* (Grand Rapids: Zondervan, 1994), esp. chap. 2, "The Meaning of Meaning," 27-45.

Daniel Fuller, in a widely circulated syllabus for a course at Fuller Theological Seminary, lauds Hirsch for his assertion that "it is wholly possible to have full knowledge of the verbal meanings of others. To know an author's language conventions . . . is to be able to know fully what he is trying to say." Hirsch is praised for espousing a "hermeneutical theory . . . not in vogue today." It is not in vogue because it has been supplanted by the theory of hermeneutics most closely associated with Hans-Georg Gadamer. Fuller dismisses what he calls Gadamer's "radical historicism." While praising Hirsch, he says that "Gadamer's point of view is not true because it counters experience and is inherently contradictory." Daniel Fuller, *Hermeneutics,* 5th rev. ed. (n.p., 1978), sec. I, 7-8, 13.

Walter Kaiser views the situation along similar lines. He writes of "the crisis in hermeneutics" and places the primary blame for "this sad state of affairs" on Gadamer, who is faulted for not giving us a "yardstick for determining which interpreter is more nearly correct if both happen to hit upon conflicting interpretations at the same moment in time." On the other hand, Kaiser praises Hirsch as one who "stand[s] almost alone in attempting to return hermeneutics and exegesis to a more objective version of interpretation." Walter Kaiser, *Toward an Exegetical Theology: Biblical Exegesis for Preaching and Teaching* (Grand Rapids: Baker, 1981), 23-34.

than to bridge the historical — and therefore cultural — gap between them and us."[76]

With its crisp distinction between meaning and significance, Hirsch's intentionalism appears to allow for a measure of interpretive liberty even as it tethers interpretation to the pole of certainty. That makes it especially attractive to conservative Christians seeking to ground their faith without either deference to tradition or recourse to a developed doctrine of the church. With the unchanging meaning of the text secured by exegetical work of the biblical scholars themselves, there is no apparent need for an understanding of the activity of God in the history of the church and its manifold interpretive practices and traditions. Hirsch argues that while our "relationship" to the meaning of a text may change over time, "one constant, unchanging pole of that relationship is what the text means." The failure to make this "simple and essential distinction" has led to endless confusion in modern hermeneutical theory and practice.[77] Following Hirsch's lead, a generation of evangelical biblical scholars has claimed that the subjective art of appropriation can be practiced but only after the objective science of interpretation has secured the unchanged meaning of the text. "There is one meaning to a text, that meaning consciously willed by the author, but the particular way that meaning affects the readers, its significance, will be quite different," asserts evangelical New Testament scholar Robert Stein, with a confidence typical of contemporary evangelical approaches to interpretation.[78]

Yet for all of their self-assurance, the evangelical promoters of Hirschian intentionalism are fighting a lonely battle. Almost two decades ago, Frank Lentricchia observed that "E. D. Hirsch stands pretty much by himself in the landscape of contemporary critical theory."[79] For two centu-

---

76. Gordon Fee, "History as Context for Interpretation," in *The Act of Bible Reading*, ed. Elmer Dyck (Downers Grove, Ill.: InterVarsity, 1996), 11.

77. Hirsch, *Validity in Interpretation*, 8.

78. Robert H. Stein, *Playing by the Rules: A Basic Guide to Interpreting the Bible* (Grand Rapids: Baker, 1994), 36.

79. Frank Lentricchia, *After the New Criticism* (Chicago: University of Chicago Press, 1980), 257. In analyzing the intellectual sources of Hirsch's intentionalism — and his abiding disdain for the Heideggerian tradition — Lentricchia also illuminates the irony of the evangelical embrace of Hirsch: "There is, in so many words, no unmediated historical knowledge. That is reserved for God, or for theorists like Hirsch who believe that objective knowledge can be acquired in a massive act of dispossessing ourselves of the only route to knowledge that we have: the historicized self. What Hirsch's readings of Heidegger and Gadamer may ultimately indicate is the traditional Anglo-

ries, the forces that Hirsch represents — and that evangelical biblical scholars have tried to muster in their battle against relativism — have been fighting a rear-guard action against the Emersonian and Hegelian hordes. Outside of the world of evangelical biblical hermeneutics, few students of interpretation or the history of ideas find Schleiermacher's strict intentionalism tenable. On seemingly every front, the advocates of *Aufhebung*, or internalization, have pressed forward and won the day. From Nietzsche and Emerson to Rorty, an air of triumphalism has informed the pronouncements of Hegel's intellectual descendants. Emerson declared with blithe confidence that "God incarnates himself in man, and evermore goes forth anew to take possession of his world"; for Nietzsche, the true interpreter is an artist, one who refuses to "[lie] in the dust before petty facts," but seeks out of a spirit of "intoxication" to transform "things until they mirror his power"; and in Rorty's words, poetic creation and strong interpretation are merely sophisticated forms of "an unconscious need everyone has: the need to come to terms with the blind impress which chance has given him, to make a self for himself by redescribing that impress in terms which are, if only marginally, his own."[80]

Rorty's glibly bleak candor helps one to understand the anxieties of those alarmed by the drift of contemporary interpretive theory. The radical allegorizing practiced by the descendants of Hegel and Nietzsche constitutes a dramatic reconfiguring of Christian practice. Allegorical interpretation first arose as a matter of apologetic concern within the Jewish, classical Greek, and early Christian traditions. From the start, allegory involved the effort to bring relevance to texts or beliefs that had been rendered obscure by historical change. Plato and the Greek tragedians employed allegory to reinvigorate the Homeric myths; in the early centuries of the Christian era, both the Jewish Philo and the Christian Origen used allegory to reconcile their respective faith traditions with Greek philoso-

---

American fear and manhandling of any sort of thought which does not work from Cartesian premises." *After the New Criticism*, 263.

Lentricchia's linking of Hirsch with Descartes is but one of many ironies of the relationship of evangelicalism to modernity. In trying to counter the rationalism and subjectivism that threaten their faith and its sacred texts, Christian scholars turn for aid to the very source of the ideas and practices they so strenuously oppose.

80. Emerson, "The Divinity School Address," in *Emerson: Essays and Lectures*, 80; Nietzsche, *Twilight of the Idols and the Anti-Christ*, trans. R. J. Hollingdale (London: Penguin, 1990), 82, 83; and Richard Rorty, *Contingency, Irony, and Solidarity* (Cambridge: Cambridge University Press, 1989), 43.

phy; and in the Middle Ages, Catholic interpreters and artists practiced allegorical interpretation in works such as Dante's *Divine Comedy,* in books of speculative and prophetic history, and in innumerable homiletical treatises.

But even though allegory was intended to sustain beliefs and practices by reinterpreting them, by the late Middle Ages it had begun to fall into disfavor, and the Reformation only hastened its demise. Allegorical interpretation had become too associated with the extravagances and abuses of medieval faith and was linked in the minds of its critics with magic and superstition. Luther and Calvin distrusted allegory, while both rationalism and empiricism discredited it.[81] The Reformers argued for the literal or plain sense of scripture over the figurative and often ridiculed the idea that there could be manifold senses of any single biblical passage. As they pressed their point about the clear and unambiguous meaning of the biblical text, the Reformers made claims about language that dovetailed neatly with the sharp distinctions being drawn by early modern philosophy and science. In the seventeenth century, for example, the British scientist Thomas Sprat called for the banishment of "Specious *Tropes* and *Figures*" from "all *civil Societies,* as a thing fatal to Peace and good Manners." Instead, he argued, the Royal Society ought to pursue "a close, naked, natural way of speaking . . . as near the Mathematical plainness as they can."[82] With language stripped to its "naked" state, there was no need for allegorical garb to conceal it.

81. "It is self-evident that Calvin would make only the most cautious use of what is called allegorizing even where NT parallels would seem to call for it directly by their *hina plerothe* ('that it might be fulfilled'). It was naturally no accident that of all the NT books he did not write a commentary only on Revelation. He hated what he called on one occasion the pleasurable playing about with every possible interpretation of the text that we can hardly avoid when it comes to Revelation." Karl Barth, *The Theology of John Calvin,* trans. Geoffrey W. Bromiley (Grand Rapids: William B. Eerdmans, 1995), 390.

Luther also excoriated the allegorists: "Origen received his due reward a long time ago when his books were prohibited, for he relied too much on this same spiritual meaning, which was unnecessary, and he let the necessary literal meaning go. When that happens Scripture perishes and really good theologians are no longer produced. Only the true principal meaning which is provided by the letters can produce good theologians." Martin Luther, "Answer to the Hyperchristian, Hyperspiritual, and Hyperlearned Book by Goat Emser in Leipzig — Including Some Thoughts Regarding His Companion, the Fool Murner," in *Luther's Basic Theological Writings,* ed. Lull, 78.

82. Thomas Sprat, as cited in Abrams, *Mirror and Lamp,* 285.

Yet later generations were to find such a "naked prose" too bracing for comfort, and they would seek once again to clothe their verbal figures in allegory. Distraught over the barrenness of a demystified world, for example, the romantic poets and philosophers redeployed allegory, this time in an effort to "re-enchant" the world. It may be true, as Hegel alleges, that "trust in the eternal laws of the gods has vanished, and the Oracles are dumb," that the statues have become lifeless stones, the hymns hollow vessels for dead beliefs, and the communion table a starving site providing "no spiritual food and drink." Yet all the same, the Spirit of Fate blesses us by showing that this loss is really a gain, for "it is the *inwardizing* in us of the Spirit which in them was still [only] *outwardly* manifested." Fully conscious of our powers, we bring life to that which seems dead outside of ourselves, whether it be the facts of history or the pages of texts.[83]

It is easy to sense the disruptive and disorienting potential of such a view of allegory. How does one hear God speak authoritatively, if the only way to understand his word is to appropriate it entirely on one's own terms? How is the church to discern and live by the unchanging standard of God's word, if the meaning of that word is never fixed but always fluctuates? And by what standard will the many competing interpretations of the Bible and Christian doctrine be judged or reconciled, if interpretation can never establish the indubitable truths that God has revealed in his word? Those who have pressed the case for authorial intention have made a valid point when they have worried about the relativizing power of interpretive appropriation. But in seeking to counter what they consider to be rank subjectivism, the intentionalists have pressed an untenable view of the interpretive process.

For almost two centuries, in short, representatives of these two interpretive traditions — the intentionalists descended from Schleiermacher and the allegorists who issued from Hegel — have pitched themselves in

83. Abrams writes, "Much of what distinguishes writers I call 'Romantic' derives from the fact that they undertook, whatever their religious creed or lack of creed, to save traditional concepts, schemes, and values which had been based on the relation of the Creator to his creature and creation, but to reformulate them within the prevailing two-term system of subject and object, ego and non-ego, the human mind or consciousness and its transactions with nature." Abrams, *Natural Supernaturalism*, 13. After Feuerbach and Nietzsche, of course, the transactions of "consciousness with nature" would seem forever altered, with nature perpetually on the verge of being devoured or obliterated by consciousness.

opposition to each other and have viewed one another as inhabitants of alien realms. Yet in reality, the allegorists and the intentionalists are hardly foreign to each other, for they are intimately related and resemble siblings squabbling about their inheritance more than anything else. For all their apparent differences, the intentionalists and the allegorists are the heirs of Descartes, who are in their markedly different ways forever re-enacting "the Cartesian moment of self-fathering."

On the basic premises of interpretation, that is, contemporary conservatives and radicals are in remarkable agreement. Both the intentionalists and the allegorists are Cartesian in that they conceive of texts as objects waiting to be operated upon by solitary subjects. They accept as a given the claim that misunderstanding and alienation constitute the normal state of affairs in hermeneutics. For the intentionalists, the text is a lifeless body awaiting the galvanizing touch of the method that will bring it to life, or it is the changeless meaning trapped inside the body of decaying human language. Only the expert, or the expert's methods, can revivify it or free it. "Exegesis is a must" for proper understanding, writes Gordon Fee, ". . . because the nature of Scripture, God's eternal Word given in human words in history, demands it."[84]

For the allegorists, texts demand nothing but yield everything under the proper caresses. Or, to use an image made popular at the height of deconstructive theorizing, the creative reader is the parasite living off the decaying body of the once vital text.[85] In many of its contemporary manifestations, allegorizing represents an effort to feed off tradition without replenishing its stores, to consume the spiritual and ethical harvests of past ages without planting new crops for future generations. Where the intentionalists are confident that the subject studying the text can extract from it the truth hidden within its language, the allegorists seek instead to bring the dead text to life by internalizing it. Intentionalists and allegorists alike are orphans contesting their legacy in a soulless Cartesian world.

---

84. Gordon Fee, "History as Context for Interpretation," in *The Act of Bible Reading*, 32.

85. "The caution amounts to saying that abnormal and 'existential' discourse is always parasitic upon normal discourse, that the possibility of hermeneutics is always parasitic upon the possibility (and perhaps upon the actuality) of epistemology, and that edification always employs materials provided by the culture of the day." Richard Rorty, *Philosophy and the Mirror of Nature* (Princeton: Princeton University Press, 1979), 365-66.

"The Shadow of Absence":
Orphans and the Interpretive Quest

Given the cultural dynamics prevailing in the early modern West, it is not surprising that orphans came to figure so prominently in the fiction of the nineteenth and twentieth centuries. As a genre, the novel offered unprecedented freedom and flexibility to explore the full range of human development and social reality. The novel also fed upon and helped to foster a remarkable appetite for the intimate delineation of inner experience, and orphans provided grist for the fictional mills. With the rise of the novel in the late eighteenth century, observes Eileen Simpson, "orphans became heroes and heroines whose feelings readers could identify with, whose orphanhood was not merely stated (as it is in Shakespeare's plays and in picaresque tales), but described as if from the inside."[86]

To put the theoretical discussion of orphaning and the Cartesian turn in perspective, we may consider the fate of orphans in three novels from the nineteenth and twentieth centuries. What happens to orphans in these novels neatly illustrates the plight of the Cartesian subject in the modern world, and in their treatment of the orphan these and other novels suggest fruitful lines of inquiry for contemporary hermeneutical discussions. In some cases, they even put forth suggestions about how to resolve key hermeneutical disputes.

Herman Melville's *Moby-Dick,* for instance, uses orphaning as a metaphor for the human condition in a world enduring the absence and silence of God. The novel is narrated by a character who tells us virtually nothing about himself, save that he is named Ishmael. The biblical Ishmael, of course, was the son of Abraham by Hagar, and he was effectively abandoned by his father. Disinherited in favor of Isaac, his younger half-brother, and cast out of the covenant, Ishmael became a wanderer and an exile.

In Hebrew, the name *Ishmael* means "God hears." In *Moby-Dick,* however, the problem is that although God may hear, he does not speak. Throughout the novel, Ishmael and Captain Ahab wrestle with the inscrutable silence of the universe. Gazing at the head of a dead whale one night, Ahab implores it to speak: "Speak, thou vast and venerable head. . . . O head! thou hast seen enough to split the planets and make an infidel of

---

86. Eileen Simpson, *Orphans: Real and Imaginary* (New York: New American Library, 1987), 181-82.

Abraham, and not one syllable is thine!"[87] As they close in on the whale near the novel's end, Ahab's first mate says of an occurrence, "'Tis a solemn sight; an omen, and an ill one." To this Ahab responds in angry disappointment: "Omen? omen? — the dictionary! If the gods think to speak outright to man, they will honorably speak outright; not shake their head, and give an old wives' darkling hint. — Begone!" (452).[88]

Yet in spite of God's silence — or perhaps because of it — we are driven to the desperate interpretation of nature and our own experience. Our insatiable hunger for meaning compels us to interpret, for without that meaning, we could not endure the burdens of living. "Some certain significance lurks in all things," Ishmael asserts at one point in the novel, "else all things are of little worth, and the round world itself but an empty cipher, except to sell by the cartload, as they do hills about Boston, to fill up some morass in the Milky Way" (358).

Though they cannot help but try to decipher the text of nature, Melville's characters have no confidence in their ability to get the reading right. They doubt themselves because their creator doubted himself, doubted God, and doubted the highly touted romantic imagination. Melville repeatedly posed the question put by Jean Paul's Christ: "If every being is its own father and creator, why cannot it also be its own destroying angel?" If the self was to become divine, that is, would it not possess the destructive powers of the Evil One as well as the creative powers of God? Even Emerson had to concede that there was a price to be paid for self-deification. In "Experience," written only a few years before Melville published *Moby-Dick*, Emerson reluctantly concluded, "We have learned that we do not see directly, but mediately, and that we have no means of correcting these colored and distorting lenses which we are, of computing the amount of their errors. Perhaps these subject-lenses have a creative power; perhaps there are no objects. Once we lived in what we saw; now, the rapa-

---

87. Herman Melville, *Moby-Dick,* ed. Harrison Hayford and Hershel Parker (New York: Norton, 1967), 264. All further references are to this edition and will be cited in parentheses within the body of the essay.

88. "In his relation to belief, Melville was like the last guest who cannot leave the party; he was always returning to see if he had left his hat and gloves. And yet he did not want to be at the party, either. It is just that he had nowhere else to be and would rather be with people than be alone. He was tormented by God's 'inscrutable' silence — this is clear from the work. Moby Dick, who is both God and Devil, flaunts his unhelpful silence as God does to Job: 'Canst thou draw out leviathan with a hook?'" James Wood, "The All of the If," *The New Republic*, 17 March 1997, 32.

ciousness of this new power, which threatens to absorb all things, engages us. . . . Every evil and every good thing is a shadow which we cast."[89]

What Emerson calls "this new power" was the human imagination as it had been defined in late eighteenth-century philosophy and early nineteenth-century poetry. In Kantian epistemology and romantic poetic theory, the perceiving and creating subject assumed an unprecedented importance. That subject was able to stand alone without the need of support from the institutional church, the scriptural record, or tradition. The autonomous human subject in Enlightenment philosophy and romantic poetry was not an abandoned orphan but a mature adult who had internalized the divine powers.

At first, that subject found within the self the same moral truths hidden within the natural world; in one of his earliest works, Emerson confidently declared that "nature is the opposite of the soul, answering to it part for part. One is seal, and one is print. Its beauty is the beauty of his own mind. . . . And, in fine, the ancient precept, 'Know thyself,' and the modern precept, 'Study nature,' become at last one maxim."[90] Yet as the passage from "Experience" demonstrates, "this new power" proved to be "rapacious," and the balance quickly shifted in its favor at the expense of nature.

As a consequence of the nineteenth century's burgeoning sense of the self — as well as of its dramatic scientific discoveries — the practice of reading the "Book of Nature" was called dramatically into question. That practice had originated in the sixteenth century and had been central to early modern efforts to replace the discredited authority of received opinion and religious dogma with a more trustworthy, universal authority. As religious sects and theological schemes proliferated alarmingly, nature spoke with one voice and in a language all could understand. What book could be clearer than this one "True Book"? From the early 1500s throughout the mid-nineteenth century, theists and deists of every kind read that book for its natural signs and, in many cases, anchored their beliefs in the meanings that it conveyed.[91]

---

89. Emerson, "Experience," in *Emerson: Essays and Lectures,* 487.

90. Emerson, "The American Scholar," in *Emerson: Essays and Lectures,* 56.

91. Ian Hacking describes this development clearly and convincingly. See *The Emergence of Probability,* 39-48. To trace the uncertainty of nineteenth-century readings of nature to problems of epistemology and the self is not to deny the enormous importance of the changes that the natural sciences were undergoing in these decades. The Darwinian critique of the argument from design fed into a skepticism already established by the romantic dilemma of consciousness.

The "Book of Nature" was meant to resolve the "problem of many authorities" by providing incontrovertible evidence of the designs of God. By the early nineteenth century, however, it had become very hard to decipher the text. With its stress upon the projecting powers of the self, romantic epistemology eventually transformed nature into a screen upon which the self was projected or a mirror which reflected that self. (Recall Nietzsche's definition of art as man's attempt to "transform things until they mirror his power.") In changing the view of nature, romanticism was abetted, to be certain, by the powerful scientific developments of the nineteenth century, particularly the rise of Darwinian naturalism. With nature drained of moral significance and the locus of meaning shifted so dramatically to the self, the "problem of many authorities" became in the romantic tradition the "problem of endless authorities." In a radically Protestant world, "every being" became not only its own "father, creator, and destroying angel," but also its own pope and authoritative interpreter.[92]

An incident in *Moby-Dick* illustrates perfectly the interpretive dilemma of the late romantic world. One day, each of the main characters stands before a gold doubloon that Captain Ahab has nailed to the mast as a bounty for the first sailor who spots Moby-Dick. Each sailor scans the symbols on the coin and reads into them whatever meaning he desires to find there. The doubloon depicted three mountain peaks in the Andes; on one there was a flame, on another a tower, and on the third, a crowing cock. Each character interprets these visual signs in light of his own most pressing concerns; there is no pattern to those concerns, so it appears to an observer that the men have not been influenced at all by what they have seen but have read into it simply what they have willed. It is left to Pip, the half-crazy cabin-boy, to sum up what the others have done as interpreters: "I look, you look, he looks; we look, ye look, they look." As another sailor puts it, having overheard the soliloquies before the doubloon: "There's another rendering now; but still one text. All sorts of men in one kind of world, you see" (362). It may be only "one world," but it is populated with "endless authorities."[93]

---

92. W. H. Auden notes that the modern devaluation of nature as a moral source has deep roots in Protestant soil: "Protestantism implies a rejection — rejection is not the same thing as rebellion — of the Mother. The doctrine of Predestination which makes the actions of God's will arbitrary from a human point of view makes the notion of necessity meaningless and thereby denies any spiritual significance to the fact that we are born from the bodies of our mothers through the necessary processes of nature." *Forewords and Afterwords*, 83.

93. James Wood comments, "His love of metaphor leads Melville marvelously

According to Ishmael, our interpretive confusion stems from our status as orphans who have no certain knowledge of either our origins or our destiny. "There is no steady unretracing progress in this life," Ishmael laments. We move through each of life's stages — through "infancy's unconscious spell, boyhood's thoughtless faith, adolescence' doubt (the common doom), then scepticism, then disbelief, resting at last in manhood's pondering repose of If" — only to have to "trace the round again . . . eternally." Where is "the final harbor" in which we might rest? What presence sustains and upholds the world? "Where is the foundling's father hidden?" Ishmael asks rhetorically. He can only conclude that "our souls are like those orphans whose unwedded mothers die in bearing them: the secret of our paternity lies in their grave, and we must there to learn it" (406).

Moby-Dick lays bare the consequences of the romantic radicalizing of Protestantism's "priesthood of all believers." When each reader of nature or scripture speaks *ex cathedra,* then there are as many denominations — and interpretations — as there are self-conscious subjects in the world. How are we to reconcile our drive for freedom of thought, expression, and interpretation with our equal hunger for the common good and our need to believe in a truth greater than ourselves?[94]

Moby-Dick also raises crucial questions about the limits of a "sign theory" of language, which holds that words are arbitrary markers that are "in principle replaceable and interchangeable."[95] In a sign theory of language, words reveal nothing more than the history of linguistic convention

---

astray, theologically. His 'wandering' love of language breaks up his God, and he encourages this; his love of language bribes him against that rival, the Original Author. . . .

"*Moby-Dick* represents the triumph of this atheism of metaphor. Or, perhaps, this polytheism of metaphor. For it is a book in which allegory explodes into a thousand metaphors; a book in which the Puritan habit of reading signs and seeing stable meanings behind them is mocked by an almost grotesque abundance of metaphor. In his book, meaning is mashed up like a pudding." "The All of the If," *New Republic,* 17 March 1997, p. 34.

94. Alfred Kazin writes, "In the struggle between man's effort to find meaning in nature, against the indifference of nature itself, which always eludes him — and this in a world suddenly emptied of God, one where an 'intangible malignity' has reigned from the beginning — Melville's ultimate strangeness is to portray the struggle from the side of nature itself." *God and the American Writer* (New York: Knopf, 1997), 96.

95. Joel Weinsheimer, *Philosophical Hermeneutics and Literary Theory* (New Haven: Yale University Press, 1991), 90. Making effective use of Gadamer's critique of semiotics in *Truth and Method,* Weinsheimer offers in this work a useful corrective to the dominant theory of words as signs.

and social practice. For both structuralism and poststructuralism, it is this arbitrariness that marks the essence of language and its relationship to whatever we would call the reality beyond or beneath it. Tzvetan Todorov correctly observes that "arbitrariness is not, for [Ferdinand de] Saussure, merely one of the sign's various features, but its fundamental characteristic: the arbitrary sign is the sign par excellence."[96] The sharp nominalism of this position resembles that of certain branches of Protestant thought; the main difference is that in the case of structuralism and its sign theory, linguistic determinism has replaced the will of God as the controlling agency. In the modern world, the assumptions of the sign theory have deeply informed the hermeneutics of suspicion and its skeptical reading of the ostensible meanings of words and actions, and they are at the center of structuralism and poststructuralism.

In their own uncertainty about the relationship of words to things, Ishmael and Ahab show themselves to be true sign theorists who take words and natural phenomena to be masks for a hidden will that works out its purposes in mystifying secrecy. But while Ahab and Ishmael may agree that signs are arbitrary, they differ markedly on how we should react to that arbitrariness. The genial and accommodating Ishmael is a pragmatist and postmodernist before his time. He would have us respond to the silence of God by seeking, at all costs, to get along with all the other orphans housed with us on our forlorn planet. With a feat of syllogistic and ecumenical legerdemain, Ishmael justifies his participation in a pagan ritual with Queequeg, his shipmate: "So I kindled the shavings; helped prop up the innocent little idol; . . . kissed his nose; and that done, we undressed and went to bed, at peace with our own consciences and all the world" (54). After all, if the earth is a prison and we never even catch a glimpse of our jailer, then Ishmael concludes that we might as well get along with one another: "It is but well to be on friendly terms with all the inmates of the place one lodges in" (16).

Like the contemporary pragmatists, Ishmael would have us abandon our ultimate concerns and get on with our practical chores. Indeed, he sounds like a prototype of Richard Rorty, the leading voice of contemporary American postmodern pragmatism. "To say that we should drop the idea of truth as out there waiting to be discovered," argues Rorty, "is to say that our purposes would be served best by ceasing to see truth as a deep matter." Like possible points of disagreement between Ishmael's Presbyterianism and

96. Tzvetan Todorov, *Theories of the Symbol,* trans. Catherine Porter (Ithaca: Cornell University Press, 1982), 268.

Queequeg's paganism, arguments about "the nature of truth" and "the nature of God" are stale and unprofitable. But in Rorty's words, "this claim about relative unprofitability, in turn, is just the recommendation that we in fact *say* little about these topics, and see how we get on."[97]

Captain Ahab rejects such pragmatic compromises. He must know the power that has created him, assailed him, and abandoned him. If "all visible objects, man, are but as pasteboard masks," then he will break through them to face the force that overmasters him (144). Ahab is one with his Enlightenment and romantic forebears in understanding God as a power lurking behind the masks he wears to encounter us. But while the Enlightenment rationalists and romantic optimists found comfort in their faith in the self that faced and read those masks, Ahab knows no such consolation. The self as he understands it is guilty and tormented, not innocent and tranquil. It must go behind the sign to learn the mind of the one who signifies: "If man will strike, strike through the mask! How can the prisoner reach outside except by thrusting through the wall? To me, the white whale is that wall. . . . That inscrutable thing is chiefly what I hate; and be the white whale agent, or be the white whale principal, I will wreak that hate upon him" (144). The pain of abandonment and divine indifference is too great for Ahab: "He piled upon the whale's white hump the sum of all the general rage and hate felt by his whole race from Adam down," Melville writes of Ahab, "and then, as if his chest had been a mortar, he burst his hot heart's shell upon it" (160).[98]

97. Rorty, *Contingency, Irony, and Solidarity,* 8.

98. Rorty acknowledges his deep debt to William James, the first and greatest of American pragmatists. In describing the difference between the pluralist and the monist, James maps out neatly the divide that separates Ishmael from Ahab. "But what at bottom is meant by calling the universe many or by calling it one?" James asks. "Pragmatically interpreted, pluralism or the doctrine that it is many means only that the sundry parts of reality *may be externally related.* Everything you can think of, however vast or inclusive, has on the pluralistic view a genuinely 'external' environment of some sort or amount. Things are 'with' one another in may ways, but nothing includes everything, or dominates over everything. . . . The pluralistic world is thus more like a federal republic than like an empire or a kingdom. However much may be collected, however much may report itself as present at any effective centre of consciousness or action, something else is self-governed and absent and unreduced to unity.

"Monism, on the other hand, insists that when you come down to reality as such, to the reality of realities, everything is present to *everything* else in one vast instantaneous co-implicated completeness — nothing can in *any* sense, functional or substantial, be really absent from anything else, all things interpenetrate and telescope together in the great total conflux." *A Pluralistic Universe,* in *William James: Writings 1902-1910,* ed. Bruce Kuklick (New York: Library of America, 1987), 776.

Ahab's complaint against God is directly related to the autonomy that he cherishes. Ahab is possessed by a Cartesian and Enlightenment desire to seal off the natural world and the human psyche from intrusions of the transcendent. To him, the malevolent arbitrariness of God was perfectly symbolized by Moby-Dick's attack upon him. With terrible fury, the divine could break into the human world without warning and with cruel intent. Yet when his consciousness afflicts him, then Ahab finds unbearable the very isolating security he has craved. It is then that he cries out for God to "come in thy lowest form of love," only to find that what had once seemed undesirable now appears utterly impossible. Fearing himself orphaned and abandoned, Ahab strikes out at "the personified impersonal" that faces him in Moby-Dick (417).

While *Moby-Dick* seems to range across the entire vast landscape of modern anxiety about the orphaning of humanity and the world, Fyodor Dostoyevsky's *The Brothers Karamazov* focuses more specifically and profoundly upon the question of "the death of God." The brothers in this novel become orphans, but only through an act of parricide. Through that act Dostoyevsky attempts to fathom the modern experience of metaphysical orphaning. Nietzsche's madman cries out in the marketplace, "God is dead. God remains dead. And we have killed him. . . . Who will wipe this blood off us?"[99] *The Brothers Karamazov* asks that question and attempts to answer it.

Of the myriad hermeneutical issues that Dostoyevsky's novel raises in its exploration of these questions, we can focus very briefly on just one fruitful line of inquiry. I have in mind the conversation that the Devil has with Ivan Karamazov near the novel's close. What Ivan comes to acknowledge in this "conversation with the devil" is that his illegitimate half-brother, Smerdyakov, murdered their father *and did so with Ivan's tacit approval.* What the Devil does is parrot back to Ivan all of the young Karamazov's radical metaphysical, moral, and political judgments. The Devil arrives at a dramatically different conclusion, however, than the one that Ivan has reached:

> "The question now," my young thinker reflected, "is whether or not it is possible for such a period [of utopian perfection] ever to come. If it does come, then everything will be resolved and mankind will finally be settled. But since, in view of man's inveterate stupidity, it may not be settled

99. Friedrich Nietzsche, *The Gay Science,* in *The Portable Nietzsche,* trans. and ed. Walter Kaufmann (New York: Penguin, 1976), 95.

for another thousand years, anyone who already knows the truth is permitted to settle things for himself, absolutely as he wishes, on the new principles. . . . The new man is allowed to become a man-god . . . [and] to jump lightheartedly over any former moral obstacle of the former slave-man, if need be. There is no law for God! Where God stands — there is the place of God! . . . 'Everything is permitted,' and that's that!" It's all very nice; only if one wants to swindle, why, I wonder, should one also need the sanction of truth?[100]

The "Devil's" rhetorical question has intriguing implications for the future of the hermeneutics of suspicion. For the past several decades, while many conservative scholars have been splitting hairs about questions of authorial intention — and have been doing so, to a large extent, on the terms established by a single book *(Validity in Interpretation)* almost thirty years ago — the mainstream theoretical world has been all but overwhelmed by the hermeneutics of suspicion and its proponents.[101] In tracing textual assertions and truth claims to their sources in economic, social, or psychological compulsions, the hermeneutics of suspicion has proved to be a powerful tool for a certain kind of critique. In ways that have often proved to be useful, it has provided a healthy critique of Christian faith and practice. And in the hands of its most ardent advocates, the hermeneutics of suspicion has been used to dismiss or discredit the idea of truthful assertion, of bearing witness, that is at the very core of the Christian faith.

Like the Ivan being queried by the Devil — ". . . if one wants to swindle, why . . . should one also need the sanction of truth?" — the practitioners of suspicion have themselves been subjected to suspicious critique in a series of recent works.[102] As Christian critics work to come to terms with the hermeneutics of suspicion, however belatedly, these works will provide substantial support for the critique of critique, the suspicious reading of suspicion.

100. Fyodor Dostoyevsky, *The Brothers Karamazov,* trans. Richard Pevear and Larissa Volokhonsky (New York: Vintage, 1991), 649.

101. See Paul Ricoeur, *Freud and Philosophy: An Essay on Interpretation,* trans. Denis Savage (New Haven: Yale University Press, 1970), 32ff.

102. See, for instance, Alasdair MacIntyre, *Three Rival Versions of Moral Enquiry: Encyclopaedia, Genealogy, and Tradition* (Notre Dame: University of Notre Dame Press, 1990); Frederick Crews et al., *The Memory Wars: Freud's Legacy in Dispute* (New York: New York Review of Books, 1995); and George Steiner, *No Passion Spent: Essays, 1978-1995* (New Haven: Yale University Press, 1996).

Of all the modern novels that treat the theme of orphaning, none explores its hermeneutical dimensions more tellingly than William Faulkner's *Absalom, Absalom!* Interpretive concerns are central to the novel's subject matter and its formal organization. Its tragic protagonist is Thomas Sutpen, a ruthless plantation builder and owner in the antebellum South. Yet though almost all of the events described in the novel occur in the nineteenth century, Faulkner has the entire story told by narrators in 1909 and 1910. In this manner, he makes the narrators' struggles to interpret the past a subject of equal importance to the tragic story they are trying to comprehend.

There are many orphans in *Absalom, Absalom!,* the most interesting of whom is Charles Bon, the firstborn son of Thomas Sutpen. Bon may not be an orphan in fact, but he is in spirit. When Bon's father, Thomas Sutpen, had discovered that his first wife had some black blood in her, he had abandoned her and their infant son Charles Bon. Sutpen refused to accept a wife and child of mixed blood, for he was desperate to establish himself as a plantation owner in the antebellum South. As he explained to one of his few friends several decades later, he had rid himself of his wife and son because "I found that she was not and could never be, through no fault of her own, adjunctive or incremental to the design which I had in mind, so I provided for her and put her aside.'"[103]

In his late twenties, Charles Bon finally meets Sutpen, but he does not receive even the slightest gesture of recognition from his father. At one point in the novel, Bon looks into the face of his half-brother Henry, Thomas Sutpen's son by his second wife, and meditates upon the mystery of his father's identity as well as his father's absence. "There — " one of the novel's narrators imagines Charles Bon thinking as he stares at his brother, "there — at any moment, second, I shall penetrate by something of will and intensity and dreadful need, and strip that alien leavening from it and look not on my brother's face whom I did not know I possessed and hence never missed, but my father's, out of the shadow of whose absence my spirit's posthumeity has never escaped" (254).[104]

103. William Faulkner, *Absalom, Absalom!* (New York: Vintage, 1990), 194. All further references are to this edition and will be cited in parentheses within the body of the essay.

104. Of the many treatments of *Absalom, Absalom!* that focus on it as a hermeneutical study, the most satisfying remains Cleanth Brooks's chapter on the novel. "Most important of all, however, *Absalom, Absalom!* is a persuasive commentary upon the thesis that much of 'history' is really a kind of imaginative construction. The

The absence of the father casts a shadow upon the spirit, and from that shadow, the "spirit's posthumeity has never escaped." Faulkner's images describe acutely the poignancy of the "post position" and allude to the theological implications of the orphan's predicament. In life as Charles Bon envisions it, we stand alone before the vast immensity of the Other, which is the source of our life but which stubbornly refuses to acknowledge us as its own. No one can mediate the experience of that Other for us, nor can anyone gain access for us to the mind and heart of the Other. Instead, each of us must struggle by "something of will and intensity and dreadful need" to strip off the mask behind which the Other, the Source, the Father, lurks in majestic silence and terrifying obscurity.

In the world of *Absalom, Absalom!,* God the Father confronts men and women without the interceding offices of God the Son. Theologically, we would call this a "Sabellian" world. In a Sabellian or modalist understanding of the Trinity, Jesus is not the god-man who *mediates* our experience of God or God's experience of us. He is instead only one of the masks that God dons for his encounter with us. We can know Jesus as a man but not as God, just as Charles Bon can know Thomas Sutpen as a man but never as the father he longs to meet. In Sabellianism, all we know is that God is on one side of the masks of transcendence, secure in his splendor and isolation. We stand on the other side, staring at them and searching for a sign. Alone on our side of the masks, we at first warmly celebrate our autonomy and then begin to feel the terrible, bracing chill of our solitude.

Helmut Thielicke traces the contemporary revival of Modalism back to Schleiermacher, among other sources. For Schleiermacher, Jesus represented the flowering of full human potential rather than God's taking on of flesh to dwell among us. *"The Redeemer,"* writes Schleiermacher in *The Christian Faith, "is like all men in virtue of the identity of human nature, but distinguished from them all by the constant potency of His God-consciousness, which was a veritable existence of God in Him."*[105] As the Redeemer, Christ saves us by taking us up into his perfected God-consciousness. He does not impart to us grace from an outside source; instead, he provokes within us a response that draws out our own innate powers. "In every work of genius we recognize our own rejected thoughts,"

---

past always remains at some level a mystery, but if we are to hope to understand it in any wise, we must enter into it and project ourselves imaginatively into the attitudes and emotions of the historical figures." *William Faulkner: The Yoknapatawpha Country* (New Haven: Yale University Press, 1963), 311-12.

105. Schleiermacher, *Christian Faith,* sec. 94, 385.

observed Schleiermacher's American contemporary, Emerson. "They come back to us with a certain alienated majesty."[106] All that one needs to do is to change the word "genius" to "divinity," and one has a perfect formula for the German theologian's understanding of the nature of Christ and his work.

But a Christ who discloses to us our own divinity is not God incarnate breaking into our state of finitude and sin. He is merely the supreme embodiment of our own capacities. In the words of Thielicke, "This . . . is shut up with us in finitude" and God reigns alone in "his transcendence . . . above it."[107] For Schleiermacher, the doctrine of the Trinity is like all other doctrines of the faith; it discloses not the particular nature of God but the specific qualities of our experience of God. *"All attributes which we ascribe to God are to be taken as denoting not something special in God,"* he claims, *"but only something special in the manner in which the feeling of absolute dependence is to be related to Him."*[108]

Between God and humanity, then, stand the masks that God always wears to meet us. On one side, God rules in isolated majesty, screened behind his manifold manifestations. As we gaze at the masks, we see not God himself but only the manipulative manner in which he has chosen to encounter us. And the more we strain to look, the more we realize that in those masks we glimpse nothing but puzzling reflections as in a mirror. Like Melville's Ahab and Faulkner's Charles Bon, we are orphaned and trapped in our finitude. Lost in our solitude without a guide, we can only guess at the nature of God behind the masks or wonder, in our more desperate moments, whether there is anything at all behind them.

It was over the course of the nineteenth century that the implications of the modern revival of Modalism became apparent. In his discussion of the history of the doctrine of the Trinity, Thielicke suggests that after Schleiermacher, the "normative role" of human consciousness increased dramatically "within the relation of God and man." It did so because in the modalist scheme of things, the history of salvation was not the record of God's entry into history but "the history of human consciousness as it reflects on God." Initially in Schleiermacher, consciousness was "a mere criterion of the possibility of appropriating revelation," but gradually it became

106. Emerson, "Self-Reliance," in *Emerson: Essays and Lectures,* 259.

107. Helmut Thielicke, *The Doctrine of God and of Christ,* vol. 2 of *The Evangelical Faith,* trans. and ed. Geoffrey W. Bromiley (Grand Rapids: William B. Eerdmans, 1977), 143.

108. Schleiermacher, *Christian Faith,* sec. 50, 194.

the "normative principle" for determining what may count as true statements about God and the scriptures. "The final result is the fully emancipated and completely autonomous consciousness of a radical secularism."

In Schleiermacher's Modalism, Thielicke notes, God reflects himself in human consciousness through the masks he puts on to encounter humanity. But before long in the nineteenth century, Feuerbach, Marx, and Nietzsche would expose those masks to be simple projections of human desire. "Now," writes Thielicke, "the consciousness reflects itself in the ideas of God that it produces." The masks become not manipulative manifestations of the hidden God but mirrors in which we see only our own countenances beamed back to us. Thielicke argues that there is an element of inevitability to the process that leads so quickly from Schleiermacher's theism of consciousness to Nietzsche's atheism of hermeneutical perspectivism. Nietzsche is merely carrying the anthropological revolution of Schleiermacher and others "to its extreme limit. As he puts it, meaning, even . . . the concept of God, is necessarily perspective, perspectivism, in virtue of which every center of power constructs all the rest of the world in terms of itself."[109]

Such is the hermeneutical journey the orphan has traveled from Descartes to Nietzsche. In his essay on skepticism, "Experience," Emerson wrote that "a political orator wittily compared our party promises to western roads, which opened stately enough, with planted trees on either side, to tempt the traveller, but soon became narrow and narrower, and ended in a squirrel-track, and ran up a tree. So does culture with us; it ends in head-ache."[110] And so, the orphans of these novels would seem to say, does the Cartesian *Cogito* in the modern world.

Beyond the Orphaned First Person

In a study of modern philosophy since Descartes, Roger Scruton concludes that "one thing is certain. . . . The assumption that there is a first-person certainty . . . has been finally removed from the centre of philosophy."[111]

109. Thielicke, *Doctrine of God and of Christ*, 149-51. For a reading of how these theological developments played themselves out in nineteenth-century literature in general and in the case of Emily Dickinson in particular, see my *Emily Dickinson and the Art of Belief* (Grand Rapids: William B. Eerdmans, 1998), 43-47, 144-50, 166-74.

110. Emerson, "Experience," in *Emerson: Essays and Lectures*, 478.

111. Scruton, *From Descartes to Wittgenstein*, 284.

And its removal, one might add, has opened the way to modes of hermeneutical reflection far more fruitful than those determined by the orphaned consciousness of the Cartesian *Cogito.*

In *Truth and Method,* for instance, Hans-Georg Gadamer has a criticism of "first-person certainty" in mind when he traces contemporary alienation back to a more pervasive form of alienation, that of historical consciousness since the Enlightenment. The "global demand" of the Enlightenment was the "overcoming of all prejudices." Driven by its desire to secure autonomy of the Cartesian *Cogito* over against tradition and external authority, the Enlightenment established its "fundamental prejudice . . . against prejudice itself, which denies tradition its power."[112]

Gadamer's observation is rich in its implications for our thinking about modern hermeneutical theory and practice. Both the allegorists and the intentionalists question the authority of historical tradition. For the allegorists, that tradition appears to be a history of arbitrary assumptions, none of which are grounded in a truth beyond the conventional uses or assumptions of their time. In this view, prejudices are preferences for which there is no justification beyond that of the provisional consensus of the moment. For the intentionalists, on the other hand, the tradition that stretches between us and the text we are trying to understand is like a desert through which we must travel if we are to drink from the clear springs of the author's mind. In this view, prejudices are like so many mirages dotting the arid landscape; we must see them for the illusions that they are and not let them deter us from our goal.

But for Gadamer, those prejudices are the very things that the interpreters of texts and human actions cannot do without as they begin the work of interpretation. "Long before we comprehend ourselves through the process of self-examination, we understand ourselves in a self-evident way in the family, society, and state in which we live," he argues. *"That is why the prejudices of the individual, far more than his judgments, constitute the historical reality of his being."*[113] Developing a line of thought first artic-

112. Gadamer, *Truth and Method,* 270. Joel Weinsheimer writes of prejudice: "We *already* know. We are always already prejudiced by tradition, which asserts its validity prior to consciousness. The fact that we never completely rid ourselves of prejudice certainly marks the finitude of historical being — but some prejudices are true. The fact that the knower's own being comes into play in his knowledge certainly betrays the limitation of objectivity and method, but it does not prevent truth." *Gadamer's Hermeneutics: A Reading of "Truth and Method"* (New Haven: Yale University Press, 1985), 258-59.

113. Gadamer, *Truth and Method,* 276-77.

ulated in Martin Heidegger's *Being and Time,* Gadamer stresses the manner in which all reading and human understanding begin with the interpreter already interested in, and prejudiced about, that which he or she is trying to interpret. For Heidegger, Paul Ricoeur explains, "hermeneutics is not a reflection on the human sciences, but an explication of the ontological ground upon which these sciences can be constructed."[114] According to Heidegger, the ground upon which those sciences can be built already has its foundation set. The task of the thinker is not, as Descartes held, to construct the intellectual edifice absolutely from scratch, but rather to build creatively with what is already there. The idea of a completely disinterested and prejudice-free interpretation becomes an impossibility for Heideggerian hermeneutics. "The illusion is not in looking for a point of departure," writes Ricoeur about the problem of human understanding, "but in looking for it without presuppositions. There is no philosophy without presuppositions."[115] Nor is there ever any point at which we can "start history over again in . . . [a] moment of self-fathering."

His convictions about the inescapable nature of prejudices and presuppositions led Gadamer to develop the idea of the "fusion of horizons" to describe the interpretive process. The reader sets out by anticipating the discovery of certain things in a text; in the process of reading, he or she finds some assumptions confirmed, some altered, and perhaps still others definitively refuted. The horizons of the text and the reader meet and "fuse," as they both focus upon their object of concern, which is the thing said or pointed to in the text. "The task of hermeneutics is to clarify this miracle of understanding, which is not a mysterious communion of souls, but sharing in a common meaning."[116] To understand another person, or a book, then, one does not put on another's glasses to see the object through entirely different lenses; instead, one looks alongside another upon an object of mutual concern and enters into dialogue in search of understanding.

C. S. Lewis says virtually the same thing as Gadamer in *The Four Loves.* In distinguishing between Friendship and Eros, Lewis offers separate images of the way that partners in these two relationships perceive one another. Under the spell of Eros, lovers stand and gaze into each other's eyes, searching for an ineffable something, while friends stand together

114. Paul Ricoeur, "The Task of Hermeneutics," in *Hermeneutics and the Human Sciences,* trans. and ed. John B. Thompson (Cambridge: Cambridge University Press, 1981), 55.

115. Ricoeur, *The Symbolism of Evil,* 348.

116. Gadamer, *Truth and Method,* 292.

and look upon a shared truth or delight. "Hence we picture lovers face to face but Friends side by side; their eyes look ahead."[117] According to the hermeneutical theory of Gadamer and Ricoeur, a "friendship" model of this kind is far more appropriate for interpretation than is the intentionalists' romantic image of isolated minds straining to reach each other across the voids of time and space.[118]

Although Gadamer's theory of the "fusion of horizons" is often referred to as the "hermeneutical circle," it might more correctly be called the "hermeneutical spiral." The circle imprecisely implies a self-enclosed finality, while the image of the spiral captures more of what Gadamer intends by *wirkungsgeschichtliches Bewusstein,* which his translators render as "the consciousness of being affected by history." What Gadamer means in using this phrase is that there is no such thing as a completely isolated reader who is uninformed by the historical tradition in which he or she is situated. There is no Cartesian moment of "self-fathering" in human understanding, for every reading of a text or human action is grounded in the history of reflection and action that language unfolds. Interpretation begins as a reader anticipates certain things on the basis of his or her tradition and proceeds as text and reader question each other, finding points of fusion in their understanding; it culminates with the production of a revised interpretation that may then shape subsequent preunderstandings of that very text. If the production and interpretation of texts are human actions, then it follows that like all other human actions, these will have both origins in the mysteries of motivation and consequences in the history we inhabit.

While ontological questions about language and tradition dominate Gadamer's phenomenological study of interpretation, the work of Ludwig Wittgenstein concentrates more upon the functions and uses of language in specific contexts of inquiry. In *Philosophical Investigations,* for example, Wittgenstein asks us to "think of the tools in a tool-box," of the hammer, pliers, saws, and nails. "The functions of words are as diverse as the func-

---

117. C. S. Lewis, *The Four Loves* (New York: Harcourt, Brace & World, 1960), 98.

118. The work of the Russian theorist and literary historian Mikhail Bakhtin is also important here. For a succinct discussion of his view of truth as dialogical — a view that overlaps at many points with the insights of Gadamer and Ricoeur — see Gary Saul Morson and Caryl Emerson, *Mikhail Bakhtin: Creation of a Prosaics* (Stanford: Stanford University Press, 1990), 59-62. "Bakhtin's ultimate image of such dialogic faith is, characteristically, a *conversation* with Christ. 'The word as something personal. Christ as Truth. I put the question to him' [Bakhtin]." *Mikhail Bakhtin,* 62.

tions of these objects," he notes. We use those words in many varied ways in the countless "language games" *(Sprachspiel)* we play in ordinary life. According to Wittgenstein, we gain an understanding of the meaning of a word, phrase, or text by examining its place in the surrounding context of human action. "The *speaking* of language is part of an activity, or a form of life," and "to imagine a language means to imagine a form of life." Even that most disciplined of human actions, the regular obeying of rules, makes sense only when we see it as part of a larger scheme of human action and communal life, for "to obey a rule, to make a report, to give an order, to play a game of chess, are *customs* (uses, interpretations)."[119]

Wittgenstein's observations about language raise serious questions about the possibility of discovering an abstract, value-neutral, and prejudice-free foundation for interpretive activity. To understand the words in a text, we must have a related understanding of the human actions involved in the use of those words, "for what makes language teachable is *its connection with observable regularities in human behavior*."[120] In spite of the grip that the ideal of the unbiased reader has on the contemporary Protestant mind, it is clear, according to Anthony Thiselton, "that concepts like 'being redeemed,' 'being spoken to by God' . . . are made intelligible and 'teachable' *not on the basis of private existential experience but on the basis of a public tradition of certain patterns of behavior*." To understand pain, we must observe and reflect upon "pain-behavior," and in like manner, to know what redemption means, we must study the "observable regularities in redemption-behavior."[121]

"Such is the circle," Ricoeur writes in one of his early hermeneutical studies: "hermeneutics proceeds from a prior understanding of the very thing that it tries to understand by interpreting it." This view of hermeneutics is similar to the understanding of interpretation that is implicit in St. Anselm's *"Credo ut intelligam"* ("I believe in order to understand"). Both views are counter to the prevailing Cartesianism of modernity. They assert that before we can understand anything — whether it be the movement of atoms, a collection of poems, a painting in a museum, or a book of the Bible — we must assume things about what we are trying to understand. As Ricoeur puts it, hermeneutics gives us "reason to think that the *Cogito* is

---

119. Ludwig Wittgenstein, *Philosophical Investigations*, trans. G. E. M. Anscombe (Oxford: Blackwell, 1953), §11, 23, 19.

120. Wittgenstein, *Philosophical Investigations*, 81.

121. Anthony Thiselton, *The Two Horizons: New Testament Hermeneutics and Philosophical Description* (Grand Rapids: William B. Eerdmans, 1980), 382.

within being, and not vice versa." If we grant that point, then "the task of the philosopher guided by symbols would be to break out of the enchanted enclosure of consciousness of oneself, to end the prerogative of self-reflection."[122]

Even if we were to argue that the Cartesian model of self-understanding — as it has been employed so relentlessly in the romantic literary tradition and the modern interpretation of the Bible — is still useful because it yields interesting readings, we still face the question of its validity. Considering the nature of language, is it ever possible for a prejudice-free reading of a text to take place? "We are always already biased in our thinking and knowing by our linguistic interpretation of the world," Gadamer observes. "To grow into this linguistic interpretation means to grow up in the world. To this extent, language is the real mark of our finitude."[123] In the larger drama of language, "the consciousness of the individual" plays a very small role.

If Gadamer is correct in his understanding of language, then none of us is ever truly an orphan as an interpreter, just as none of us is ever the sole author of his or her life or the meaning of that life. ("We are never more [and sometimes less] than the co-authors of our own narratives," explains Alasdair MacIntyre. "Only in fantasy do we live what story we please."[124]) When we read, we do so both as individuals with particular needs and expectations and as members of communities whose beliefs inform our understanding. When we read, that is, we do so as people who belong, seek, and act. We belong, to a great extent through language, to the theological, ethnic, and cultural traditions that have molded us as subjects and without whose mediation we could understand nothing; we seek the beauty and truth of the world we inhabit, even as we also seek, through stories and images, to conceive of the world we should like to create and the kinds of persons we should like to become; and we act as readers whose interpretations have both histories and consequences. As it is with the life of the spirit, so it is with reading: there is no finding without seeking. Of course we may discover things that challenge our expectations, but we would discover nothing at all were we not to search.[125]

122. Ricoeur, *The Symbolism of Evil*, 352, 356.

123. Hans-Georg Gadamer, *Philosophical Hermeneutics*, trans. and ed. David E. Linge (Berkeley and Los Angeles: University of California Press, 1976), 64.

124. MacIntyre, *After Virtue*, 213.

125. Ricoeur has written extensively on the tension between reading as a rule-governed activity and reading as an active, creative engagement with the fixity of a

This is not to argue for a form of interpretive determinism. We are not fated to discover only what we have anticipated, for any particular act of reading may overturn the assumptions that we brought to the interpretation of the text. But our very possibility of being changed by the texts we read depends upon our being active seekers rather than disinterested recipients. When we read, we are not isolated subjects who either endanger texts or worship them. Instead, we are members of multiple communities whose traditions make possible our very understanding of what we read, even as those traditions open themselves to the risk of being changed by what we discover when we read.

Neither is this to argue that the questions raised by the ideal of objectivity have no place within our theory of reading. If we dispense with notions of falsification and verification, we are left in the seductively lonely worlds of Stanley Fish's "interpretive communities," in which competing traditions arbitrarily constitute the meanings of texts for their private purposes.[126] We may adjudicate interpretive disputes and test the validity of individual interpretations without having to claim that a single interpretive method exists to resolve all disputes. To interpret with confidence in our ability to acquire an adequate understanding of meaning, as well as an adequate grasp of the truth, we do not need to fall prey either to the impossible drive for certainty undertaken by the intentionalists or to the beguiling liberty promised by the allegorists. If a "text had but one right interpretation and many wrong ones, or many right interpretations and no wrong one, there would not be a problem," explains Joel Weinsheimer.[127] As he points out, in interpreting, we always live with the tension of correctness and creativity.

Martin Luther understood this tension well. In a study of Luther's theology, Paul Althaus notes that Luther was not preoccupied with the

---

text. In "The Bible and the Imagination," he writes, "I would like to consider the act of reading as a dynamic activity that is not confined to repeating significations fixed forever, but which takes place as a prolonging of the itineraries of meaning opened up by the work of interpretation. Through this first trait, the act of reading accords with the idea of a norm-governed productivity to the extent that it may be said to be guided by a productive imagination at work in the text itself." *Figuring the Sacred: Religion, Narrative, and Imagination,* ed. Mark I. Wallace, trans. David Pellauer (Minneapolis: Fortress, 1995), 145.

126. Stanley Fish, *Is There a Text in This Class? The Authority of Interpretive Communities* (Cambridge: Harvard University Press, 1980).

127. Weinsheimer, *Philosophical Hermeneutics and Literary Theory,* 87.

pursuit of certainty, a pursuit that overtook the European mind less than a century after his death. Scripture was not for Luther the pure and sole foundation for the Christian life, but it served instead as the "standard of what can and cannot claim to be good tradition of the church." The Bible set the standard by which the traditions of the church were to be judged, according to Luther. Yet the "'no' to tradition is not a basic and universal 'no,' but is always spoken in a specific situation and based on Scripture."[128]

In hermeneutical terms, this would mean that tradition grounds our reading of texts and opens up the very possibility of understanding them; the principle or standard of criticism — in Luther's case, the scriptures — provides a check upon that tradition. That means that our distancing from tradition is subsequent to our belonging to it. It is in that process of distancing ourselves from our assumptions that our prejudices are tried and modified. A great deal of this inevitable process of testing and confirmation takes place in the silent transaction between reader and text; it also occurs in our dialogue with others, from the past and the present, who have interpreted this same text. "The text presents a limited field of possible constructions," Ricoeur explains. "The logic of validation allows us to move between the two limits of dogmatism and skepticism," between the poles of correctness and creativity, and between the methodical rigidity of the intentionalists and the formless fluidity of the allegorists. In Ricoeur's words, "It is always possible to argue for or against an interpretation, to confront interpretations, to arbitrate between them and to seek agreement, even if this agreement remains beyond our immediate reach."[129]

That is one truth that all who seek to understand hermeneutics would do well to realize. Perfect agreement may be beyond our immediate reach, but that is not cause for despair. Like texts themselves and those who seek to understand them, interpretations are a part of our history. As such, they have pasts that have shaped them and futures that open before them and beckon them. And as one form of human action, interpretation requires of us the same diligence, trust, and perseverance that all our responsible actions do.

---

128. Paul Althaus, *The Theology of Martin Luther,* trans. Robert C. Schultz (Philadelphia: Fortress, 1966), 335.

129. Paul Ricoeur, *Interpretation Theory: Discourse and the Surplus of Meaning* (Fort Worth: Texas Christian University Press, 1976), 79.

Confessing Our Part

I wish to conclude this section with an edifying note. But first a question: To what degree might the condition of the orphan explored by the writers treated in this essay be the product of what one might call complex cultural decisions made in the Western world over the past several hundred years? Is the orphan's experience bound to be the experience of present and future generations? Are Nietzsche's questions perhaps *the* questions for our age?: "Who will wipe the blood off us? . . . Is not the greatness of this deed too great for us?"

The answer of the Christian faith to Nietzsche's question is Yes, this deed is too great a burden for humanity to bear. But, that faith asserts, that burden has already been borne for us. The "greatness of this deed" may be too much for us to bear through heroic self-striving, but it is not too great a burden for confession to carry.

As the Benetton ad for hiking boots so tellingly illustrates, however, we postmoderns have become positively casual about claiming solidarity with Christ's sufferings. Long before those ads appeared, W. H. Auden provided a sharp critique of our glib attempts at identifying with Christ. He did so in a long poem, *Horae Canonicae,* that sets the activities of a typical day within the structure of the canonical hours of worship in the Anglo-Catholic tradition. That typical modern day, in turn, is related anachronistically throughout the poem to the events of Good Friday. Nones, for example, is traditionally observed at three o'clock in the afternoon. And on this day, something tragic has happened suddenly at midday. As the narrator of "Nones" remarks, "We are surprised / At the ease and speed of our deed . . . / It is barely three, Mid-afternoon, yet the blood / Of our sacrifice is already / Dry on the grass."

In a later poem in the cycle, the speaker describes the moment of dropping off to sleep, that "instant of recollection / When the whole thing makes sense." But, he admits, instead of sense,

> All
> I recall are doors banging,
> Two housewives scolding, an old man gobbling,
> A child's wild look of envy,
> Actions, words, that could fit any tale,
> And I fail to see either plot
> Or meaning; I cannot remember
> A thing between noon and three.

As the speaker gropes for the meaning of this single day, of his own life, and of the whole of the history into which he has been thrust, he finds at first that

> Nothing is with me now but a sound,
>   A heart's rhythm, a sense of stars
> Leisurely walking around, and both
>   Talk a language of motion
> I can measure but not read: maybe
>   My heart is confessing her part
> In what happened to us from noon till three . . .

Here, in the mystery of the cross, Auden argues that we cannot know the satisfactions of allegorical coherence without the discipline of confession. The story of the death of Christ, and all the stories of human suffering that flow into and out of that death, will not make sense and will not correspond to our realities until "my heart" confesses "her part / In what happened to us from noon till three."[130]

In *Horae Canonicae* Auden is effectively asserting that if we have been orphaned and abandoned, then, as Paul says in his letter to the Romans, it is to our own desires that God has abandoned us, even if those desires involve killing God himself: "They boast of their wisdom, but they have made fools of themselves. . . . For this reason God has given them up to their own vile desires." In a work written two decades ago, the Nobel prize-winning poet Czeslaw Milosz writes of the modern age, "I did not expect to live in such an unusual moment. / When the God of thunders . . . / would humble people to the quick, / allowing them to act whatever way they wished." Given over to their own desires, Milosz writes,

> People, afflicted with an incomprehensible distress,
>   were throwing off their clothes on the piazzas so that nakedness
>   might call for judgment.
> But in vain they were longing after horror, pity, and anger.[131]

As a word of judgment, the Christian faith claims first that the distortions of the human will drove Christ to the cross. If God has been killed

130. Auden, *Horae Canonicae,* in *Collected Poems,* ed. Edward Mendelson (New York: Random House, 1976), 484-85.

131. Milosz, "Oeconomia Divina," in *The Collected Poems, 1931-1987* (New York: Ecco, 1988), 235-36.

and humanity abandoned, then it is we who have wielded the weapon. As Anthony Thiselton writes at the close of this book, the law is meant to expose human responsibility for the "failure, evil, suffering, and fallenness" of the world. Confession is a part of Christian hermeneutical endeavor, because our self-understanding and interpretive skills share in the brokenness of our condition. As readers, we need to be redeemed.

Yet as Thiselton goes on to point out, the gospel of the Christian faith is the news of our liberation from bondage to sin and the law. "The covenant of *promise* is a dispensation of *grace: of change by divine agency, giving and given,*" Thiselton explains. As a word of promise, Christian faith affirms that God is not trapped in his tomb and sealed off from his world. The good news is that when the heart confesses "her part in what happened to us from noon till three," we, the orphans of our age, may begin to learn how to read — both our experiences and our books — as the heirs of eternity.

II

Narrative Hermeneutics

CLARENCE WALHOUT

Texts as Objects of Action

Because the writing and reading of texts are actions that occur in the context of social and historical life, texts and the language that composes them are never autonomous and context-free. Thus, a theory of hermeneutics needs to show how language and texts function in relation to human actions. This is the main topic for the second section of our book. In this essay I will be chiefly concerned with written texts and, more specifically, with fictional narratives.

I will also be using Nicholas Wolterstorff's distinction between texts as objects of action and texts as instruments of action.[1] We perform many actions, Wolterstorff notes, with the goal of producing objects, and among these objects are written texts. Since texts are objects produced by actions, we must see them in relation to the actions that produced them. Texts acquire meaning by virtue of their place within complex chains of actions.

But texts can be instruments of action as well as objects of action. By means of texts, authors and readers perform certain additional actions, such as communicating with others, describing nature, expressing emotions and beliefs, and interpreting the implications of a story. Hermeneutics, thus, should not be limited to viewing texts simply as objects that have

---

1. Nicholas Wolterstorff, *Works and Worlds of Art* (Oxford: Clarendon Press, 1980), x, 15-16; and *Art in Action: Toward a Christian Aesthetic* (Grand Rapids: William B. Eerdmans, 1980), 14.

certain properties. We need to explore what it means to say that a text is both an object and an instrument of action.

Texts and Contexts

The word *meaning* often connotes the concept of a self-contained "sense" lodged within the sentences of a text. Since this conception of meaning is what I will later bring into question, I should say at the outset that an action theory of texts concentrates on function, that is, on the role of a text in chains of action initiated by authors and readers. Meanings are not simply lodged within a text to remain there inert until they are extracted by readers; the meaning of a text is not something that is cut off from and made independent of the actions involved in producing and interpreting a text. One of the first questions for hermeneutics is this: "What actions are performed in the making and in the use of a text?" Actions acquire meaning from their functional relationship to other actions in a chain of interdependent actions, and the objects produced by or used in these actions need to be understood in relation to these actions. In order to grasp the meaning of a text, therefore, we need go outside the text as well as inside it.

To clarify why this is the case, let us examine the relation of the structure of a sentence to its semantic function, using the models of speech-action theory. Every sentence has a subject that identifies what the subject stands for and a predicate that indicates what is being predicated about the subject. But in addition the sentence as a whole may be used to say something, that is, to form a proposition. For example, take the sentence "David will go tomorrow." We may use this sentence to identify a person, David, about whom we predicate something, namely that he will go tomorrow. But in addition we may use the sentence as a whole to say that David will go tomorrow. These three things — identifying, predicating, and saying — are distinguishable. We use the predicate to say of David that he will go tomorrow, but we could use these words to predicate the same thing of Joe or Bill or anyone. Similarly, we use the subject to identify David, but we could use that same subject to identify any number of persons or things named David. What we do by way of the sentence as a whole, however, is to say that David will go tomorrow. We use the combination of subject and predicate to perform an action (saying) which is distinguishable from the actions of identifying and predicating.

The need for these distinctions is evident in two ways. First, many sentences include indexicals: elements such as demonstrative pronouns, first-person pronouns, proper names, certain adverbs, and time indicators. The reference or designation of these indexicals can be understood only if we know their context of use; they cannot be understood from the subject and predicate alone. For example, if someone utters the sentence "David Jones will go tomorrow," we know that he is predicating of someone identified as David Jones that he will go tomorrow. But if we are to understand what he is saying by way of the sentence, we will have to know who David Jones is and the specific time designated by the word *tomorrow*. And these things we cannot learn from the subject and predicate alone or from the syntactic relationship of the subject and predicate. We cannot understand the meaning of the sentence unless we know its function in the specific situation of the sentence utterance. Indexicals are important elements in the sense or meaning of many sentences, but their meaning or semantic function cannot be fully discerned from the words and syntax of the sentences themselves.

Furthermore, the sense of a sentence depends also on what speech-action theorists call the illocutionary force of the sentence, that is, the purpose for which the sentence is used. Sentences are used not only to assert but also to ask, command, promise, insist, concede, forgive, and the like. For example, the sentence we have been using — "David Jones will go tomorrow" — could be used to insist, concede, or promise as well as to assert. But its use in any particular situation can be known only if we know the context of its use. The illocutionary force of a sentence cannot be determined from the language or syntax alone. Thus, because of the presence of indexicals we will in many instances have to look beyond the sentence in order to understand what is being said by the sentence; and always we will have to go beyond the sentence in order to determine the illocutionary force of its utterance.

Another general principle that is relevant for an action theory of hermeneutics has to do with the temporal nature of actions. They begin at a given moment, move through subsequent moments, and come to an end. The objects that are produced by our actions cannot be fully understood apart from the sequence of actions which produces them. The import of this principle can be seen clearly when we move from sentences to the text as a whole. Earlier hermeneutical models which claim that meanings are wholly contained within the structures of a text are fraught with difficulties.

One of the most rigorous of these earlier attempts to define a text as an object possessing self-contained meanings can be found in Roman

Ingarden's book *The Literary Work of Art*.[2] Ingarden argues that the meaning of a text is contained in the "many-layered structure" that constitutes the text as an intentional object. His view is that language projects "purely intentional correlates" that serve as the objects to which the words and sentences refer. In the case of real judgments or scientific descriptions, the intentional correlates are the existing objects that we encounter in actual experience. However, in the case of literary or fictional judgments and descriptions, the intentional correlates only simulate real objects; they are "quasiobjects," *analogues* of real objects and states of affairs. A fictional text as a whole, then, projects via its language an imagined world made up of imagined objects and states of affairs. It seems evident, however, that words and sentences do not of themselves have intentions or intentional correlates but have them only as a consequence of the speech actions of those who utter the words and sentences. As Wolterstorff concludes in his recent book *Divine Discourse*, sentences considered only in the context of a text are "not enough to determine the noematic content of that act of discourse."[3] When we speak, we often do correlate words and things so that the words themselves appear to hold or "intend" certain meanings: the word *apple*, for example, designates a certain kind of fruit, not just any kind. But words acquire these dependable or "intended" meanings only because we habitually associate them with certain objects and use them for certain purposes. The meanings are not lodged in the words per se but in our continued use of the words for certain purposes and in certain ways. We could, for example, use the word *apple* to refer to a city or a recalcitrant child.

In support of his view, Ingarden argues that the meanings of a fictional text are established for us by the complex internal relationships of language structures through the entire text. These linguistic interdependencies create in the text various "strata" or structures of meaning that fix the meanings the author intends. The result is that the language structures contain an "intentional" meaning apart from the author. An analysis of the "many-layered" strata of a text will, in Ingarden's view, reveal the intentional meaning of the text. Such a position seems also to be implied in Paul Ricoeur's early view of the distantiation of the text from its author. A written text, Ricoeur says, ex-

---

2. Roman Ingarden, *The Literary Work of Art*, trans. George G. Grabowicz (Evanston: Northwestern University Press, 1973).

3. Nicholas Wolterstorff, *Divine Discourse: Philosophical Reflections on the Claim that God Speaks* (Cambridge: Cambridge University Press, 1995), 152.

ists at some distance from its author and hence must be interpreted as a language structure independent of its author. Since the author is no longer present to be questioned, the meanings must be derived from the language of the text.[4] For Ricoeur, as for Ingarden, this is not a disastrous situation, for they believe that the text has certain structures that will disclose the "sense" of the text. On this point Wolterstorff disagrees. There is, he argues, "no such thing as the sense of a text,"[5] that is, no sense of a textual meaning self-contained in and accessible from the text alone.

We can illustrate the difficulties with a textual theory such as Ingarden's with an example taken from Keats's "On First Looking into Chapman's Homer." Keats writes,

> Much have I travell'd in the realms of gold,
>   And many goodly states and kingdoms seen;
>   Round many western islands have I been
> Which bards in fealty to Apollo hold.
> Oft of one wide expanse had I been told
>   That deep brow'd Homer ruled as his demesne . . .[6]

Every gloss on this poem takes the word *Homer* in line six as a reference to the Homer who stands behind *The Iliad* and *The Odyssey*. Yet on Ingarden's view, the Homer of line six could only be an analogue of the actual Homer, since a literary text refers only to intentional or "quasi" objects, not to actual objects. Furthermore, if the intentional correlate of the word *Homer* exists as a quasi object distinct from the real "object" that is the Greek poet Homer, then every literary text which uses the word *Homer* must project a distinct quasi object. In that case, there is potentially (in literary texts) an infinite number of intentional correlates for the word *Homer*, each one of which is distinct from all the others and none of which is identical with the Greek poet named Homer. Even if such a conception were possible, the relationships among those distinct correlates and among the recurrences of the word *Homer* would remain problematical.

4. Paul Ricoeur, *Hermeneutics and the Human Sciences: Essays on Language, Action, and Interpretation*, ed. and trans. John B. Thompson (Cambridge: Cambridge University Press, 1981), 131-44, 197, 221; and see Ricoeur, *Interpretation Theory: Discourse and the Surplus of Meaning* (Fort Worth: Texas Christian University Press, 1976).

5. Wolterstorff, *Divine Discourse*, 172.

6. John Keats, "On First Looking into Chapman's Homer," in *The Complete Poetry and Selected Prose of John Keats*, ed. Harold Edgar Briggs (New York: Modern Library, 1951), 35, lines 1-6.

It appears more intuitively correct to hold that all uses of the word *Homer* (when designating the Greek poet) have as their correlate the Homer that stands behind *The Iliad*. But in that case, the correlate of the sixth line of Keats's poem is not contained exclusively in the "intentional" world of the text but appears in the actual world that exists outside the text. In more ordinary terms, the word *Homer* in line six of Keats's poem refers to the Greek poet Homer. If this is the case, we may identify certain of the referents of a literary text with the real objects of history. In those cases the "intentional correlates" of a literary text are actual objects in the real world.

The view that the words and sentences of a text gain their meaning from their internal structure has a certain attractiveness, but its weakness is evident even more clearly when we consider the role of authorship in textual interpretation. Theories of textual autonomy typically underplay the importance of authorial intention and frequently ignore the significance of authorship altogether. Ingarden deals with the question of authorial intention by treating it as a problem of narrative voice. He distinguishes several kinds of narrative strategies, but he thinks the narrator is always within the world of the text.[7] Even when the narrator is not a character in the narrative, as in the case of the third-person omniscient author, Ingarden holds that "It is as if an invisible and never determinately represented person were wandering through the represented world and showing us the objects as they appear from his point of view."[8]

The pervasive influence of this view in midcentury formalist literary criticism is evident in a 1950 essay by Walker Gibson, in which he comments,

> It is now common in the classroom as well as in criticism to distinguish carefully between the author of a literary work of art and the fictitious *speaker* within the work of art. . . . It is this speaker who is real in the sense most useful to the study of literature, for the speaker is made of language alone, and his entire self lies on the page before us in evidence.[9]

But since texts do not autonomously contain all the data needed for interpretation, the narrative voice of a text, in whatever form it takes, may be

---

7. Ingarden, *The Literary Work of Art*, 230.
8. Ingarden, *The Literary Work of Art*, 130.
9. Walker Gibson, "Authors, Speakers, Reader, and Mock Readers," *College English* 11 (1950): 265-69.

considered in relation to the real author, whose actions in forming the text are relevant to textual understanding. In speech-action theory the issue of authorship once again assumes importance, and new ways of dealing with it become possible. Not only do we concern ourselves "with the meanings of words and their place in the text," but we also "must bring into play considerations of what the author would and would not have wanted to say."[10]

Knowledge about an author's intentions is not *necessary* for interpretation, but an awareness of the author's actions in forming a text makes us more conscious of the author's presence in a text and more willing to recognize the potential value of a knowledge of those intentions. Even aside from intentions, however, what an author *does* in forming a text is always crucial to hermeneutics, and we can analyze these actions apart from what the author subjectively intended. In that analysis, we can examine the ways in which an author uses language and the ways in which the author's actions enable language to function.

In the following sections I will examine how the meanings of texts are related to their structures and language. But I have no desire or reason to efface the author, supplanting him or her with a concept of textual intentionality. I am abandoning the notion of textual intentionality, then, and focusing rather on how textual structures arise out of the actions and intentions of authors.

Reference and Mimesis

The foregoing discussion raises questions about how texts are related both to the actions of authors and to the world outside the text. These knotty questions are focused in discussions of two controversial concepts: *reference* and *mimesis*. Ever since Plato and Aristotle established *mimesis* (imitation) as a key concept in textual understanding, the term has proved to be elusive and protean.[11] In the twentieth century, the term *mimesis* has generally been suspect because of a pervasive philosophical skepticism. If reality as it is in itself is unknowable, what does it mean to say that texts imitate reality? In modern discussions of literary criticism, the term *refer-*

10. Wolterstorff, *Divine Discourse,* 229.
11. Cf. Gunter Gebauer and Christoph Wulf, *Mimesis: Culture, Art, Society,* trans. Don Reneau (Berkeley and Los Angeles: University of California Press, 1995).

ence tends to replace the term *mimesis,* and many theoretical debates have focused on the problem of the referentiality of language. Thus, in order to evaluate the concept of *mimesis,* we need also to examine the much-debated concept of *reference.*

Most of the words in a fictional text do not refer to entities or states of affairs in the real world, and thus questions pertaining to the referents of the language of fiction do not directly raise questions about the nature of reality. The snake that bit Jim in Twain's novel *Huckleberry Finn* does not exist in the actual world, at least not in the same sense that an ordinary snake does. We may bypass, therefore, the ontological conundrums centering on the nature of reality and the nature of the referents. The question for the understanding of a fictional text is, Can its language have reference at all, and if it can, how can that referentiality be understood?

Some literary theorists have suggested that fictional texts require a notion of *self-reference.* On this view the referent is available in language itself: words have meaning because their referential power is grounded in their relationships to other words within a language system. Tzvetan Todorov, for example, says,

> Literature enjoys, therefore, a particularly privileged status among semiotic activities. It has language as both its point of departure and its destination; language furnishes literature as its abstract configurations as well as its perceptible material — it is both mediator and mediatized.[12]

Other literary theorists have made the claim that fictional language is *nonreferential.* If *reference* designates the relationship of words to things, then fictional language is different from ordinary language because fictional language has no referents that actually exist. This view may be seen in John Ellis's *The Theory of Literary Criticism: A Logical Analysis:*

> Nowhere in current theory of literature is it clearer than in the dispute over the problem of definition [of literature] that the reference theory of meaning is the barrier to progress. . . . Of these [commonsense notions of the logic of language], the most pervasive, and therefore the most pernicious for literary theory, has been the reference theory of meaning.[13]

12. Tzvetan Todorov, *The Poetics of Prose,* trans. Richard Howard (Ithaca: Cornell University Press, 1977), 20-21.

13. John M. Ellis, *The Theory of Literary Criticism: A Logical Analysis* (Berkeley and Los Angeles: University of California Press, 1974), 12, 26.

A variant of this view is evident in the position taken by Michael Riffaterre, who suggests that in literary texts the referential aspect of language must be transcended:

> This is proof at least [the point here concerns a critic who was too pre-occupied with literal or referential meaning] that no matter what the poem ultimately tells us that may be quite different from ordinary ideas about the real, the message has been so constructed that the reader has to leap the hurdle of reality.[14]

Thus, what makes the poem, what constitutes its message, has little to do with what it tells us, that is, with referentiality. It has everything to do with the way the poem twists the referential codes out of shape by substituting its own structure for their structures.

The denial of referentiality stems from the desire to avoid the metaphysical problems that focus on the relationship of language to reality. A more general strategy for dealing with referentiality in fiction is possible, however. By introducing a conception of *descriptive reference,* we may place metaphysical problems at one remove from the problems of textual interpretation. This term suggests that language points to or designates objects or states of affairs, but it does not require us to specify the ontological status of those objects that are descriptively pointed out. We may say that the snake in *Huckleberry Finn* is the one that bit Jim and that the word *snake* in the novel refers to or designates that particular snake. We can do this without having to raise the issue of this snake's relation to real snakes in the actual world. (This relation is what we will subsequently treat as an issue of mimesis rather than of reference.)

Using this conception of reference, we may say that all language has reference and that words designate or point to objects and states of affairs in a descriptive way. In the case of fiction, the words *Huck Finn* designate the person Huckleberry Finn, the main character of Twain's novel. The issues surrounding the relation of this fictional character to people in the actual world may be held in abeyance. By restricting the term *reference* in this way, we may distinguish reference, as the designating function of language, from mimesis, which concerns the relation of words to reality. The strategy of suppressing issues of mimesis and focusing instead on the issue of referentiality turns out to be unproductive and ob-

14. Michael Riffaterre, *Semiotics of Poetry* (Bloomington: Indiana University Press, 1978), 7.

fuscating. Both terms are needed, and the relation between them needs clarification.

Let me propose a way of seeing the relationship between *reference* and *mimesis*. The language of a novel descriptively refers to or designates the fictional objects and states of affairs that the author picks out or projects by means of the language. We may regard these objects and states of affairs as constituting the world of the novel. As long as we limit our concern to the descriptive references of the novel's language, we are only surveying or mapping out its fictional world, that is, seeing clearly the states of affairs that are being descriptively pointed out. For example, the language of *Huckleberry Finn* refers descriptively to the states of affairs in which Huck Finn finds himself in Mark Twain's novel. Our concern with reference is a concern only with an accurate understanding of what these states of affairs are.

After the world that Huck Finn inhabits has been surveyed, however, there arise other interesting and important questions for textual criticism. Such questions concern, for example, the cultural significance of the novel, its social and moral value for readers, its relation to its historical milieu, its relationship to the reader's historical situation, and the like. These subsequent questions involve the ways in which the fictional world of the text is related to the actual world of authors and readers, and these are questions of mimesis. I am proposing, then, that the term *reference* be used to indicate the relationship of the language of the text to the world that is projected by the language, and that the word *mimesis* be used to indicate the relationship of the fictional world projected by the text to the actual world that we inhabit. Questions about referentiality are questions about the fictional world projected by the text; questions about mimesis are questions about the relation of the fictional world to the actual world. While the two concepts are interrelated, they are also distinct and can be examined independently. All fictional texts are referential because they designate characters, events, and situations, and all fictional texts are mimetic because their fictional worlds stand in a certain relationship to the actual world of authors and readers.

The failure to distinguish clearly between reference and mimesis lies behind certain problems in contemporary literary theory, problems that can be exemplified by Wolfgang Iser's *The Act of Reading*. Iser repeatedly calls attention to the fact that fictional texts cannot refer to real things and that the referents must be constructed in the minds of readers according to the directions given by the linguistic signs of the text. The lack of reference to real objects leads Iser to believe that the fictional work exists in the interaction between the language of the text and the consciousness of the reader. In the process of reading, the reader actualizes the potential meanings of the linguistic signs: "Text and reader converge by way of a situation which depends on both for its 'realization.'"[15]

Iser wants to deny the referential function of a work of fiction while retaining the notion that it can provide in its structural patterns "the thought systems which it has chosen and incorporated in its own repertoire."[16] The power of a novel to present "thought systems or models of reality" apparently comes from the fact that in fictional language reference is suspended. Thus, while the text presents no "reality" in the sense of reference to "real" things, it can offer us a view or model of reality. But if reference is suspended because there is no reference to "real" things, then there is also no mimesis, no "imitation" of reality. Iser presents a model in which the work of fiction exists in the minds of readers in the acts of reading. Because of the structure of its linguistic signifiers, readers are able to actualize the potential meanings of the text. These meanings are "thought systems" or "world-pictures" that offer readers a model of reality but not a picture of reality.

What is it that has led so many literary critics in the twentieth century to suspect or attempt an escape from the concepts of reference and mimesis? Is it possible to escape these concepts even on their own terms? Many of the problems they raised seem now to be specious ones created by certain formalist principles. First, even if we conceive of texts as sign systems that guide the actualizing of the fictional world in the minds of readers, is not the world that is actualized the one designated by the language of the text? And if this world is the one designated by the signifiers of the text, is this not what we mean by "reference"? "Reference" in this neutral sense does not commit us to metaphysical judgments about the nature of reality.

Second, if the text produces in our minds "models of reality" or "world-pictures," how would we recognize these as models unless we had some prior notion of reality or of a world? How is it possible to identify what fiction gives us as a world-picture unless we have some idea of what a world-picture is? The only source of and basis for that prior idea is the ac-

---

15. Wolfgang Iser, *The Act of Reading: A Theory of Aesthetic Response* (Baltimore: The Johns Hopkins University Press, 1978), 68.

16. Iser, *The Act of Reading*, 72.

tual world we encounter in our experience. But this relation is what is designated by the term *mimesis.* While it is true that mimesis has been defined in many specific ways that reflect many different views of reality, in a broad sense mimesis concerns the relation between the worlds projected by texts and the actual world of our experience. In itself the term does not imply a view of reality, even though a particular theory of mimesis may involve a view of reality.

Since any theory of fictional texts as objects necessarily involves the relation of language to the projected or imagined world of the text on the one hand (reference) and the relation of that imagined world to the actual world of our experience on the other hand (mimesis), it is not possible to escape questions of reference and questions of mimesis. The challenge is to give substantive definition to these relational terms. How can we understand *reference* and *mimesis* as the key terms in understanding texts as objects?

I have indicated how the term *reference* can be detached from particular views of reality. We need to do the same for the term *mimesis.* Historically, mimesis has not always implied that the world of the text is a realistic copy of actual states of affairs. It has implied for some that fictional states of affairs exhibit structural patterns of action which stand in a relation of resemblance (similarity or difference) to structural patterns of action that exist outside the text. When Aristotle described literature (art) as an imitation of an action, he was not implying that language is a copy or mirror of actual states of affairs. Instead, he held that the particular events designated by the language of a text exhibit a structural pattern that in turn exemplifies a paradigmatic or universal pattern of action. The language of *Oedipus Rex,* for example, gives us the story of Oedipus. The story of Oedipus in turn exhibits a particular pattern of tragic action that we can identify and understand because of its relationship to a universal paradigmatic pattern of tragic action. Mimesis, then, specifies the relationship of the actions depicted in *Oedipus Rex* to the pattern of tragic action that can be defined extratextually as a "model" or "system." In our terminology, the language of the text is used to project and thus to refer to an imagined world. And this imagined world stands in a certain relationship — a mimetic relationship — to the actual world outside or behind the text.

The term *mimesis,* however, need not entail Aristotle's metaphysics, and the patterns of action that the text "imitates" need not be conceived of as universal or ideal paradigms. Gebauer and Wulf, in their encyclopedic book on mimesis, make this clear. After reviewing the history of the concept from Plato to Derrida, the authors make a number of general conclusions, including the following one: "Mimesis construes anew already construed worlds. . . . Mimetic new interpretation is at the same time a new perception."[17] With regard to fictional narratives, mimesis involves a relation between the imagined world of the text and the actual world as it is perceived and interpreted by the author of the text.[18] The actual world we have been speaking of is a world that is already interpreted, and mimesis need not therefore be conceived of as an "imitation" of a fixed or finalized world. Mimesis may be detached from an Aristotelian or other metaphysical theory of the nature of the actual world.

Mimesis in this basic sense is inescapable. The world that the author projects in a fictional narrative can only be imagined in relationship to the actual world as the author experiences and construes it. But if the concept of mimesis is in this broad and neutral sense inescapable, what is the source of our modern difficulty with the concept? The difficulty, I think, is not with the concept of mimesis per se but with our hermeneutical thinking about texts, and specifically our thinking about the mimetic relation of text to world. And this hermeneutical problem arises from our various understandings of the actual world as much as from our various readings of the text itself. If we as authors and readers have differing views of the actual world, how can we say that the imagined world is an "imitation" of the actual world or stands in some kind of mimetic relation to the actual world? What actual world do we mean? If we have no fixed or determinate concept of the actual world, how can we give the concept of mimesis any credence? If our conceptions of the actual world are fluid and diverse, there can be nothing definitive that can be imitated, and hence the concept of mimesis becomes suspect. As long as the actual world was conceived as a stable and knowable entity, the concept of mimesis could flourish. But in an era in which common assumptions about the nature of reality have been deconstructed and destabilized, how can the concept of mimesis still be a tenable one?

My argument here is that if the concept of mimesis can be loosened from Aristotelian and all other theories of reality, then the problem speciously associated with mimesis can be recognized as a hermeneutical problem of interpreting our world and not a problem with mimesis per se.

17. Gebauer and Wulf, *Mimesis*, 317.
18. Gebauer and Wulf call this imagined world a "mimetic world," whereas I believe it is more accurate to speak of mimesis as a relation between worlds.

Mimesis is concerned with the *relation* among worlds rather than with a determinate understanding of the actual world. How we construe this mimetic relationship in the case of a particular text depends, of course, on our theories about reality and the actual world, but the concept of mimesis is not itself thereby under attack. Our interpretations of the mimetic relation of particular narratives to the actual world will vary according to our understandings of the actual world, but the mimetic relation persists irrespective of our conceptions of the actual world.

When we recognize that our conflicting views of a text often arise out of our conflicting views of actual life and experience, then we see also that mimesis is not, properly speaking, a relationship between the unstable or variable worlds of fiction and the fixed or determinate actual world. Ironically enough, the opposite is the case. Mimesis involves a relation between the fixed worlds of fictional texts and the variable and unstable conceptions of the actual world. Once the fictional narrative has been completed, its imagined world is unchanging and unchangeable. The actual world of experience, on the other hand, is subject to time and change, and our conceptions of the actual world vary over time in response to the historical and cultural circumstances of our experience. While we may differ in our interpretations of the imagined world of the novel (that is, of the text as object), our hermeneutical differences owe much more to the strong differences in how we interpret the actual world of our everyday experiences.

The concept of mimesis has been suspect in much twentieth-century critical theory because of our movement away from Aristotle's metaphysics more than from our movement away from his conception of art and imagination. Even though definitions of the term *mimesis* have taken many forms throughout history, Aristotle seems incontrovertibly right in the *Poetics* when he says that poetry (or imaginative literature) is defined by mimesis. If we liberate the concept of mimesis from fixed paradigms of reality, we may interpret mimetic relationships hermeneutically without rejecting the concept of mimesis per se. We need not throw out the baby with the bathwater.

To conclude, the mimetic relationship of imagined worlds and actual worlds is a necessary property of fictional texts, and it is this relationship that accounts for the historical variety and flexibility that we discover in fiction. The mimetic relationship creates hermeneutical difficulties, but it also prevents us from conceiving of texts as linguistic objects cut loose from their moorings in an actual world and allowed to drift in some detached sea of aesthetic autonomy. The fictional text is not to be thought of as a carbon copy or mirror of the world, but it is nevertheless anchored in the world. To show how mimesis results from this necessary anchoring of fiction in the actual world is the subject of the next section.

Imagined and Actual Worlds

In the previous section I separated the concept of mimesis from the concept of referentiality and suggested that both are important concepts in the hermeneutical understanding of texts, and in particular of fictional texts. I suggested, further, that a mimetic relationship of a fictional or imagined world to the actual world is a relation of resemblance, one of similarities and differences. We turn now to a further clarification of how this mimetic relationship can be understood. Our understanding of narrative fiction involves an analysis of how its imagined world is related to the actual world that we inhabit; understanding cannot be based solely on an analysis of the internal states of affairs presented in the fictional text.

The mimetic relationship may be clarified by the observation that all knowledge is grounded in the comparisons we make among the states of affairs that we encounter or observe. In everyday life we interpret new experiences and events in relationship to those that are already known to us. Objects, persons, words, and situations remain strange to us until we can place them in a frame of reference that is already familiar; our understanding of new or strange phenomena depends on our ability to bring them into familiar contexts.

We might better understand the mimetic function of imagined or fictional worlds by considering first an example of how we arrive at understanding in the case of ordinary or nonmimetic relationships. Consider the problem of understanding personal identity. How are we able to recognize a person at successive moments in time, and, indeed, over long periods of time? We recognize a person whom we have not seen for twenty years as the identical person we knew twenty years earlier in spite of the many changes that have occurred. To conceive of identity as an unchanging essence presents us with difficulties, as Paul Ricoeur demontrates in *Oneself as Another*,[19] for every moment alters, however slightly, the ele-

---

19. Paul Ricoeur, *Oneself as Another*, trans. Kathleen Blamey (Chicago: University of Chicago Press, 1992), 27-39.

ments that constitute a person. And the conception of identity as the "essential" properties of a person still would not explain how we recognize changes in a person over time. The physical appearance of a person, of course, helps us recognize him or her, but our sense of a person's identity is only partly based on physical appearances. Certainly our sense of someone's "personhood" or "personality" is not simply a matter of physical recognition.

How, then, do we distill and recognize a person's identity from that person's many and varied actions, none of which may be exactly like any other? We do so by observing those actions, comparing them, and marking certain patterns of action. Over time, we correct or modify or enlarge our understanding on the basis of new observations and comparisons. Our conception of a person's identity is never final, since the person is constantly performing new actions; yet our conception is reliable because certain patterns of action become familiar. As Anthony Thiselton shows in *Interpreting God and the Postmodern Self*, this feature of identity is clearly evident in narrative. A narrative, fictional or biographical, "traces the destiny and responsibility of 'the same' self amidst changes which may sometimes render it almost unrecognizable as this same self."[20] In spite of changes in a person, courts of law, for example, as well as friends and acquaintances, recognize that an identity endures through the changes in a person's life.

In addition to this, we grasp a person's identity because we recognize every individual as like or unlike other persons. Jane is Jane because she is different from Jill or because she is like Joan. Without our complex sense of other persons, we could not grasp the identity of a particular person. Not only this. We also imagine hypothetical situations to enrich our understanding of a person's identity. We imagine what a certain person would do in a certain situation, what it would be like to be another person or to act as another person. We fantasize about other persons, real and imaginary, as a means for understanding others and ourselves. We are constantly creating models of persons and modifying and enriching our models in an effort to gain ever more confident understanding. Anthony Thiselton writes, "Part of the safeguard against self-deception and manipulation is the task of listening to other selves in mutuality and self-criticism. This belongs to that aspect of selfhood which has to do with

---

20. Anthony C. Thiselton, *Interpreting God and the Postmodern Self: On Meaning, Manipulation, and Promise* (Grand Rapids: William B. Eerdmans, 1995), 74.

intersubjectivity and more especially with moral and political responsibility in the context of community and traditions."[21]

This account of the process of understanding identity will help us grasp what is involved in the understanding of narrative fiction. All actions are historical, occurring in time and having a temporal structure; understanding occurs when we see the relation of prior acts and prior moments to subsequent acts and subsequent moments. Such is the case even for our understanding of mathematical and logical propositions, for such propositions cannot be understood discretely but only in relation to our prior understanding of related propositions. The relations themselves among logical propositions are atemporal and exist apart from human acts of understanding, but we can understand them only through a process of discovering, proposing, testing, and accepting or rejecting. Understanding, in short, occurs as a temporal process wherein new propositions are proposed and tested in relation to propositions that are already familiar. New theories, as Thomas Kuhn and others point out, can be proposed and evaluated only in the context of theories already held. Such is the condition that history places on understanding.

If the historicity of actions implies that all understanding is based on a relation of resemblance between the new and the familiar, then all understanding is also dynamic or progressive. Every moment introduces new perceptions and contexts in which the new and the familiar are continuously interacting. Usually these interactions are so pervasively regulated by conventions and habits that we hardly notice the constantly changing patterns of our experiences and thoughts. Nevertheless, we are constantly absorbing, evaluating, and using new experiences. And we do so by relating them, consciously or not, to the patterns of experience that we have previously developed. We may describe this as a process of *modeling*. Most of our models for action are conventional — we simply do things as we have become accustomed to doing them. But if we modify the typical patterns of our actions, we do so by imagining and choosing among alternative possibilities for action. Our choices may range from the automatic to the deliberately self-conscious, but in every case a pattern of relationships or a *model* for action is operative. Without such models our actions would be random and purposeless.

The process of understanding just described also operates in our understanding of fictional texts. Fictional worlds function as models whereby

21. Thiselton, *Interpreting God and the Postmodern Self*, 71.

we explore the possibilities of understanding and living in the actual world. Without a familiar or given sense of what the world is like, we could not imagine new possibilities in fiction or in reality, but without the ability to imagine new possibilities we could not expand our understanding or use it creatively.

If fictional worlds have a mimetic relationship to the actual world and function as models do, then fictional works serve us as interpretations of the actual world. Fiction is itself hermeneutical: it offers new ways of seeing and thinking about the world. And if this is so, fictional works also serve a heuristic purpose: they open up for us new ways of reflecting on the world. To interpret fiction hermeneutically is also to use fiction heuristically as a means for helping us to understand the world in which we are always living and acting. Every fictional text implies the question "What if the world were like this?" We reflect upon fictional events in relationship to our sense of actual events, and our interpretation of fictional events helps us to reflect on the significance of actual events. In this way, works of fiction present us with new models for our thinking about the actual world. They become meaningful to us because we are able to compare their fictional worlds with the world that is already familiar to us.

Our understanding of texts and our comparing of worlds are often intuitive and not self-conscious activities. Much of our understanding of texts, in fact, is pretheoretical in the sense that it does not involve problems which need to be mediated by self-conscious hermeneutical methods. A large body of traditional and shared experience shapes our intuitional or pretheoretical understanding of texts, and this body of understanding provides the context for our more self-conscious efforts to understand when we encounter or raise interpretive problems. Often, thus, we may understand a work of fiction and its significance, to a degree at least, without having to engage in self-conscious hermeneutical analysis. But because fictional worlds are mimetically related to the actual world, we are always *able* to use fictional texts as a means for self-consciously reflecting on the fictional world and its relationship to the actual world. Fiction is interesting and valuable to us not only because we enjoy imaginative activities and aesthetic experiences but also because fictional texts present us with alternative ways of seeing or thinking about the world.[22]

---

22. The word *alternative* is potentially misleading. Not every fictional work presents us with a worldview that is different from the worldview we hold prior to the reading. Many stories will confirm our established ways of seeing the world; indeed, many

We are able to understand the events of a fictional story because we have encountered and witnessed numerous events, fictional or actual, in our previous experience. But whether the persons and events are fictional or actual makes no difference as far as the *processes* of understanding are concerned. The comparisons we make among objects and actions are not "world bound" but cut across the boundaries of worlds. We compare Huck Finn and Tom Sawyer to boys that we have known in actual life even though we have no uncertainty whatsoever about which of the boys are fictional and which are actual. In this way fiction illuminates life and life illuminates fiction. Without this mimetic relationship, fiction could neither exist nor be of interest to us. Far from being autonomous worlds grounded in the autonomy of literary language, fictional works derive their meaning and value from their anchorage in the actual world. We encounter fictional persons who live in fictional worlds, and we discover that they are like (or unlike) us and that their worlds are like (or unlike) our world. And through the resemblance — through the mimesis — we discover the value of the encounter.[23]

Two further implications of this view help to clarify some issues pertaining to understanding the mimetic character of fictional texts. First, if we can imagine new possibilities only on the basis of what we already know, then new fictional worlds have a necessary relationship to the worlds already familiar to us. Only because authors have some knowledge of the actual world can they project a new fictional world. Although the fictional world is not a copy of the world familiar to the author (the case of

---

stories have this as one of their main purposes. I am using *alternative* in a more neutral way to indicate that a new story presents us with a set of characters and situations which we have not encountered in that way before. A new story presents us with an alternative way of seeing the world in the sense that we have not confronted or viewed the world through this means before. Our beliefs about the world remain unchanged, but the novel gives a new — that is, alternative — means for seeing it and reflecting on it.

23. It is perhaps worth pointing out that, in a sense not indicated so far, fictional texts do exist within the actual world and that their fictional worlds are included in the actual world. Rather than conceiving of textual worlds as totally discrete and independent of one another, we should perhaps have in mind a model of "worlds within world." In this sense it may also be said that the world of *Don Quixote* is included within the world of John Barth's *The Sot-Weed Factor* when we read that Henry Burlingarne III, one of Barth's characters, is reading *Don Quixote*. But this qualification does not change the hermeneutical model being proposed, for it is still the fictional world of the novel that is seen in relation to the actual world, however the scope and overlapping of these worlds be understood.

fantasy would surely be enough to discredit a naive conception of mimesis as copy), neither is it possible for the fictional world to exist apart from a mimetic relation to the familiar world. This is one of the reasons why historical considerations are part of hermeneutics. The way authors perceive the world and the way their perceptions are influenced by their historical situations shape the fictional worlds they are able to imagine and project. Historical matters will never absorb hermeneutics because throughout the hermeneutical process we are interested in the text and the world it projects. That world of the text is not itself subject to interior change and has no ongoing interior history. Nevertheless, our understanding of historical backgrounds — that is to say, of the actual world to which the text stands in a mimetic relationship — may often be illuminating and even necessary for an adequate understanding of the text.

A second implication concerns the reading of a text. If the new must be seen and understood in relation to the familiar, then readers will inevitably understand the new world of a fictional text in relation to worlds already familiar to them, including both the fictional worlds they have previously encountered and the world they actually inhabit. Hermeneutics cannot escape the fact that texts are interpreted in the cultural contexts of readers. This does not make hermeneutics an entirely subjective or relativistic enterprise, but it does entail an important consequence for the reading and interpreting of texts: the task of hermeneutics can never be finished. Although the worlds of fiction cannot change — the world of Shakespeare's *Hamlet* is the same for all readers in all ages — the way we interpret the relationship of fictional worlds to the actual world is constantly changing because our interpretive contexts change. History makes interpretive tasks very complex, but if history frustrates us by offering no end to the interpretive process, it also blesses us with the possibility of growth.

Textual Analysis

Although a work of fiction is not an autonomous work and cannot be fully understood apart from its mimetic function, it is nevertheless also an object in itself and needs to be analyzed as such. I would suggest that analysis of a text follows the pattern of the actions that occur in the forming of the text. The action of forming a text (writing a novel, for example) is not a singular action but one that involves many subordinate or contributing actions. The various actions that go into the forming of a text provide a pattern for distinguishing the kinds or levels of analysis that are relevant to interpretation. In this section, I will identify five basic or primary contributing actions. Each of these actions, of course, is itself made up of many subordinate chains of contributing actions.

At the first level we recognize that the author uses language in forming a text. Our understanding of the text, therefore, depends on our ability to understand the language and the various linguistic devices that an author uses. At this level we use some of the components of what W. K. Wimsatt has called "our inherited grammar of criticism."[24] We identify and describe the diction, imagery, figures of speech, and other rhetorical devices of prose, or the meter, rhyme, alliteration, and other characteristic uses of language in poetry. Since the author patterns the language in a text, we also include at this level the formal designs in the work: plot, devices of characterization and description, stanzaic forms, style, and the like. When we analyze a text at this level, we are focusing on the formal elements of the text, not on the world that is projected by means of the text or on how the author is using these elements to give significance to the work. By itself this level of analysis is incomplete and must lead to other levels, but it is important to note that much of our pleasure in reading comes from the delight we take in experiencing the formal elements of a text. Indeed, the pleasure of reading is often simply the aesthetic delight we take in the formal artistry of the text.

A second thing that the author does in forming a text is to use language to project the imagined world of the text. At this second level of analysis we examine the imagined world that the author projects in the language of the text. Our interest at this level is not so much the author's deployment of the language as it is the descriptive references of the language, the states of affairs it presents or designates. Before we can go on to answer further questions about the meaning of the text, we must know what the text says, which in the case of narrative fiction is the story that is told. So at this level we attempt to give an accurate accounting of the characters, events, and situations in a narrative text. Sometimes we think of this as the text's literal meaning — what it literally says. Because of the ambivalence of the term *literal,* however, it is better to speak of the states of affairs (the objects, events, actions, situations) that are designated by the lan-

24. William K. Wimsatt, *Hateful Contraries: Studies in Literature and Criticism* (Lexington: University of Kentucky Press, 1965), 217.

guage. Analysis at this point is sometimes controversial, as, for example, when we ask whether Jay Gatsby really loved Daisy Buchanan in Fitzgerald's *The Great Gatsby* or whether Ligeia came back to life in the body of Rowena in Poe's story "Ligeia." In such cases our interpretation of the evidence at this level will influence our interpretation at the other levels. With respect to most of the occurrences in a work of fiction, however, most readers are in agreement.

A third thing the author does in forming a text is to give significance to the components of the world he or she projects. When we move to this third level of analysis, we ask questions not just about what happened or who did what but about how we are to understand the significance of the characters and their actions. We ask, for example, questions about a character's motivation: Why did Jay Gatsby pursue Daisy Buchanan? Or why did Ligeia struggle against death? Such questions focus on the *why* rather than the *what* of the text. At this level we must interpret the significance of what takes place in a narrative. *Significance* is an elusive term because it often suggests relativism in interpretation: significance for whom? We should distinguish clearly, therefore, between significance for the author and significance for the reader. Although we cannot totally separate these concerns, many controversies occur because interpreters conflate them.

A helpful discussion of how authors give significance to the worlds they project is found in Nicholas Wolterstorff's *Art in Action:*

> But what must now be noticed is that there is more to the workings and significance of his [the author's] use of those words than just that thereby he projects the world of the work. A simple way of putting the point is this: fictional discourse has significance beyond *story,* where "story" is understood as designating the world of the work. For one thing, not only does the discourse give us the story; it gives us the story in *a certain way.* But secondly, fictional discourse often bears a significance beyond even that of giving us the story in a certain way.[25]

By the phrase "gives us the story in a certain way," Wolterstorff means simply that the events which constitute the story may be told in different ways by different narrators without the story itself becoming a different story. Three eyewitness reports of a traffic accident, for example, will not be identical word-for-word, even if they are in essential agreement about what happened. Sophocles' *Antigone* and Anouilh's *Antigone* tell the same

25. Wolterstorff, *Art in Action*, 134-35.

story, but each text tells the story "in a certain way." In any particular telling of a story, however, an author uses certain narrative strategies that indicate how he or she sees the significance of the story. This use of strategies may be called the formation or management of the events of the story. By analyzing how these strategies function in a text, we move toward an understanding of the significance of the story as the author sees it. The expression (usually implicit in fiction) of the significance of the story may be called the authorial stance.

We should here distinguish the term *authorial stance* from the term *point of view*. In formalist practice, the term *point of view* is typically used to designate the "narrative voice" in a story; it identifies the "teller of the tale." Formalist critics often go on to assume that we need not inquire further into an authorial point of view or stance, because the "narrative voice" belongs either to a character within the story or to an anonymous, implied narrator who is to be distinguished from the author of the text. But if the author of a text stands behind the work establishing *all* of its narrative strategies, then limiting the term *point of view* to the "narrative voice" of a character or persona can lead us to ignore or minimize the importance of the author's actions in forming a text. The issue here is partly one of preferred usage, but the formalist usage often hides the crucial issue of the author's presence in the text. To highlight this presence, we might better use the term *authorial stance* to include *all* the strategies the author uses to give significance to the story.

In addition to narrative voice, or point of view in the narrow sense, the authorial stance includes, as Wolterstorff observes, the following narrative strategies the author uses to form or manage the events of the story: the reliability or unreliability of the narrative point of view; pacing, or the manipulation of the temporal order of the story; the knowledge/ignorance contour, or the giving and withholding of information; focus, or the highlighting or minimizing of details; evaluation, or the exhibition of authorial attitudes toward characters and events in the story; the use of symbols and of allusions to things and events that occur outside the imagined world; and the expression of beliefs concerning the actual world.[26] Much of our understanding of a text depends on our alertness to these strategies that constitute the authorial stance.

A fourth level in the analysis of fictional texts involves their mimetic function. By projecting an imagined world through the language of the

26. Wolterstorff, *Art in Action*, 139-42.

text, the author is also establishing a relationship between the fictional world and the actual world. In part, our interpretation of the fictional world of a text rests on how we construe its mimetic relationship to the actual world. The methods we use to analyze the fictional world are usually and understandably analogous to those we use for analyzing the actual world. Consequently, our choice of critical methods and our theories or biases concerning methodologies are reflected in the ways we analyze the mimetic function of texts.

The methods of analysis we use to understand the world around us are indicated by the familiar disciplines that appear in our universities. We examine the world as physicists, sociologists, psychologists, philosophers, or linguists, for example. Analogously, we inquire into the psychological, social, political, ethical, or linguistic dimensions or implications of the world that is projected in a novel. To some extent, various types of criticism can be understood as giving priority to one or more of these categories: Freudian criticism stresses the psychological level, Marxist criticism the political-economic, Christian criticism the religious-ethical. Literature is amenable to these types of criticism because in literary works we are confronted with worlds that reflect the contours of actual experience.

One of the general concerns of hermeneutics, therefore, is uncovering the relationships among the many dimensions of our experience. For us to interpret a fictional world at the mimetic level, we need some kind of systematizing theory of the nature and kinds of human actions. Such a comprehensive theory — whether Marxist, Freudian, Christian, deconstructionist, or other — is necessary as we strive for a full understanding of what it is to interpret a world. Our own view of the structure and unity of our actual world will shape the way we interpret fictional worlds.

Complications appear at this level of analysis, however, even aside from the problem of our own methodological biases and theories. One complication is that fictional worlds are never given in their full extension but are what Wolterstorff calls "world segments." This means that an author may, by a selection of material, choose to highlight one aspect or dimension of experience and ignore others. When an author highlights certain aspects of experience — as Poe, for example, highlights psychological terror — we may not conclude from that fact that he fails to recognize or acknowledge other dimensions of experience. We may not, for example, conclude that Poe highlights psychological terror because he is insufficiently aware of the religious or economic dimensions of life. A conclusion such as that would depend on our assessment of the entire scope of Poe's work, of his principles of selection, of his authorial stance, and of all the other levels of analysis. Because our analysis of texts at the level of their mimetic function depends on our own conception of the dimensions of experience and the appropriate methods of analysis, we are highly susceptible to hasty interpretive generalizations. Determining the scope of the text's world segment is one check on our tendency to generalize too broadly.

But in spite of the difficulties at this level, the mimetic function of texts also opens up and enables us to understand the importance of a fifth level of analysis, one involving the authorial stance. In establishing a mimetic relationship between the fictional world and the actual world, the author is also establishing an evaluative perspective on the experiences that are depicted in the fictional world. Authorial evaluations may range from judgments on relatively trivial events and situations to larger philosophical and moral judgments. Because these judgments are more often implicit than stated in a fictional text, historical and biographical data may be very helpful at this level of analysis. But the text itself will — through its narrative voice, plotting, pacing, focus, symbolism, allusions, and so forth — provide the basis for this as well as the previous levels of analysis.

Here a cautionary note is in order. In dealing with issues of evaluation and perspective, it is of crucial importance to distinguish between the author's evaluation and the reader's evaluation. Because readers bring their own perspectives to the reading of a text, it is difficult if not impossible to establish an unbiased interpretation of the author's perspective. And since we read not just to peer into the imagined world or to observe the author's perspective but also to gain something for ourselves from the text, that is, something beyond the pleasure of reading, we tend to nudge the work into positions that are most useful for our purposes, and our own purposes can bias our analysis. Any evaluation we make needs to follow an analysis of what is given in the work itself as an object of the author's making.

At this point it may be useful to summarize the levels we have discussed. (None of the levels of analysis distinguished here can be isolated from the others, and therefore the term *levels* can be misleading as well as useful.)

1. Through the deployment of language, the author forms a text. At this level we analyze the formal features of a text.

2. Through the descriptive references of the language, the author projects an imagined world. At this level we aim accurately to survey the details, structure, and scope of the fictional world.

3. Through the use of narrative strategies, the author establishes a point of view. At this level we try to understand how the author gives significance to the imagined world, how he or she interprets it.

4. Through its anchorage in the actual world, the fictional world acquires a mimetic function. At this level we compare the fictional world to the actual world, inescapably employing the models we use in our understanding of the actual world.

5. Through its linguistic form, its projected world, its point of view, and its mimetic function, the text presents us with a model or paradigmatic way of viewing the world or some aspect of it. At this level we analyze the author's perspective on the events given in the text.

The actual process of interpretation, of course, is not as simple or programmatic as this analytic scheme makes it appear.

Texts as Instruments of Action

So far we have been concerned with the text itself as an object produced by an author's actions. But texts are also used by readers in various ways that are pertinent to our understanding of them. We use them to entertain ourselves, to confirm or challenge our beliefs, to impose discipline on our children, to provide illustrations for our lectures, to reinforce our arguments in a debate, to give us source material for our scholarly work, to advance our professional goals, and so on. Our analysis of a text is in part dictated by the purposes we have in doing the analysis. To study all of these uses would involve us in a sociology of texts. But in a more general way we may speak in hermeneutical terms of a teleology of texts, that is, a theory of the purposes that texts serve. Whether one engages in a sociology of actual uses or a hermeneutics of purpose, however, one would still have to account for a huge range of types of texts — economic, political, religious, historical, scientific, and so forth. For our purposes we will again focus on fictional texts.

A teleology of fictional texts has been undervalued in much literary criticism, especially in formalist, structuralist, deconstructionist, and other forms of criticism that focus more on the text as object than on the text as instrument. Hence, in our day reflection on the value and function of texts as instruments is just as important as reflection on the analysis of texts as objects.

I will propose a general teleology of fictional texts by exploring more fully several questions that I have touched on earlier as well as some additional questions: (1) Does the diversity of perspectives that various readers bring to texts mean that relativism reigns in the interpretive process? (2) How can fictional texts speak to the real conditions of actual life? (3) What is the value of fiction for us as readers? and (4) How is the structure of narrative related to the structure of our experience?

Relativism in Interpretation

The mimetic function of a fictional text brings the imagined world of the text into relation with the actual world of readers as well as with the actual world of authors. But the world of the author and of the reader is always an already interpreted world, and the fact that different readers hold different interpretations of the world means that interpretations of a text will also differ. We naturally adapt our models for understanding the actual world to our understanding of imagined worlds. If we employ Marxist or Freudian or Christian models in our analysis of actual societies, we tend to examine fictional societies also from a Marxist or a Freudian or a Christian point of view. Is the understanding of a text, then, simply relative to the reader's worldview? Is a reader-response theory inescapably relativistic?

Much of contemporary thinking about philosophical hermeneutics can be characterized as a debate over the issue of relativism. Is it possible after the demise of Cartesian foundationalism to establish rational standards that escape the epistemological dilemmas that the relativists point out? On the skeptical side we find such influential thinkers as Lyotard, Derrida, Foucault, Rorty, and Fish. On the other side we find equally influential thinkers who, in spite of their differences, reject the conclusions of the radical relativists: Levinas, Gadamer, Ricoeur, Habermas, MacIntyre. None of these thinkers on either side believe that a return to Cartesian foundationalism is possible, but the latter group seeks to establish a basis for thought on firmer ground than is suggested by Rorty's call to "continue the conversation" in the face of unanswerable questions. What emerges in all of these thinkers is a strong sense of the historical and cultural limits that are placed on understanding, but in the latter group there is as well the belief that history and cultural experience provide new ways of conceiving of our search for normative and even universal standards of thought and action. Historical dependence limits our understanding to something less than the Cartesian ideal, but it also enables us to reach beyond extreme forms of relativism and subjectivism.

It is not my purpose here to sum up the ideas of all of these thinkers. Such summations are readily available in a variety of sources. Rather, I will examine some of the ideas put forward by two Christian philosophers, Nicholas Wolterstorff and Alvin Plantinga, that bear upon this issue.

Using speech-act theory for his own purposes in his recent book *Divine Discourse*, Wolterstorff makes the case that speech acts, that is, the utterance of sentences that have illocutionary force — or, more simply, sentences that have intended purposes and are not simply the mouthing of sounds — such sentences have a "normative standing" that is moral in nature. The utterance of sentences in acts of communication entails rights and duties on the part of the speakers. To speak, in short, is to engage in a moral action.

Wolterstorff's examples are simple and commonplace. If a worker requests a fellow worker to give him a drink of water, he "has altered the moral relationship between himself and his fellow worker."[27] The argument is (1) that in speech actions (as well as in other kinds of actions) we implicitly ascribe to the speaker the status of one who makes a claim or request or promise, etc., and (2) that the ascription of that status to a speaker puts the person spoken to under an obligation to respond in some way. All person-to-person discourse is normative in this way because speaking is a means of establishing relationships among persons. A sentence functions not simply as an independent linguistic entity but as an action performed by a speaker. It acquires meaning because it gives the speaker a certain status that is normative, that is, a status that is generally recognizable and not arbitrary or relativistic. The worker who forms the sentence "Would you hand me a drink of water?" acquires the status of a person who has requested a drink of water. And in doing so he has altered the moral relation with another person in such a way that both parties in the discourse acquire certain rights and duties.

The status that is gained by a speaker occurs via ascription, that is, by our common social recognition of the meaning and implication of the sentence uttered. The illocutionary meaning of a sentence, in other words,

27. Wolterstorff, *Divine Discourse*, 84.

comes from the sentence as formed by a speaker in a social act of communication. The sentence is understood as an utterance by a speaker, and in acts of discourse this recognition leads us to ascribe a certain status to the speaker such that speaker and hearer acquire certain rights and obligations. In his intricate analysis and illustration of these features of discourse, Wolterstorff is arguing that speech actions are normative in nature and moral in their social implications.

Implicit in this view is an assumption that discourse takes place in social and cultural contexts and that the meaning of sentences is therefore historically conditioned. The norms for ascription and the rights and duties thereby acquired are developed historically in specific cultural and social situations. But if the normative authority of discourse is derived from tradition and cultural form, the issue of relativism has not disappeared. A further question is whether any of the norms applicable to speech actions are universal in the sense of being crosscultural or even transcultural. Wolterstorff clearly thinks that there are such universal norms, and the basis for thinking so is that speech actions are actions involving persons. Rather than grounding universal norms in the structure of reason or the structure of language, Wolterstorff establishes the relation of speech to persons and then finds in that relationship the normative universals that ground meaning and obligation. This general line of thinking can be found in the work of many other philosophers as well. Emmanuel Levinas, for example, begins his debate with postmodern skepticism from the relation of one person to another. In this relationship Levinas finds normative and binding ethical ties:

> The alterity of the Other is the extreme point of the "thou shalt not kill" and, in me, the fear of all the violence and usurpation that my existing, despite the innocence of its intentions, risks committing. Here is the risk of occupying — from the *Da* of my *Dasein* — the place of an Other and, thus, in the concrete, of exiling him, dooming him to a miserable condition in some "third" or "fourth" world, bringing him death. Thus an unlimited responsibility would emerge in this fear for the other person, a responsibility with which one is never done, which does not cease with the neighbor's utmost extremity . . . even if the responsibility amounts to nothing more than responding "here am I," in the impotent confrontation with the Other's death, or in the shame of surviving, to ponder the memory of one's faults. This is so despite all the modern denunciations of the inefficiency and the easiness of "bad conscience"! It is a responsibility that, without doubt, keeps the secret of sociality, whose total

gravity — be it vain to the limit — is called "love of the neighbor" — that is, the very possibility of the unicity of the unique one (beyond the particularity of the individual in a genus). It is a love without concupiscence, but as irrefragable as death.[28]

Paul Ricoeur in his *Oneself as Another* develops a similar analysis. His book, he writes in his introduction, does the following:

> [It] suggests from the outset that the selfhood of oneself implies otherness to such an intimate degree that one cannot be thought of without the other, that instead one passes into the other.... To "as" I should like to attach a strong meaning, not only that of a comparison (oneself similar to another) but indeed that of an implication (oneself inasmuch as being other).[29]

If the question of norms is placed in the context of human beings who have social relationships with one another rather than in the abstract realm of "pure reason," we can understand the recent shifts in epistemology from the classical foundationalism of Descartes, with its appeal to self-evident principles of reason, to various contemporary ways of dealing with the justification of one's beliefs. Since human beings operate within history, not outside it, our understanding of ourselves and our world is always subject to modification or correction. Instead, therefore, of speaking of knowledge and truth in absolute terms, current philosophers emphasize that knowledge must be defined as beliefs that we are justified in holding in our historical circumstances or as beliefs that are properly normative for us in our historical situation. Understanding, in short, is a matter of knowing what can be believed or affirmed by human beings in their socially conditioned experiences of the world. Normative universals arise and take shape within the context of human societies and need to be justified within that frame of reference.

The term *justified belief* has itself, however, become a disputed term because of deep differences over what constitutes justification. Instead of speaking of justified beliefs, Wolterstorff prefers to speak of beliefs that we are entitled to hold. The shift from justification to entitlement moves the basis for affirming normative beliefs from purely propositional criteria to

---

28. Emmanuel Levinas, "Diachrony and Representation [1982]," in *Time and the Other*, trans. Richard A. Cohen (Pittsburgh: Duquesne University Press, 1987), 109-10.

29. Ricoeur, *Oneself as Another*, 3.

practical experiential criteria. We find our basis for normative principles for thought and action in the experiences of people who form social dependencies. All people have beliefs and are constantly seeking proper ways for judging the merits of these beliefs. In general terms, Wolterstorff describes the ways in which we sort out our beliefs as follows:

> We implement ways of finding out about new things. We implement ways of ousting false beliefs. And we implement ways of forestalling the emergence of false beliefs, or rather, of diminishing the frequency of their emergence, so that various components of the flow become more reliable. Some of these ways we learn on our own, from experience. But massively it's the case that we learn them from others. For many are established in our society; they are *social practices*, in Alisdair [*sic*] MacIntyre's sense; and we are inducted into them, by modeling and by explicit instruction. We learn from our parents how to determine more reliably the colors of things, from our art teachers how to look at paintings, and so forth.[30]

Not all of what we learn from experience yields beliefs that we are entitled to hold as reliable and binding beliefs, for we may be in error or may lack sufficient evidence. But the process of learning from the social practices that serve to guide our experiences provides the basis for moving toward the beliefs that we are entitled to hold. More specifically, we employ *doxastic* practices to gain and test our entitlement to more specific beliefs. If a belief is supported by the doxastic practices that pertain and is not undercut by any of these practices, then we may claim that we are entitled to hold such a belief. And if we are entitled to a belief, that means that we are also obligated to believe it and to do what is entailed by it. For example, the doxastic practices of physics entitle us to the belief that the moon is a certain distance from the earth, and as long as the doxastic practices of physics support this belief, we are obligated to believe it and to carry on the practice of physics in a way that does not contradict that belief. Beliefs that meet the criteria of entitled belief, thus, are what we mean when we speak of normative and universal claims. They are always socially and culturally situated, as Wolterstorff insists: "Whatever be their nature, it's important to realize that the obligations in question are *situated* obligations, in that which obligations of this sort actually apply to a given person is a function of various aspects of the

---

30. Wolterstorff, *Divine Discourse*, 270.

particular situation of the person in question."[31] But their situational character does not undermine their normative and obligatory character. We are entitled to hold certain beliefs because they are grounded in the common practices that structure human societal experience.

An even stronger case for a nonrelativist stance with respect to understanding is made by Alvin Plantinga in the first two works of his planned trilogy on the subject of warranted beliefs: *Warrant: The Current Debate* and *Warrant and Proper Function*. The argumentation in these volumes is beyond the scope of this work, but a few implications for our hermeneutical theory can be examined. Plantinga, too, rejects the term *justified beliefs* because the tradition of thinking which established that term is the tradition of classical (Cartesian) foundationalism, the view he aims to refute. He selects the term *warrant* as his preferred term in speaking about beliefs that human beings have a rightful claim to affirm and to act upon. In his first volume he argues against various versions of what he calls "internalism," that is, theories that attempt to ground the notion of justified beliefs in one or another of the properties that are "internal" to human beings. In the second volume he develops his own view of warrant, a view which holds that warranted beliefs are based on the notion of proper function, that is, on the notion that warrant is achieved only when cognitive faculties are functioning properly in a congenial epistemic environment. He argues that our minds have a normative (not, in this instance, a morally or deontologically normative) way of functioning and that this normative functioning requires a normal or congenial context or environment. Further, if this is the case, there must be what he calls a "design plan" that specifies what normative functioning is. A function can be "proper" only if there is a design plan that defines or determines what is proper. In his words,

> *Design plan* and *proper function* are interdefinable notions: a thing (organism, organ, system, artifact) is functioning properly when it functions in accord with its design plan, and the design plan of a thing is a specification of the way in which a thing functions when it is functioning properly.[32]

How can we know what the design plan is and therefore what kind of functioning can be called proper? For our purposes, we can refer to two

31. Wolterstorff, *Divine Discourse*, 272.
32. Alvin Plantinga, *Warrant: The Current Debate* (New York: Oxford University Press, 1993), 213.

ideas that Plantinga discusses. First, proper function and design plan are not self-evident or evident on the basis of introspective analysis. They are evident on the basis of experience:

> According to our design plan, obviously enough, *experience* plays a crucial role in belief formation. *A priori* beliefs, for example, are not, as this denomination mistakenly suggests, formed prior to or in the absence of experience. . . . Of course experience plays a different role here [in logical thinking] from the role it plays in the formation of perceptual beliefs; it plays a still different role in the formation of memory beliefs, moral beliefs, beliefs about the mental lives of other persons, beliefs we form on the basis of inductive evidence, and the like. . . . Further, our design plan is such that under certain conditions we form one belief *on the evidential basis* of others.[33]

Plantinga's emphasis on experience as the source of cognition is important for his view that warrant depends on the proper functioning of our cognitive faculties in relation to experience. He claims to be developing thereby a naturalistic view of warrant, that is, one that is grounded in analysis of the experiential conditions for human thought, or, to put it another way, in the proper functioning of thought in its natural experiential environment. This is part of his rejection of classical foundationalism and the Cartesian effort to ground knowledge and warrant in the noetic structures of propositional thinking. But while his theory of warrant is naturalistic in this sense, Plantinga also argues that this epistemology does not support a naturalistic metaphysics. Indeed, he argues the opposite — that, as he puts it, "naturalistic epistemology flourishes best in the garden of supernaturalistic metaphysics. . . . This view of warrant is a *naturalistic* one, but one that requires, for its best flourishing, to be set in the context of supernatural theism."[34]

A second idea relevant for us is his emphasis on the social aspect of the cognitive environment:

> The human design plan is oriented toward a certain kind of cognitive environment. . . . But from the point of view of the individual person, other people are part of the cognitive environment; the design plan does

---

33. Alvin Plantinga, *Warrant and Proper Function* (New York: Oxford University Press, 1993), 15.
34. Plantinga, *Warrant and Proper Function*, 237.

not cover my cognitive faculties in isolation from yours or yours from mine: as it applies to my faculties it presupposes that you and *your* faculties will function and react in certain ways.[35]

This view provides a basis for the warrant we gain from the testimony of others but also for the warrant we have for moral beliefs. Because of our relationships to one another, we hold basic beliefs about what is right and wrong. These beliefs have warrant for us not just because they are based on a chain of noetic propositions about the moral obligations of human beings, but because they arise intuitively out of social experience. Warrant derives from the proper functioning of moral beliefs in the cognitive environment that is formed by the social relations among human beings.

Some moral beliefs are properly basic beliefs, that is, not dependent for warrant on the process of propositional thinking. Such beliefs become the ground for propositional thinking rather than vice versa. Plantinga writes,

> We [people in general] do not think a well-formed, properly functioning human being could honestly arrive at the view that it does not matter how one treats his fellows, that if inflicting suffering on someone else affords me a certain mild pleasure, then there can be no serious objection to my so doing. We do not think a person could honestly come to the view that all that matters is his own welfare and pleasure, other persons being of value only insofar as they contribute to that end. It is not, of course, that we think it *logically* impossible (in the broad sense) that there be persons who honestly arrive at such views; it is rather that we think it simply would not, more exactly, could not happen, given ordinary circumstances and what is in fact the nature of human beings. A theist will be likely to view this as a matter of God's having created us in such a way that we can simply *see* that heinous actions are indeed heinous; nontheists will account for the same fact in some other way.[36]

Plantinga's views, we may conclude, offer support from the analytical tradition in philosophy for certain aspects of hermeneutical thinking that are found in the tradition of continental phenomenology, namely the emphases, found in the thinking of Levinas, Gadamer, and Ricoeur, on the ex-

---

35. Plantinga, *Warrant and Proper Function*, 82.
36. Plantinga, *Warrant: The Current Debate*, 17-18.

periential and historical contexts for understanding, the social and moral dimensions of experience, and the relationship of language and texts to the worlds of authors and readers. What Plantinga offers in this respect is a basis for believing that although interpretations are historically contingent, they need not be thought of as relativistic in a debilitating sense; one may speak about knowledge and truth as criteria for interpretation in a way that need not fall into the skeptical and relativist traps set by postmodernists like Derrida and Rorty. Interpretations may be historically contingent and yet be judged in relation to our stock of warranted beliefs about the social and moral conditions of our experience. The fact that beliefs and interpretations do not have the kind of propositional certainty that the rationalistic tradition aimed to establish does not mean that they do not have merit which reaches beyond the conditions set by the relativists or that the cognitive conversations which we engage in do not make steps in the direction of truth and knowledge.

As a first step in our understanding of texts as instruments, thus, we may state that hermeneutics can affirm the concept of purpose in a way that is not stymied by the notion that purposes are totally relative to the cultural situation of the interpreter. While no one denies that cultural situations are central to the enterprise of interpreting texts, we need not succumb to the currently popular notion that all thought and value are entirely culturally determined. Some beliefs about matters that transcend cultures are warranted. This principle is argued in Plantinga's epistemology and is practiced in the hermeneutics of Gadamer and Ricoeur. We have good reason, therefore, to look both within and beyond culture in our reflections on how texts purposively serve us as instruments to understand the cultural and historical conditions of our experience. And we have good reason to suggest that interpretation of texts should be done in relationship to those beliefs that we think are warranted beliefs. Our hermeneutics needs to be grounded in our warranted beliefs. We may dispute which of our beliefs are warranted and consequently dispute our hermeneutical theories, but only if hermeneutical theory and the practice of interpretation are placed in the context of our stock of warranted beliefs will we find means for resisting the lure (if indeed we want to resist it) of the relativism and faddishness that reign in contemporary textual criticism.

Truth and Fiction: Authorial Stance

We need now to reflect further on how fictional texts can be related to our beliefs. How do beliefs about our everyday world pertain to the imagined worlds presented to us in fiction, or, to put it in contrary fashion, what does fiction have to do with our beliefs about the real world?

Earlier we discussed the view that all fictional narratives are mimetic, that is, they establish a relationship of resemblance (similarities and differences) between the imagined world and the actual world. It is this mimetic relationship that makes it possible for authors to use narrative texts to express their beliefs about the actual world. How and for what purposes authors use the mimetic qualities of narratives to give expression to their beliefs is what we designate by the term *authorial stance*.

We can clarify authorial stance by comparing it to the broader concept of authorial intention. In the past, debates over authorial intention have been vehement, and the concept was often regarded by formalist critics as an irrelevant if not misleading one in literary criticism. The dismissal of intention as a critical concept was an offshoot of theories that focused on the text as object and relegated to sociology the concern with the text as instrument. But in a larger account of hermeneutics, particularly in hermeneutical theories that take seriously the historicity of texts and their production, the issue of authorial intention is both relevant and important. It may be true that an author's actual intentions are unknown or that they are multiple and diverse (including such things as the intentions to gain fame, to make money, to hurt a rival, to please a friend, to demonstrate stylistic skill, and so on). But the difficulty in dealing with intention does not justify eliminating it from the hermeneutical task. Since texts and sentences are the products of certain kinds of speech acts, the role of the author/speaker is crucial in understanding them. Authorial stance in a narrative text corresponds to the illocutionary force of a sentence utterance. The meaning of sentences and texts depends upon illocutionary force and authorial stance, and both are expressive of the author's/speaker's intentions.

In order to avoid the problems surrounding the concept of intentionality, I will limit discussion to the narrower concept of authorial stance. This term refers not to all of the intentions of an author but only to the kinds of purposes an author may have in mind for readers and the kinds of claims about the actual world that an author may be making. These purposes and claims may be explicit or implicit, but in either case they are present because texts have authors who aim to fulfill their intentions.

In order to show more specifically how fictional narratives can, via their authorial stance, make claims and express beliefs, I will compare fictional texts with historical texts. Like fiction, historical works are narrative in structure and express what they have to say by means of the stories they tell. Unlike fiction, historical works describe and make claims about events in the actual world. The differences between historical and fictional narratives are differences in the function of authorial stance in the two genres.

The importance of authorial stance in both cases becomes evident when we observe that the differences between history and fiction are not always obvious in the narrative events themselves. If we had only the narrative events, we would have a hard time telling whether the narratives in novels like Stephen Crane's *The Red Badge of Courage* and John Steinbeck's *The Grapes of Wrath* were intended as accounts of what actually took place or as fiction. And the same pertains to historical works such as Esther Forbes's *Paul Revere and the World He Lived In* and Francis Parkman's *The Oregon Trail*. At times authors deliberately attempt to hide or minimize their stance in a text. In some realistic fiction — say, the novels of Henry James — there is an effort to create an "illusion of reality" and thereby to blur the distinction between fiction and history. Likewise, some historians attempt to write in a purely narrative way, giving us few clues that would enable us to identify the text as history or fiction. When the differences between history and fiction are blurred in this way, we feel the need for more than the narrative events themselves. It is because narrative texts have authorial stances as well as stories (the narrated states of affairs) that we can identify and interpret them appropriately as history and fiction. A narrative without a clear authorial stance complicates our hermeneutical task. Authorial stance is a necessary element in our understanding.

Many factors in addition to the narrated events themselves help us to recognize an authorial stance. Some of these are extratextual, such as our knowledge about history in general, about the author and the author's stated intentions, about the characteristics of genres, about publishers and marketing and reviewing, and so on. Some of these factors are intratextual, such as the ways in which the narrative is managed and the authorial comments that are often part of the text. All of these factors enable us to recognize the author's stance and to interpret the author's aims and beliefs.

The differences between history and fiction can be seen in relation to the kinds of truth claims that historians and fiction writers make. In a historical text the historian makes the claim that the events in the historical narrative count as a story of events as they actually occurred. We are interested in the story the historian tells in his or her text, but our interest is tied to our assumption that the events in that narrative correspond to events in the actual world. We conclude that if (or since) there is such correspondence, the historian is telling us the truth.

Such is obviously not the case with fiction. Since the fiction writer is not claiming that the events of the narrative correspond to events in the real world, many readers conclude that the fiction writer is not telling the truth. One of the persistent misconceptions among common readers is the correlation of the history-fiction distinction with the truth-falsity distinction. What is historical and actual is taken to be truthful, and what is fictional and imagined is thought to be false.

Let us examine this misconception in a little more detail. In the cases of both history and fiction, the question of truth or falsity tends to be focused exclusively on the events (or states of affairs) that the text presents. But if we are more precise, we can see that the terms *true* and *false* are not properly used with regard to the states of affairs presented in a fictional text. This is what lies behind Sir Philip Sidney's well-known remark that poets never tell lies. Sidney was observing that (using our terminology) poets in their fictions never make truth claims about the states of affairs in their works. Because they never claim that those states of affairs occurred in the actual world, they speak no falsehoods. Sidney did not think of truth or falsehood as applying to the states of affairs in fiction. Truth and falsity pertain to the claim of historians that the events of their narratives correspond to events that actually took place, but since fiction writers make no such claims, the term *falsehood* is not appropriate for the events in their fictions. Fiction is not in this regard the same as falsehood.

We can use the terms *true* and *false* not only in relation to the historian's claims about the states of affairs in a historical narrative but also in relation to the beliefs that the historian expresses via authorial stance. With respect to authorial stance, fiction is like history; it, too, can make claims that are true or false. This is evident in two ways. First, authorial stance is seen in the management of the narrative events themselves, in how a writer sets up and construes the relationships among the events (in ways we discussed earlier). Second, authorial stance is seen in the expression of beliefs about the significance of the narrative events for us as readers, in the conclusions the author states (more common in history) or implies (more common in fiction) about the significance of the narrative for our understanding of ourselves, our society, our traditions, our duties, and the like.

102

Let us look at these two aspects of authorial stance in succession, taking first the management of events in the narrative, the interrelationships among the events as the author presents them. In addition to claiming that the events of the narrative have actually occurred, the historian claims implicitly if not explicitly that his interpretations of how events are interrelated are correct and truthful. Like the former claim, this latter claim can be judged to be true or false because it is possible for others to make independent assessments of the use of evidence and of the interpretive criteria. Such is not possible in the case of the fiction writer. There is no debating that Huckleberry Finn went down the Mississippi River and had the many experiences he did have in just the way Mark Twain describes them. The events of a fictional narrative occur only in the imagined world, and they occur exactly as the author describes them. No independent or alternative judgment can be formed about a fiction writer's way of managing and interpreting the relationships among the events of the narrative, since there is no corresponding set of actual events. Whether the author has formed and interpreted fictional events truthfully is not an issue, since there is no other alternative. In contrast to the historian, the author of fiction is, to quote Wallace Stevens, "the sole artificer of his world." Neither in his presentation of the fictional states of affairs nor in his management or formation of those states of affairs does the fiction writer perform actions that are properly judged by standards of truth or falsity. (Note: If the issue of truth pertains at all at this point, it does so in a different sense: it is true, we might say, that the events occur in the imagined world of the text.)

Sometimes critics say that fictional events are "true to" reality or the patterns of events in the actual world. But this claim is quite different from the claim that the narrative as given in fiction is an account or description of a set of events that occurred in the actual world. The question of fiction's being "true to" reality is a question of mimesis (resemblance to the actual world); the question of history's descriptive account of real events is a question of truth or falsity. On the question of mimesis a reader might judge that a writer of fiction has, as a manager of the events, been deep or shallow, profound or superficial, insightful or trite, but not whether the writer has given a true or false description of the happenings. The telling may be regarded as mimetically "true to" or "not true to" the patterns of actual life as we see them as readers, but the events and their ordering cannot be judged true or false as renditions or interpretations of events in the actual world.

A second aspect of authorial stance is the claim that a narrative may have a certain significance or value for readers. Historians may suggest, for example, that their interpretations of the historical narrative yield insights into certain aspects of human nature or human behavior or contemporary social life. Such claims may be the most important of the three claims that we are identifying. It could be argued that the ultimate value of historical research and writing is to be found in the ways in which it illuminates human behavior generally and/or the kinds of behavior we find in our contemporary culture. If so, authorial stance, the author's uses of the text that he or she forms, is of crucial importance for hermeneutics. Analysis of a text as an object is, in a sense, but the preliminary step in the process of interpreting the text as an instrument.

A reading of such books as *The Varieties of History* and *The Philosophy of History in Our Time* confirms the importance of authorial stance in historical writing.[37] Most of the more than fifty historians represented in these anthologies express in some form the view that the ultimate purpose of the historian is to speak to our understanding of human life in general or to specific problems in our social environment. It may be of interest to cite the way two historians speak about the ultimate purpose of writing history. In 1828 Thomas Babington Macaulay wrote,

> The perfect historian is he in whose work the character and spirit of an age is exhibited in miniature. He relates no fact, he attributes no expression to his characters, which is not authenticated by sufficient testimony. But, by judicious selection, rejection, and arrangement, he gives to truth those attractions which have been usurped by fiction. In his narrative a due subordination is observed: some transactions are prominent; others retire. But the scale on which he represents them is increased or diminished, not according to the dignity of the persons concerned in them, but according to the degree in which they elucidate the condition of society and the nature of man.[38]

In 1893 Frederick Jackson Turner wrote,

> It [history] is more than past literature, more than past politics, more than past economics. It is the self-consciousness of humanity — humanity's effort to understand itself through the study of its past.... The study has a utility as a mental discipline, and as expanding our ideas re-

37. *The Varieties of History: From Voltaire to the Present*, ed. Fritz Stern (New York: Vintage, 1972); *The Philosophy of History in Our Time: An Anthology Selected*, ed. Hans Meyerhoff (Garden City, N.Y.: Doubleday, 1959).
38. Stern, *The Varieties of History*, 86.

garding the dignity of the present. But perhaps its most practical utility to us . . . is its service in fostering good citizenship.[39]

These are only two of a host of differing and often conflicting ideas about the ultimate aims of historical scholarship, but in most of the selections given in these volumes, one can find statements that confirm the importance of what we are calling authorial stance. The interpretation of how events are interrelated and the expression of beliefs about those events are the goals that are served by the accurate rendition of evidential data.

A historian's view of the significance of a narrative for us as readers will be influenced by his or her beliefs about the real world. These beliefs may involve an entire worldview, or they may derive from a more pragmatic and immediate view of some aspect of social life, a belief about the importance of freedom, for example, or of justice for minorities, or of some political or economic theory. An authorial stance can be shaped by many factors that arise out of the author's experiences in his or her own social environment. Because authorial stance grows out of and reflects the author's beliefs about the real world of the present, the author's view of the narrative's significance can be judged to be right or wrong, true or false.

Thus, with regard to historical texts, we are able to see and to judge the accuracy of the events that the historian narrates, the adequacy of the historian's interpretation of the events, and the value of the view of the work's significance for us as readers. At all three levels these actions can be judged by criteria of correctness and incorrectness, truth and falsity.

Like historians, fiction writers can at the third of these levels express, implicitly or explicitly, a view of the significance of their narratives for us as readers. While fiction writers make no claims that the events presented and arranged in their narratives occurred in the actual world and therefore do not make the same kinds of claims about events that historians make, fiction writers stand in the same situation as historians with regard to the instrumental uses of a narrative. Fiction writers as well as historians may use their narratives as a means for expressing their beliefs about the extratextual significance of their stories.

Here we need a few examples to clarify. It is generally agreed that in his novels Faulkner is saying (or implying) that a burden of guilt hangs over his native South because of the history of slavery and segregation in the southern states. Nothing in his novels, however, says this directly; the

39. Stern, *The Varieties of History*, 207.

novels present characters and events that are, by and large, purely fictional and do not make explicit claims about the actual states of affairs in the South. Yet Faulkner can and does use these novels as a means for expressing beliefs about the history and social life of the South. Hemingway's novels imply certain beliefs about male-female relationships and the experience of love, as is evident in the common feminist critique of Hemingway. Flannery O'Connor's stories imply beliefs about what ails modern society and what remedies are needed. The kinds of beliefs expressed in fiction are as multifarious as the writers of fiction. If it were not for their expression of beliefs about our actual world, works of fiction would not play the role they do in our lives and in our educational institutions. Without the expression of beliefs, fiction would be of value only as "mere entertainment."

Beliefs are not usually stated in fiction explicitly, but they are the focus of attention in the interpretations that readers and critics give to fictional works. These implied beliefs or claims, when they are identified, become, like the similar claims of the historian, subject to the criteria we have for truth and falsity, for they are expressions of belief about actual states of affairs. In fiction, then, authors use their texts to project an imagined world, but they also use these imagined worlds to assert something about the actual world. They may do so explicitly in the text, but ordinarily they will do so implicitly by their choice of narrative strategies and by the mimetic patterns they establish (that is, by the relationships between the imagined world and the actual world that are implied). As a consequence, we may legitimately say that fiction writers are concerned with truth. Although Sidney is correct in saying that poets (or fiction writers) never lie with respect to their presentation of the imagined events in their fiction, he is wrong to imply that poets are not capable of lying or telling the truth at all. By virtue of the authorial stance they adopt, fiction writers can tell the truth, or they can lie. Of course, some fiction writers may not be interested in using their authorial stance to express beliefs about the actual world; they may intend simply to craft narratives for purposes of entertainment.

A hermeneutical theory that distinguishes between imagined worlds and the actual world, between reference and mimesis, between texts as objects and texts as instruments will help to cut through those Gordian knots that have tied together history, referentiality, reality, and truth on the one hand and opposed them to fiction, nonreferentiality, imagination, and falsity on the other. Instead of separating history from fiction, reality from imagination, truth from fancy, it is more accurate to conceive of history and fiction as related kinds of texts that can be true and false in some respects if not in all of the same respects.

Even so, the truth-falsity criterion may not be the most important criterion that we as readers use in our responses to fictional texts. This possibility will be examined more closely in the next two sections.

Truth and Fiction: The Text and the Reader

We have examined the view that an author can make claims by means of his or her narrative, that is, an author can via narrative give expression to beliefs about life and society. This view involves the reader in a response to authorial stance as well as to narrative events. But the reader brings his or her own beliefs to the text, too, and the interaction between the author's beliefs and the reader's beliefs is of central importance for hermeneutics. By encountering the author's perspectives in the text, whether the text be historical or fictional, the reader is drawn into reflection on his or her own perspectives. Through this relationship between author and reader via the text, the reader may be challenged, educated, reassured, distressed, pleased, disappointed, enlightened, saddened, and so on. The reader's response to a text at this point in the hermeneutical process is so important that it has become the focus of various kinds of critical theories that fall under the rubric of reader-response criticism. Although the hermeneutical interpretation of texts involves much more than what is usually meant by the term *reader-response criticism,* the interaction of the reader with the perspectives of the author is the culmination of the hermeneutical process. It is important, therefore, to explore some of the principles involved in this relationship.

We will begin with a question related to our previous discussion of truth in fiction: What place does the discovery of truth have in our total response to the experience of reading? The view that narratives have value for us because they dramatize and teach truths has linkages to hermeneutical traditions going back to Plato and Aristotle. It has also been strong in Christian traditions of biblical hermeneutics and literary theory. Theories of mythical and sacred narratives have often appealed to the truth-value that myth has for the culture in which the myth is born and nourished. This concern with truth in fiction has often focused on how fictional narratives can give expression to universal or transcendent truths — how, in other words, a story that is infused by temporality (both in its telling and in its internal sequences of events) can express something of permanent or eternal or universal meaning.

In view of these traditional ways of thinking about truth, Helmut Thielicke's opening paragraph in the first volume of his *The Evangelical Faith* is striking, to say the least. Because theology is by nature historical, he writes, it "has nothing whatever to do with timeless truth."[40] The subversion of the belief that human beings can know "eternal truth" has been the aim of much postmodern thought for decades now, and most philosophers and cultural theorists have abandoned the classical foundationalism of the Cartesian tradition. In the light of observations about our historical and epistemological limitations, even Christian theologians are rethinking theology. Today, truth is conceived of not as propositions that are grounded in rational necessity but as beliefs for which we have sufficient epistemological warrant. Consciousness of the historicity of thought does not, of course, lead everyone to the skeptical positions taken by Derrida and Rorty; as we have seen, other alternatives have been suggested. To the viewpoints of Levinas and Ricoeur, of Wolterstorff and Plantinga, cited earlier, we may add the views of such theologians as Jürgen Moltmann, Helmut Thielicke, and Wolfhart Pannenburg.

In *The Future of Hope*, Moltmann writes,

> It appears to me that one can say in somewhat general terms of the phenomenology of religion that today transcendence is experienced more and more as historical boundary of the future. . . . Already in the transition from the model of "physics and metaphysics" to the modern model of "existence and transcendence" many had the feeling that "God is dead." Actually, however, it was merely the boundary of the experience of God that had changed.[41]

Moltmann develops a new approach to the understanding of truth by focusing on the theological categories of eschatology and hope, categories that reshape Christian teachings in the light of our historical existence.

Thielicke, while abandoning the notion of "timeless truth," discovers in fresh ways the notion of experiential truth:

40. Helmut Thielicke, *Prolegomena: The Relation of Theology to Modern Thought Forms*, vol. 1 of *The Evangelical Faith* (Grand Rapids: William B. Eerdmans, 1974), 23.

41. Jürgen Moltmann et al., *The Future of Hope: Theology as Eschatology*, ed. Frederick Herzog (New York: Herder & Herder, 1970), 159-60.

> Only if the validation of the truth takes place in dealings with it can appropriation cease to be a mere form of reflection which presupposes possibilities and methodological conditions in virtue of which the content of faith can be integrated into my self-consciousness. Now the possibilities are learned only in action, in dealings with the truth. . . . Thus to be in the truth is to let the truth work on us, to expose ourselves to it, to surrender to it, to let it shape our lives. Only in this doing of the truth, which means surrendering to it and living with it, can it be manifested and have the chance to validate itself.[42]

Thinking about truth is based on thinking about the patterns of our daily actions; epistemology is closely tied in with ethics.

Pannenberg, in the first volume of his *Systematic Theology*, writes,

> For one thing, Christian doctrine is from first to last a historical construct. Its content rests on the historical revelation of God in the historical figure of Jesus Christ and on the precise evaluation, by historical interpretation alone, of the testimony that early Christian proclamation gives to this figure. The terminology, which has evolved since apostolic times in attempts to formulate the universal scope of the divine action in the person and history of Jesus, cannot be understood apart from its place within the history of these attempts. . . . As regards the truth claims raised in the investigation and presentation of Christian doctrine, historical and systematic reflection must continually permeate one another.[43]

A new awareness of the historicity of human thinking and the importance of theological traditions, in contrast to the absolutist language deriving from the rationalistic philosophers, permeates the thinking of many recent and influential theologians.

We can explore the consequences of this "historical turn" for a hermeneutics of narrative through a close examination of Hans-Georg Gadamer's conception of art and aesthetics. We can see in Gadamer the tension between older conceptions of truth and modern conceptions of historicity. In the first part of *Truth and Method*, Gadamer sets out to distance himself from the subjectivism of the Kantian tradition of aesthetics and Kant's view that knowledge and art are as unmixable as oil and water.

---

42. Thielicke, *Prolegomena*, 154.

43. Wolfhart Pannenberg, *Systematic Theology*, trans. Geoffrey W. Bromiley, vol. 1 (Grand Rapids: William B. Eerdmans, 1991), x-xi.

In contrast, he asserts his view "that art is knowledge and the experience of the work of art is a sharing of this knowledge."[44] Our responses to art are cognitive as well as aesthetic, and therefore we "hope to understand better what kind of truth it is that encounters us there" (89).

Gadamer draws an analogy between works of art and games as forms of structured play. Several observations in his analysis of play are surprising. He says, for example, that play "has no goal which brings it to an end; rather it renews itself in constant repetition" (93) and that "play is not to be understood as a kind of activity" (93). What he wants to insist on is that because play is structured it is not to be understood simply as activity in which players subjectively determine the movements and goals of their play. Players perform movements prescribed by the game itself. The significance of play is seen in the game that is played rather than in the players: "It is the game that is played — it is irrelevant whether or not there is a subject who plays. The play is the performance of the movement as such" (93).

The "primacy of the game over the players engaged in it" (95) enables Gadamer to reinstate representation as an ontological property of games. Games are representations in structured forms of the "to-and-fro movements" found in our observations and experiences in the natural world. He further argues that the aim of playing is simply to play the game successfully and that "to perform a task successfully 'represents it'" (97). Just as we might say that a performance of Mozart's Symphony #40 is a representation of Mozart's Symphony #40, we can say that the playing (performance) of a game is a representation of that game. But since representation in the sense of performance (playing) is successfully done in and through the performance itself, the representation does not exist for or serve a purpose outside of the performance. Players lose themselves in the play of the game (92). Gadamer concludes that "Play is really limited to representing itself. Thus its mode of being is self-representation. . . . Only because play is always representation is human play able to find the task of the game in representation itself" (97).[45] Thus Gadamer's drive to transcend subjectivism yields an objectivist account of art in which a work of

44. Hans-Georg Gadamer, *Truth and Method* (New York: Crossroad, 1982), 87. All further references are to this edition and will be cited in parentheses within the body of the essay.

45. For a more nuanced analysis of representation, see Wolterstorff, *Works and Worlds of Art*.

art is a kind of structured play that exists independently of human subjects.

Like a game, an art work "has the structure . . . of a closed world" (98). An art work is a self-contained structural unity that "has its telos within itself" (101):

> But, above all, what no longer exists is the world, in which we live as our own. Transformation into a structure is not simply transposition into another world. Certainly it is another, closed world in which play takes place. But inasmuch as it is a structure, it has, so to speak, found its measure in itself and measures itself by nothing outside it. Thus the action of a drama — in this it still entirely resembles the religious act — exists absolutely as something that rests within itself. It no longer permits of any comparison with reality as the secret measure of all copied similarity. (101)

Gadamer seems to think that insistence on the separate structural integrity of art is a necessary hedge against the subjectivist location of the meaning of art in the aesthetic consciousness of authors and readers:

> Neither the separate life of the creating artist — his biography — nor that of the performer who acts a work, nor that of the spectator who is watching the play, has any separate legitimacy in the face of the being of the work of art.
>
> What unfolds before one is for every one so lifted out of the continuing progression of the world and so self-enclosed as to make an independent circle of meaning that no one is motivated to go beyond it to another future and reality. The spectator is set at an absolute distance which makes any practical, purposive share in it impossible. (114)

What is the self-contained telos of art? Gadamer describes it as "the joy of knowledge" (101). In his view, what is being represented in our encounter with a work of art is to be found not in the specific states of affairs in the work of art but in the structural relations that form these states of affairs into a "game," that is, into a form of structured play. And it is in these structural relations that we discover the possibilities for knowledge and truth in art. Let us take the case of fictional narratives. The states of affairs in fiction are obviously not states of affairs that occur in the actual world, even though they may resemble real states of affairs. What then is represented? Gadamer answers that a literary work of art "has in common with all other literary texts that it speaks to us in terms of the significance of its contents. Our understanding is not specifically concerned with the achievement of form that belongs to it as a work of art, but with what it says to us" (144-45). The events of the fiction cannot represent actual events. What can be represented in narrative fiction, however, is what is represented in all written texts — namely, the content, "what it says to us." The connection between the work of art and the real world, thus, is found in what is represented by means of the structure of the work. "All literary works," Gadamer writes, including but not limited to narrative fictions, "have a profound community in that the linguistic form makes effective the significance of the contents to be expressed" (145).

Because art is structured, we recognize that the essential relations among things in the work of art are like the relations among things we know in our experience. And because these relations are not merely copies of what is already familiar, our recognition of them can expand and illuminate our understanding. Art expands our horizons by presenting variations on the structural relationships that we can recognize. These structural relationships are the primary concern of hermeneutics because it is through our recognition of them that we are able to judge their similarity (or lack of it) to the structures of life, that is to say, we are able to judge their truthfulness. "What one experiences in a work of art and what one is directed towards is rather how true it is, i.e. to what extent one knows and recognises something and oneself" (102). Gadamer sums up these primary concerns as follows:

> Thus imitation, as representation, has a clear cognitive function. Therefore the idea of imitation was able to continue in the theory of art for as long as the significance of art as knowledge was unquestioned. But that is valid only while it is held that knowledge of the true is knowledge of the essence, for art supports this kind of knowledge in a convincing way. For the nominalism of modern science, however, and its idea of reality, for which Kant drew the conclusion that aesthetics has nothing to do with knowledge, the concept of mimesis has lost its aesthetic force.
>
> Having seen the difficulties of this subjective development in aesthetics, we are forced to return to the older tradition. If art is not the variety of changing experiences whose object is each time filled subjectively with meaning like an empty mould, representation must be recognized as the mode of being of the work of art. This was prepared for by the idea of representation being derived from the idea of play, in that self-representation is the true nature of play — and hence of the work of art also. The playing of the play is what speaks to the spectator, through its

112

representation, and this in such a way that the spectator, despite the distance between it and himself, still belongs to it. (103-4)

The nature of the truth, or the joy of knowledge, that we glean from art — that quality of an art work that exists beyond its aesthetic qualities — is for Gadamer, as for the formalists, difficult to describe. It appears that the all-absorbing experience of a work of art, which takes the "spectator" out of his own world, provides an expansion of understanding that has beneficial effects when the spectator reassumes his identity and activity in the world of experience. Gadamer writes,

> But the distance is, in the literal sense, aesthetic distance, for it is the distance from seeing that makes possible the proper and comprehensive sharing in what is represented before one. Thus to the ecstatic self-forgetfulness of the spectator there corresponds his continuity with himself. Precisely that in which he loses himself as a spectator requires his own continuity. It is the truth of his own world, the religious and moral world in which he lives, which presents itself to him and in which he recognises himself. Just as the parousia, absolute presence, describes the ontological mode of aesthetic being, and a work of art is the same wherever it becomes such a presence, so the absolute moment in which a spectator stands is at once self-forgetfulness and reconciliation with self. That which detaches himself from everything also gives him back the whole of his being. (114-15)

The "ecstatic self-forgetfulness" of one's experience of art seems more mystical than definitive, but its value is "the joy of knowledge" (101). This knowledge is not scientific, but it is knowledge nonetheless. It is more akin to the knowledge of the historian than the knowledge of the natural scientist, for the historian aims to understand particular events through the interrelationships of the particular details of a narrative rather than, like the scientist, through "the subsumption of the individual thing under universal concepts" (446).

Like all other written texts, then, the literary work of art "speaks to us in terms of the significance of its contents" (144-45). Our understanding of the work of art, in contrast to our aesthetic experience of it, "is not specifically concerned with the achievement of form that belongs to it as a work of art, but with what it says to us" (145). And what it says to us has the character of a truth that is represented in the work.

Now if we are able to recognize the content or truth of fiction on the basis of our knowledge of truth in our experience, then the truths of fiction must be seen as parallel to the truths of actual life or heightened variations of those truths. The claim that the truths of art are grounded in its representational or structural character is the basis for claiming that art has a validity different from but equal to scientific truth. That means that the truths of art cannot be simply the private opinions of the author but must have some universality beyond persons. And in fact Gadamer claims a greater degree of universality for the truths of art than the author's opinion: "The free invention of the writer is the presentation of a common truth that is binding on the writer also" (118). Art as "an increase of being" (135) represents truths whose validity does not rest in individual authors or readers but is embedded in traditions of thought. It is here that Gadamer's understanding of history has an important relationship with his hermeneutics of art. The content or truth of art works is not to be thought of as the eternal truths of a foundationalist philosophy, or as the relativistic "truths" of the postmodernists, but as the truths that are formed by and tested in the history of traditions. While not final or absolute, these truths nevertheless have validity beyond the subjective consciousness of individuals. They are warranted by the testimony of history even though they are subject to the changeable structures of historical traditions.

This view of the truth of art has some attractive features. If the truths of art are generated in historical traditions, we escape the clutches of classical foundationalism and perhaps of Kantian subjectivism. But Gadamer's model is also unsettling. It seems to limit hermeneutics to interest in the truth claims of art and to suggest that the truths warranted by the expanding horizons of history are the criteria for recognizing and judging those truth claims. Art, in short, has cognitive value because it represents or heightens those universal truths that are familiar to us in our historical experience. Gadamer, of course, acknowledges that art also serves also our aesthetic interests and needs, but the truths of art are the primary concern of hermeneutics.

Even if we grant the dubious separation of aesthetics and hermeneutics, does this view of the truth of art hold up? Is our concern with truth focused on discovering the common or universal truths of our historical experience? Is it not the case, rather, that in the history of art we find contents (in Gadamer's sense of the term) that are extremely diverse, and not only diverse but conflicting and even contradictory? What are the common truths, for example, that we can find in works by, say, Theodore Dreiser, Ernest Hemingway, and Norman Mailer on the one hand, and by Flannery O'Connor, Walker Percy, and John Updike on the other? The philosophical perspectives in these works are so different that one is impressed with the contrasts more than with the commonalities. And even if we do find certain common truths about human behavior in all of them, are these common truths what we find most interesting and valuable? And are we to judge the hermeneutical value of all writers on the basis of the common truths that are represented in their fictions? On the contrary, we are often deeply moved and challenged by works whose views ("contents" in Gadamer's sense) are alien to our own. What interests us in art is the range of diversity and the distinctiveness of each artist's viewpoint, not just the common and universal qualities.

Furthermore, in the history of fictional narratives, it is not the case that works are forgotten or their value is diminished because they exhibit different and conflicting views of life. Nor is it the case that works survive simply on the basis of their aesthetic qualities in distinction from their content. It appears, rather, that in our experience of art, as suggested above, form and content, events and truths, aesthetics and hermeneutics are not as sharply distinguished as they are in Gadamer's model. Or, to put it in other words, our hermeneutical interest in art is not comprehended by the truth value of art.

Gadamer's account of the truth that encounters us in art escapes the subjectivism of the Kantian tradition, but in doing so it develops affinities with the objectivism that is characteristic of formalist theories of art. The formalist, too, situates the meaning or truth of a work of art in its structural integrity and examines that structure independently of authors and readers.

Like the formalists, Gadamer does not in every sense escape the Kantian tradition, for that tradition still sets the terms of the discussion. The formalists want to claim, contra Kant, that we can have knowledge in art, but they are still working within the Kantian model of aesthetics. They conceive of their task, therefore, as the need to distinguish knowledge in art from knowledge in science and to justify knowledge in art on grounds other than those that justify knowledge in science. This strategy leads to the objectivism of a structural theory, but in the end, the losses in formalist theory outweigh the gains. We can see this in two main ways. First, it does not account adequately for the actual experience of reading, and second, it limits the value that art has beyond its aesthetic value to the realm of common truths, that is, to our cognitive appropriation of the content of the work. Let us examine these two points more fully.

First, when we read a fictional narrative (or any other work of art), we are absorbed by the drama of actions more than by any common truths that may be implicit in the narrative. The problems, dilemmas, emotions, uncertainties, and so forth of the characters as well as the power of the descriptions move us and engage our emotions. Our interest in ideas is submerged in our encounter with the events of the story. And it is not the case that our interest in the story (the events and how they are structured) is simply an aesthetic interest that is propadeutic to our hermeneutical interest in the truths expressed in the narrative. In real life our ideas about life are constantly being formed and tested by the totality of our experiences; our experiences and our thoughts are interdependent in ways that are not easily separated, and in fact there is no desire, need, or reason to separate them. In a narrative, there is the same kind of interdependence of thought and experience that we find in real life; and in our reading of a narrative we do not separate our aesthetic experience of the work from our reflection on the truths the work may be dramatizing.

Furthermore, there is a natural interaction between our experiences in reading and our real-life experiences. We are delighted or saddened by the lives of fictional characters in the same ways that we are delighted or saddened in real life; we laugh or cry while reading; we have hopes for and disappointments about fictional characters; we become angry at villains and admire heroes; we sympathize with the oppressed and desire to emulate the courageous. Our emotions and thoughts are often intensely engaged even when our own beliefs about life differ from the author's. In short, our experiences in reading are not characterized by the aesthetic distance that the formalist critics prize, nor is there a separation of our aesthetic and our hermeneutical interests. Stories, whether drawn from real life or from fiction, engage our imaginations and thoughts in more holistic and interactive ways than formalist models of aesthetics acknowledge. The theory, in other words, does not account for the actual experience of reading.

Second, formalist or structural models do not give a large enough account of the truths of art. In the formalist model, the truths of art tend to be identified with the themes or ideas that are represented in the story, themes that can be articulated as propositions. But in real life our understanding of truth is much more complex. Understanding takes many forms, from the forming of logical propositions and scientific generalizations to the practical know-how needed to fix a leaky faucet, from knowing rules of etiquette to the empathetic counseling of an alcoholic, from the calculated guesswork of the experienced gardener to the proficiency of an experienced chess player. Knowledge takes many forms, and understanding grows out of a diverse and complex range of experiences that take place over a period of many years. What we encounter in a fictional narrative is a world of similarly complex experiences, and our understanding of that fictional world is as complex as our understanding of our actual world. To suggest that our understanding of the truths of art is in essence our cognitive recognition of the common truths of experience fails to account for the full richness of the knowledge that inspires our interest in works of art. Our knowledge of life in all its diversity is what art appeals to, and the knowledge that is represented in art in all its diversity is what keeps us coming back to art as a source of understanding. The truths of life and the truths of art are not distinct in the way that the formalist model suggests; in actuality there is a constant interaction between life and art such that the emotions and thoughts associated with them are similar and interdependent.

Gadamer's aim was to develop an ontology of works of art. He was searching for the common essence that all works of art share: "The intention of the present conceptual analysis . . . is not aesthetic, but ontological" (121). He concluded his discussion of portrait painting as follows:

> The picture — and with it the whole of art that is not dependent on reproduction — is an ontological event and hence cannot be properly understood as the object of aesthetic consciousness, but rather is to be grasped in its ontological structure when one starts from such phenomena as that of representation. The picture is an ontological event — in it being becomes meaningfully visible. (126-27)

If, however, we leave behind a preoccupation with the ontology of art and the need to justify the truth value of art over against the Kantian subversion of that notion, we can see more clearly the advantages of building a model of art on the basis of action theory. To see art works in relation to the processes of their creation and use and to see all of these processes in a holistic way is more productive than focusing only on the ontology of the art work itself. The ontology of the work of art as an object can be more clearly understood when art is seen in relation to authors and readers, that is, in relation to the real-life processes of creating and responding to art rather than in terms of a spurious aesthetic distance that formalist theories place between art and life. While Gadamer has developed a strong theory about the historical nature of hermeneutical thinking, in his aesthetics he tries to reconcile it with a view that traditionally has attempted to escape the conditions of our historicity. In attempting to define the work of art as an object, he has underestimated the work of art as an instrument.

But if this is the case, can we describe more fully this interaction that takes place between the work and the reader? Our model, which is based on action theory rather than on Kantian premises, at least offers an alternative approach. It focuses first on how narratives are related to the personal actions and historical situations of authors and readers, and it develops an ontology of art consistent with those considerations. When we bring together our dual concerns with the work as object and the work as instrument, we can see that our concern with truth and knowledge is but one of our concerns in the understanding of art, and perhaps in our ordinary reading it is not the primary concern. In the next section we explore what may be a more basic concern: the ethical dimension of hermeneutics.

Ethics and Fiction: The Reader's Response

Thielicke's view that "the validation of the truth takes place in dealings with it" is a view that in general is shared not only by the writers cited in the previous section but by many others as well, including Karl Apel, Richard Bernstein, and Alasdair MacIntyre. This is a general and broad principle that blurs the important differences among these writers, but the point here is in fact the general one that there is a sizeable body of philosophical and theological work that addresses hermeneutical issues in ways that are distinctly different from those of whom we have called the radical postmodernists. The new emphases on historical and cultural contingencies in the views of these thinkers give them some common ground with the postmodernists, but the historicity of experience and knowledge does not lead them to epistemological skepticism. Their willingness to reconceptualize what it means to make truth claims and to have knowledge tends also to give to hermeneutics a pragmatic and ethical emphasis that is just as important as if not more important than the cognitive one of seeking correct or truthful interpretations.

Understanding is based on the patterns of our actions as well as the patterns of our thoughts. Truth may be the end of a noetic response to a text, but truth may also serve as a means to further ends, more specifically to the cultivation of a well-directed life. We formulate our understanding of the truth propositionally, but these formulations may also serve a further end, the promotion of good and virtuous actions. This emphasis does not denigrate knowledge or cognitive understanding, for obviously we need to understand if we are to use our understanding for ethical ends, and obviously at certain stages of the hermeneutical process, the arrival at a true or reasonable understanding is the proximate end of our interpretations. But the final end looks beyond knowledge per se. We interpret not just to increase understanding but to live more fully and wisely in our particular social environment. We might put the relationship of understanding and ethics this way: hermeneutics goes hand in hand with heuristics. The significance of hermeneutics as our understanding of the texts of the past is that this understanding serves the further purpose of assisting us on our journey into the future. In this section, then, we will inquire into the ethical dimensions of narrative hermeneutics.

Broadly speaking, the ethical response to texts overarches or embraces all other kinds of response, since responses are themselves actions and therefore carry with them ethical implications. Ricoeur writes, also in a very broad sense, "there is no ethically neutral narrative."[46] Specific hermeneutical tasks, such as philological analysis, historical research, bibliographic description, and the like may not be directly ethical, but none of these tasks is self-contained. They all serve further purposes, and as they move closer to these purposes, the ethical implications of the hermeneutical tasks become more and more definite and clear.

Before getting too far into the discussion of ethics, however, it will be helpful to clarify a couple of points. In discussing ethics in fiction, I do not intend to talk about the lives of authors or about censorship and the social influences of fiction. Those are sociological rather than hermeneutical issues. Here we are concerned with the way in which narrative hermeneutics draws us into ethical reflection on human actions, actions that take place both inside and outside of the story.

What links narrative hermeneutics to ethics is the fact that both are concerned with actions and events that occur in time. And since actions and events have a temporal structure, both narratives and ethics are concerned with the relation of the past to the future, with how a set of existing circumstances leads to a subsequent set of circumstances. In real life we are constantly thinking about the purposes that inspire and motivate our actions. We feel distress when we can see no purpose in the actions and events that occur in our lives, and when we have no sense of purpose, we also have no sense of ethical meaning or significance. Our ethical sensitiv-

---

46. Ricoeur, *Oneself as Another,* 115.

ity is dependent on our sense of purpose — in other words, ethics is tied to teleology. When we ask about the ethical value of our actions, we ordinarily ask about the teleological ends or purposes the actions serve or how those ends were contravened.

The debates over ethics and teleology that have shaped the history of moral philosophy are beyond the scope of this book, and only a few remarks will be needed before we turn specifically to the ethics of reading fictional narratives. First, we may observe that the question of teleology in ethics embraces a variety of philosophical positions, from Aristotle's view of the essential or intrinsic good to Kant's view of duty and right action to Mill's view of the utilitarian or instrumental good. Teleological ethics, which in the philosophical tradition focuses on the idea of goodness, can be contrasted to deontological ethics, which focuses on duty, but the term *teleology* can also be used in a broader and more neutral way, referring generally to the purpose of any action whatsoever, regardless of its goodness or rightness. In a broad sense, all actions (in contrast to events) are purposive, whether for good or bad, right or wrong. As David Carr notes, "In a significant sense, when we are absorbed in an action the *focus* or direction of our attention, the center of our concern, lies not in the present but in the future."[47] In *Ethics after Babel*, Jeffrey Stout observes that the *telos* or end need not be "a fixed conception of the good, derived once and for all from a philosophical view of the human essence."[48] The concept of telos may be used in a more neutral sense to indicate a purpose that is "actually achievable under our social-historical circumstances by acceptable means," leaving the question of what is acceptable for later ethical debate.[49] Many actions that are teleological in this broad sense, such as tying one's shoelaces or weeding the garden, do not seem to be ethical actions at all, except perhaps when linked to a much larger chain of actions. For our purposes, this general conception of teleology will serve. More detailed study of ethics and narrative would require more refined engagement with various ethical theories; our discussion will focus only on the broad question of how fictional narratives can in general be related to ethics. What we want to see is the connection between teleology and ethics in the actions of fictional narratives.

47. David Carr, *Time, Narrative, and History* (Bloomington: Indiana University Press, 1986), 39.

48. Jeffrey Stout, *Ethics after Babel: The Languages of Morals and Their Discontents* (Boston: Beacon, 1988), 237.

49. Stout, *Ethics after Babel*, 226.

Second, we need to note the close ties between teleology, eschatology, and utopia. In Christian theology, the understanding of the teleology of particular actions is ultimately related to the teleology of history in general, which is the concern of eschatology. Eschatology is at times limited to a belief about the "second coming" and life after death, but in a broader sense it is a belief that the ultimate end of life does and should influence the way we think about the proximate ends of all of our actions. Jürgen Moltmann, the leading advocate of this view, writes, "From first to last, and not merely in epilogue, Christianity is eschatology, is hope, forward looking and forward moving, and therefore also revolutionizing and tranforming the present. The eschatological is not one element *of* Christianity, but it is the medium of Christian faith as such, the key in which everything in it is set."[50] In the Christian view, as Moltmann indicates, the concept of hope is an important concept in teleology and therefore also in the ethical understanding of experience.

A similar concept is that of utopia. Utopian reflection in philosophy and utopian societies in fiction are, like Christian eschatology, efforts to see particular social actions in the light of a larger vision of an ideal society. Paul Ricoeur argues in *Lectures on Ideology and Utopia* that societies have always needed an integrative vision of the unity and coherence of their cultural experiences, a vision that provides a rationale for moving into the future.[51] This vision of the future was originally provided by religion and is now often provided by utopian thinking. The social and moral visions that are articulated in eschatological and utopian thinking are grounded in our need to think teleologically. The teleology of particular actions leads eventually to ethical thinking about the complex chains of interrelated actions that constitute social life.

Teleology, eschatology, and utopia, because of their concern with ends and purposes, are related to our discussion of narrative in two ways: (1) in regard to the chain of events in the narrative itself, and (2) in regard to the uses of texts by authors and readers. A narrative, as indicated earlier, may by virtue of its authorial stance be used to express themes and ideas. But the story itself is an account of actions and events and not a set of noetic propositions. We may ask, therefore, about the function and value

50. Jürgen Moltmann, *Theology of Hope: On the Ground and the Implications of a Christian Eschatology* (New York: Harper & Row, 1967), 16.

51. Paul Ricoeur, *Lectures on Ideology and Utopia,* ed. George H. Taylor (New York: Columbia University Press, 1986).

of a story apart from its thematic implications. Is the story of interest to us only as a vehicle for the truth that is thereby expressed? Clearly not. If we are avid readers, we read for the story as well as for the themes that are implicit in it, and perhaps at times we read for the story rather than for the themes. We may return to a work again and again not just to discover the themes but because the story itself has some compelling interest for us. Why does the story itself seem to have this power over us as we read? What is the nature of that interest that is not satisfied by the noetic content of the work?

The interest is as varied as our interest in life itself. It includes an interest in people (in emotional and psychological experiences), an interest in description (in natural and social environments), and an interest in the design of the plot and the quality of the language (an aesthetic interest). But embracing all of these is an interest in how people act in the specific situations and environments that the story depicts. These specific situations are always ones in which choices must be made or problems must be solved. Our interest in the people, places, and plots of stories is related to our insatiable curiosity about how people act in situations of conflict. That interest is natural, of course, because that is so much of what life is about: how to deal with the problems and stressful situations that come our way. Our uncertainties and fears drive us to seek answers beyond ourselves and our immediate circumstances. If everything in life would go smoothly or if there would be no questions or hesitations about what we should do, we would have no compelling interest in the conflicts and actions of other people. But because we do not have all the answers, we turn naturally to the experiences of others for what we can learn. It is this unending socialization process that sustains our interest in others as well as ourselves.

This is also the basis for our interest in stories. Life is so diverse and complex and so full of possibilities that we look to fictional stories as well as to actual life and history to give us examples that will confirm or guide or explain or point out new directions for our actions. We read for many reasons, but underlying them all is that in fictional narratives we are encountering patterns of action that help us understand or come to grips with conflicts and issues that we face in real life.

Emmanuel Levinas gives this experience an ethical explanation. In the face of the other, he says, we see ourselves. That is to say, when we see the face of the other, we come to understand our own situation as well as the situation of the other. The identity of the self depends on a recognition of the other, and thus the concern for self depends also on responsibility for the other. If there is no responsibility for the other, there will be a loss of understanding of oneself. Concern for oneself demands concern for the other. In the mutually dependent relationships of the self and the other lies the ethical foundation of human action. Paul Ricoeur, in *Oneself as Another,* carries the analysis of this relationship even further, arguing that Levinas leaves a gap between the self and the other that needs to be bridged by the recognition that the consciousness of the other comes not only from the outside but also from within the self: our sense of otherness "belongs . . . to the ontological constitution of selfhood."[52] In nontechnical language, this means roughly that we understand ourselves by identifying deeply with others; our own identity is formed by the presence of others in our lives; we find the other within ourselves as part of our self-understanding and self-identity; we can speak not only of oneself *and* another but of oneself *as* another. Thus our responsibility for ourselves is inseparable from our responsibility for others, and vice versa.

Following these insights, I would suggest that our interest in the lives of fictional characters is more than an emotional or psychological empathy. It is an interest in the ethical relationships that are a necessary part of human interaction. The characters of fiction, like human beings in real life, form and discover their identities through their relationships with other characters. And more than this, they discover that their identities are dependent on the identities of others — in other words, that personal identity is shaped by the social interaction of interdependent selves. The search for identity or the quest for the self is, in short, not the quest for autonomy and independence but the quest for others. There is no self apart from the selves of others, and therefore no personal identity apart from social interaction with others. We are accustomed to thinking of our interest in the great works of fiction as an interest in strong individuals — Oedipus, Lear, Captain Ahab, Thomas Sutpen, and the like — but these characters are striking individuals only through their relationships to others in their social world. The contextual situations of these characters are what make them strong individuals, not their alleged self-determination or self-definition. Strong individual characters in fiction appear only when the social context for their actions is equally strong, that is to say, when their identities as individuals are fully and deeply immersed in the identities of others in a specific cultural situation.

A good example is the character of Hester Prynne in Hawthorne's

---

52. Ricoeur, *Oneself as Another,* 317.

The Scarlet Letter. Hawthorne writes near the end of that novel that Hester had become a strong woman as a result of her experiences. This strength is often taken to be an individualistic kind of strength, the power of self over antagonistic circumstances. Hester is seen as an early celebration of democratic individualism asserting itself in a hostile environment formed by a political and religious establishment. But Hawthorne's point is that Hester's strength is formed positively as well as negatively by her society. In the paragraph where Hawthorne speaks about Hester's strength, he observes also that she "had wandered, without rule or guidance, in a moral wilderness," and that although her experiences in separation from the Puritan community "had made her strong," they had also "taught her much amiss" (chapter 18). She does not gain her full stature until she participates in the personal struggles of the others in the community who have shaped her own life. Not until she acts openly and freely with Dimmesdale and Chillingworth and the community as a whole does she become the individual heroine that we admire. And this does not happen until the end of the book, when she returns to the Puritan community to live out the rest of her life doing charitable deeds. In the end "there was a more real life for Hester Prynne, here, in New England" than anywhere else. Hawthorne sees this return not as a concession or a failure but as Hester's recognition that her identity is a social identity, formed and fulfilled in the relationships with others that have made her life what it is. It is in the acceptance of the particular moral relationships of her particular social context that Hester achieves her true strength. The social nature of individual identity is evident also in the fact that the Puritan society is altered for the better by Hester's personal strength.

The range of human relationships in fiction is, of course, as broad as it is in life itself, but it is always the case that our interest in individual characters is deeply embedded in the total story, in the specificity of the particular social environment in which the characters live out their struggles and hopes. And since the particular relationships with others that define the identity of individual characters are broadly ethical in nature, our interest is grounded in our interest in the ethical relationships of human beings. Of course, we are also interested in the emotional, psychological, social, economic, political, and other dimensions of the characters' lives, but these dimensions are all embraced within the larger category of the ethical. The individual seeing the face of the other, the individual seeing oneself as another, the individual as nothing apart from relationships with others — this individual, whose identity arises out of particular social relationships with others, is what commands our interest in narrative fiction.

Like the actions in real life, the actions in fictional narratives are tele-ological: plots move forward in time with the purpose of reaching an end. A good part of our interest in fiction, thus, is in the resolution of the con-flicts of the characters. But why are we interested in these resolutions? Aes-thetically we look for completion and wholeness; we have a sense of fulfill-ment when the threads of the plot are drawn together in the tapestry of the story. But more fundamentally, we are interested in how characters deal with their crises and aspirations, and thus we are interested in the authorial stance of the narrative, that is, the author's beliefs about how the situations of the characters can or cannot reach satisfactory resolution. The ways in which characters respond to and deal with their problems provide images for reflection on our own situations. Whether drawn from real life, as in historical narratives, or from fiction, the actions of other people provide the stories we need to continue our own efforts to under-stand our personal and social experiences.

It is at this point that our previous distinction between the noetic and the ethical implications of narrative comes into play. How or what do we gain or learn from the stories of other people, whether actual or fic-tional? If we emphasize noetic responses, we tend to look for models or ex-amples that can yield knowledge about human relationships. We look for themes or ideas that can be formulated as truths about human life, truths that we can appropriate for our own understanding of life. But this com-mon and traditional view is too limiting; it does not adequately account for our endless fascination with the experiences and stories of others. Our struggles and hopes are not resolved and our curiosity is not allayed simply as a result of the truths that we learn from observing the lives of fictional characters. While we do respond noetically to stories, we need more than the knowledge of the truth in our personal journeys. Our concerns are with actions more than with truths, and therefore the ethical implications of stories grip us more deeply than the noetic implications.

Do fictional narratives, then, provide us with ethical models for our own actions? Here we need to make an important distinction. When we speak of models, we sometimes see them as prescriptive patterns for be-havior, as examples that can or should be followed. But models can also be thought of as possible ways of understanding something, as hypothetical ways of construing a set of related instances. In the latter case, models are not presented as prescriptive or exemplary but as heuristic, as sketches for

125

possible ways of understanding something. Fiction offers models of human action in the second sense. If and when stories attempt to present prescriptive models, we usually reject them as too didactic.

Fiction, as indicated earlier, gains meaning from its authorial stance. This implies that the models of action that may be presented in fictional stories are models formed by the beliefs of authors. They are, in effect, interpretations of human action and have a status comparable to hypothetical models. Ricoeur's formulation of this idea is stated coldly but correctly: literary fiction, he writes, "proves to be an immense laboratory for thought experiments in which this connection [between agents and actions] is submitted to an endless number of imaginative variations."[53] Fiction explores the possibilities of human action and possible ways of moving human actions toward resolution. The primary aim of fiction is not to give us knowledge of the truth about human actions but, in Frank Kermode's happy phrase, to "educe the forms of a future."[54] Fictional narratives explore ways of understanding the teleology of action, the possibilities for moving from conflict to resolution.

We learn (if that is the right word) from fiction by comparing the relationships of actions in the narrative to our own sense of how actions are interrelated in our own experience and observation. As Wayne Booth writes in *The Company We Keep*, "Every appraisal of narrative is implicitly a comparison between the always complex experience we have had in its presence and what we have known before."[55] In real life much of our understanding is gained by the exchange of stories, by our narrations of actual or imagined events. We interpret our situations and actions by listening to the stories of others, seeing in these stories examples of how events and actions are intertwined in the experiences of others. It is through this kind of narrative modeling more than through didactic formulations of truth that we gain insight into our own lives. David Carr puts it this way:

> The actions and sufferings of life can be viewed as a process of telling ourselves stories, listening to those stories, and acting them out or living them through. And here I am thinking only of living one's own life, quite apart from the social dimension, both cooperative and antagonis-

53. Ricoeur, *Oneself as Another,* 159.

54. Frank Kermode, *The Sense of an Ending* (London: Oxford University Press, 1967).

55. Wayne Booth, *The Company We Keep: An Ethics of Fiction* (Berkeley and Los Angeles: University of California Press, 1988), 71.

tic, of our action, which is even more obviously intertwined with narration.[56]

Stories, fictional as well as actual, function as models that we use in assessing the stories of our own lives.

In comparing the stories of fiction with the stories of our own lives, we see more clearly the ethical dimension of narrative hermeneutics. Our personal life stories are always in process, never completed while we have the capacity for further action and further thought. Thus, we are constantly thinking about the future, about the teleology of our actions. We are preoccupied with the purposes of our actions, for without a sense of purpose, we have a sense of emptiness. Fictional stories, in contrast, are completed; they arrive at resolution. Accordingly, fictional narratives provide a way of thinking about both the consequences and the purposes of actions. In fiction we can envision resolutions and completions in ways that we cannot fully achieve in our own historical odysseys. Although these resolutions in fiction cannot prescribe models for our own actions, they can serve as models for our reflection. Ethically we move toward understanding through this kind of modeling as well as through the cognitive understanding of moral principles. We interpret the ethical contours and implications of our actions with the help of both narrative and theoretical discourse.

As we explore the ethical dynamics of life, we need to understand the possibilities of evil as well as the possibilities of good. And hence some of the most compelling fictional stories are tragedies, stories of failure and suffering. Many are stories of violence, depravity, and crime. While such stories may be regarded as depressing, offensive, or degrading by readers who want to enjoy uplifting stories with happy endings, our teleological conception of narrative as the exploration of the ethical possibilities of experience explains the value of these stories. Actions arise out of conflict, and the heuristic value of tragic fiction is that it enables us to confront the violent and depraved possibilities of life as well as the peaceful and beneficial possibilities. In narrative fictions we encounter the whole range of human actions and the whole range of emotions, thoughts, and attitudes that accompany and shape actions.

Because these fictions are heuristic rather than prescriptive models for thinking about the ethical patterns of our actions, our interpretations

56. Carr, *Time, Narrative, and History,* 61.

of the narratives are influenced by our own beliefs about ethics. If we believe that ethics is the application of absolute transhistorical principles governing human behavior, we may look to fiction for exemplary instances of those principles. If we are skeptical about moral as well as noetic absolutes, we may engage in deconstructionist analyses of fiction. If we are followers of Aristotle or Kant or Mill, or of Freud or Marx or Nietzsche, we may examine fictional narratives in the light of their theoretical models. Our interpretations of the goodness or badness, the rightness or wrongness, the justice or injustice of the actions of characters will reflect our own beliefs about ethics. But it is because of the underlying ethical import of narrative fiction that it can make sense to reflect ethically on fictional actions. It is because fictional narratives have a mimetic relationship of resemblance to actual life and because the actions of life are fundamentally teleological and ethical that a hermeneutics of fiction is ultimately grounded in the ethical character of our living and our thinking. It is at this point, too, that hermeneutics moves toward moral philosophy as such. This move, however, is beyond the scope of this volume.

Before ending this section, I want to say a few words about the implications of our book's hermeneutical model for Christian thinking, since our authorial stance is a broadly Christian one. Two points will help to suggest the value of our model for Christian theorizing.

First, the model acknowledges the open-endedness of history. The stories of our personal lives and the story of history are never completed within our own allotted time. We are always engaged in a quest. We achieve resolution with respect to specific conflicts and ventures in our lives, but we never see the final design or resolution of the whole. There is always more to come, and time and history never allow things to occur exactly in the same way. Patterns appear, and hence we can speak of purposes and ends in meaningful ways, but our understanding is constantly developing and adapting itself to new circumstances. There are always new ends to consider; teleology is, ironically, our endless preoccupation.

But recognition of the historicity of experience and thought does not, as we have observed, lead inevitably to epistemological skepticism. In a Christian worldview, certain beliefs are taken to be truthful and authoritative, but these beliefs do not have to be understood in a non- or antihistorical way. The meaning of Christian beliefs is found in their application to the particular situations of our lives; they demand constant interpretation in the light of historical situations. For a Christian, therefore, the reading and criticism of fiction is not identical with a search for "eternal truths." Fiction for Christians, as for all of us historical creatures, is a means for envisioning the possibilities of action and a means for achieving greater insight and flexibility in understanding. Fiction is not prescriptive, nor are there "lessons" to be learned, if one thinks of lessons as finalized dogmatic or doctrinaire teachings.[57] Fiction gives us all a chance to explore the possibilities of life and to reflect on the implications of our own particular beliefs about life.

In a Christian context, these possibilities can be seen as explorations of the world that God has created for our use and enjoyment. The worlds of fiction are not identical with the actual world of creation, and hence to read fiction is not to encounter God's world directly. It is rather to encounter the rich and varied ways in which human beings respond to God's world. But in exploring those human responses, by entering those imagined worlds that authors create for us, we develop our ability to interpret God's world. We develop our sensitivities and our understanding by encountering alternatives, and in fiction we are encountering alternative worlds, that is, alternative renditions or interpretations of the world. Fiction has no controlling or binding power over us in the way that the actual world has, and fiction does not reveal to us the workings of the divine Creator in the way that the actual world does. Thus, while Christians should not fear or shun fiction, neither should they think that in the creation of literary fiction writers share in some transcendent way in the activity of the divine Creator.[58] Fiction comes to us with an authorial stance (the author's beliefs about life and the world), and in our responses to and interpretations of fiction we have our own stance (our own beliefs about life and the world). Literary fictions are through and through, as objects and instruments, products of human actions. But in spite of their human shortcomings, fictional narratives — in all of their richness and variety, in all of their expression of conflicting and disparate beliefs — are among the means we have for exploring and reflecting on our own beliefs and for developing our sensitivity to the world created for us by the God in whom we believe.

Second, because the worlds of fiction are not prescriptive or normative, the reading of fiction can for Christians be an experience of hope.

57. There are some genres of fiction that are didactic by intent, e.g., fables, parables, and some allegories. But even in these genres, the truth or moral is embedded in the story as well as in the accompanying statement.

58. This view has been made popular among some Christian critics by such works as Dorothy Sayers' *The Mind of the Maker.*

Christian readers empathize with disillusioning, depressing, demoralizing kinds of fiction as strongly as do any other readers, but the values that are operative in the worlds of fiction, nihilistic or pessimistic as they sometimes are, are always and only possibilities that human beings imagine and dramatize. Fictional narratives do not offer final truths about life; they explore for our imaginative encountering the possible ways of interpreting human experience. For every reader, fiction offers opportunities for deepening one's sensitivity and understanding of human conflicts, emotions, struggles, and beliefs. And out of such engagements with fictional narratives comes a more profound awareness and understanding of one's own beliefs. Fiction, of course, has the potential for influencing the reader's beliefs, and that is why some Christians are wary of fiction. But beliefs are things that need to be influenced. Beliefs need constantly to be made responsive to new situations and responsibilities. Fiction can have the effect of enhancing one's beliefs and of developing them in more fulsome ways even if the author's beliefs are very different from one's own.

It is in this sense that reading fictional narratives can support a Christian understanding of hope. Out of the matrix of innumerable narratives expressing the full range of human experiences, aspirations, and disappointments arises an unending flow of possibilities for seeing and interpreting the world of God's creation. We may judge some of them as inadequate, slanted, or wrong, but they all help us by enabling us to examine our own ways of seeing and interpreting. From a Christian point of view, the world and the God who created it are full of infinite possibilities for flourishing, possibilities that can never be exhausted by the finite resources of our history. To engage in the reading of fictional narratives is for Christians to participate in this unending and hopeful exploration of the possibilities of living in the world and thereby in our own living to discover and enjoy more fully the faces of others and the face of the Other. In *The Trinity and the Kingdom*, Jürgen Moltmann expresses this perspective theologically:

> A world which is created for this end [the glorification of the triune God] has to be understood as an "open system". . . . Creation "in the beginning" can only be the commencement of God's creative activity — an activity which also includes creation's continuance. . . . The interpretation of providence must be expanded correspondingly: providence . . . means that God keeps the world's true future open for it through the gift of time, which works against all the world's tendencies to close in on itself, to shut itself off. This must be understood as *the divine patience*.

God has patience with his world because he has hope for it. God's hope is manifested in his readiness to endure the apostasy of the men and women he has created, their self-withdrawal and closed-in-ness. In the patience of his love he keeps the world's future open for it. . . . Creation is the first stage on the road to liberty.

. . . the truth of freedom is love. It is only in love that human freedom arrives at its truth. I am free and feel myself to be truly free when I am respected and recognized by others and when I for my part respect and recognize them. I become truly free when I open my life for other people and share with them, and when other people open their lives for me and share them with me. Then the other person is no longer the limitation of my freedom; he is an expansion of it. In mutual participation in life, individual people become free beyond the limits of their individuality, and discover the common room for living which their freedom offers. That is the social side of freedom. We call it love and solidarity. In it we experience the uniting of isolated individuals. In it we experience the uniting of things that have been forcibly divided.

Freedom in the light of hope is the creative passion for the possible. . . . It is directed *towards the future,* in the light of the Christian hope for the future of the coming God. The future is the kingdom of not yet defined potentialities. . . . Creative passion is always directed towards a project of a future of this kind. People want to realize new possibilities. That is why they reach forward with passion. In hope, reason becomes productive fantasy. People dream the messianic dream of the new, whole life that will at last be truly alive. They explore the future's possibilities in order to realize this dream of life.[59]

59. Jürgen Moltmann, *The Trinity and the Kingdom: The Doctrine of God,* trans. Margaret Kohl (San Francisco: Harper & Row, 1981), 209-10, 216, 217.37. *The Varieties*

III

Communicative Action and Promise in Interdisciplinary, Biblical, and Theological Hermeneutics

ANTHONY C. THISELTON

The Unity and Coherence of the Argument throughout This Study

Autonomy? Or Respect for the Other's Otherness as Given and Giving

Roger Lundin has exposed the fragile, brittle foundations on which the philosophy of the *orphaned individual* rests in Descartes and in the pervasive legacy of Cartesian and Enlightenment rationalism. He traces the persistence of the individualist strand through the Kantian notion of *autonomy* and the expressionism of much romanticist literature and art. By contrast, hermeneutics does not place the individual human self at the center of the stage in heroic or illusory self-isolation. It substitutes a paradigm of listening to the Other in give-and-take, or, more strictly, a triadic relation between the Other, the self, and a content that emerges from the dialogue and from the self-transformation or self-transcendence which results from it. Whereas Kant locates respect for the human person in autonomy and supposed freedom, hermeneutics nourishes respect as *respect for the otherness of the Other*. Hans-Georg Gadamer observes as he looks back over his life's work, "It is the Other who breaks into my ego-centredness and gives me something to understand. This . . . motif has guided me from the beginning."[1]

Such a shift of focus coheres profoundly with biblical hermeneutics and with Christian theology. On one side, the historical finitude of fallen humanness characterizes every "Other" with a givenness that calls into question all notions of unconstrained autonomy found in liberal optimism. More to the point, interpreters conditioned by their own embeddedness in specific times, cultures, and theological or secular traditions need to *listen,* rather than seeking to "master" the Other by netting it within their own prior system of concepts and categories. This premature assimilation of the Other into one's own prior grooves of habituated thought constitutes the "control" and advance commandeering that Gadamer calls "Method." In a theistic context, listening to the God who is Other remains dependent on the priority of the Other as Giving and Given. Unless God chooses to give himself as One who is given, we listen in vain, and can "master" nothing by constructing a prior "method" in advance of understanding who it is who addresses us.

This deeply theological principle, however, defines all hermeneutics. To borrow Lundin's phrase, "a parentless, autonomous thinking agent who is dependent upon nothing outside himself" remains deaf to the giving and given Other.[2] Paul Ricoeur comments, "The idea of myself appears profoundly transformed, due solely to my recognizing this Other."[3] Whereas Descartes presupposes an isolated, individual self, hermeneutics presupposes an interactive, relational, intersubjective self. Whereas the Cartesian legacy focuses on a thinking self abstracted from history, hermeneutics focuses on the whole self, an agent who experiences, understands, and performs actions, embedded in time and in historically conditioned developing traditions and pre-given "worlds."

The two exponents of hermeneutics who have achieved the greatest weight in the twentieth century, namely, Gadamer and Ricoeur, stand together in stressing the role of *listening* and of *practical action* in hermeneutics. Gadamer observes, again at the end of his long career, "Hermeneutics is above all a practice, the art of understanding and of making

---

1. Hans-Georg Gadamer, "Reflections on My Philosophical Journey," in *The Philosophy of Hans-Georg Gadamer,* ed. Lewis E. Hahn (Chicago: Open Court, 1997), 46; cf. 3-63.

2. Lundin, 3 above.

3. Paul Ricoeur, *Oneself as Another,* trans. Kathleen Blamey (Chicago: University of Chicago Press, 1992), 9.

something understood to someone else. . . . In it what one has to exercise above all *is the ear*, the sensitivity for perceiving prior determinations, anticipations, and imprints that reside in concepts" (my italics).[4] Similarly, Ricoeur discusses illocutionary speech-acts (of which promise offers a major example) with the comment that these "consist in which the speaker *does in* speaking. . . . Facing the *speaker* in the first person is a *listener* in the second person to whom the former addresses himself or herself" (Ricoeur's italics).[5]

Descartes and the Enlightenment on the one side, and Gadamer, Ricoeur, and hermeneutics on the other, represent respectively the self-sufficient, isolated, autonomous, thinking self, and the interactive self who discovers self-identity and understanding in the to-and-fro of thought and action regulated by respect for the otherness of the Other. Lundin has not only exposed the fragility and vulnerability of the Cartesian perspective, but has also traced some of its negative effects in literature, politics, and human life. The self stands at the center of its own horizons and seeks to achieve knowledge by deduction and control.

Clarence Walhout has examined the other side of the coin: if speech and language are interactive and social, utterances and texts are produced by the actions of agents who address persons, and further actions generate processes whereby utterances on texts may *count as* history or fiction, warnings or promises, heuristic explorations of possible scenarios or mimetic representations or refigurations of an extralinguistic world.[6] Walhout calls attention to the multilayered, multifunctional nature of language, which performs many acts, or many types of action. Thereby he provides the material that suggests an approach to the very question which Lundin asks in his first two pages. How can we "say something new" if part of our agenda may be also, in other terms, to "say the same old thing"?[7] This has constituted the dilemma of biblical expositors and systematic theologians since the era of the New Testament church. Indeed, Walhout's exposition of *fiction* as projecting worlds of *possibility* (i.e., of how things *might* be or *could* be, rather than of how they *are*) recalls the way frequently chosen by Jesus to proclaim the promissory realities of the kingdom of God.[8] Jesus told fictional nar-

4. Gadamer, "Reflections on My Philosophical Journey," 17.
5. Ricoeur, *Oneself as Another*, 43.
6. Walhout, 67-71, 79-84, 100-107 above.
7. Lundin, 1-2, 11-12 above.
8. Walhout, 79-84 above.

ratives that project possible worlds.[9] This is how things *might* be if people lay hold of the promises of God and act on them; this is how it might be if they turn away from these possibilities.

It takes little imagination to perceive that the two modes of approach to literature, to texts, and to human life bear some correlation respectively to the orientations of the natural sciences or technology, and literature or art. Descartes (1596-1650) sought instances of certainty and security in mathematics and the physical sciences. Gadamer compares this starting point with that of Giambattista B. Vico (1668-1744), who published *The New Science* in 1725 (revised, 1730).[10] Vico attacked Descartes for neglecting the importance of history and social community. All life and thought, Vico urged, are governed by the primordial power of "imagination" (Italian, *fantasia*), and traditions mediated by communities offer the invaluable resource of "poetic wisdom" *(sapienza poetica)* for questions of understanding and truth. Vico's thought was largely neglected until it was taken up especially by Coleridge, Benedetto Croce, and Max Horkheimer.

Gadamer recalls the very different paths taken by his father, who "was a researcher in the natural science," and his own pursuit of the humanities, literature, and the arts, and those whom his father regarded as "those 'chattering professors'" *(Schwätzprofessoren)* at Breslau and Marburg.[11] In his article published in the *Frankfurter Allgemeine* in October 1989, Gadamer discloses his early passion for Greek philosophy, especially for Plato's dialectic, in which "intelligence" *(Geistigkeit)* certainly could not be reduced to knowledge *(epistēmē)* or technical "know-how" *(technē)*, but rather invited "wisdom" *(phronēsis)* in a context of understanding *(sophia)* and rational judgment *(nous)*.[12] The natural sciences too often reflect a tendency to transform technical instrumental scientific method *(technē)* into a comprehensive worldview (communal, *phronēsis*). Yet the assimilation of everything, including theology and biblical interpretation, under the model of "science" or Cartesian "method" verges on the plausible only in an industrial age of mechanistic Newtonian science and tech-

---

9. Anthony C. Thiselton, *New Horizons in Hermeneutics: The Theory and Practice of Transforming Biblical Reading* (London: HarperCollins; Grand Rapids: Zondervan; Carlisle: Paternoster, 1992), 566-75.

10. Hans-Georg Gadamer, *Truth and Method,* trans. William Glen-Doepel, 2nd ed. (London: Sheed & Ward, 1979), 19-26.

11. Gadamer, "Reflections on My Philosophical Journey," 3.

12. Hans-Georg Gadamer, "Gadamer on Gadamer," in *Gadamer and Hermeneutics,* ed. Hugh J. Silverman (New York: Routledge, 1991), 17; cf. 13-19.

nology. Dieter Misgeld and Graeme Nicholson write, "Only an age of engineering would suppose that the application of a science or a theory would take the results of a theory erected in its own domain, and then impose it somewhere, hoping to produce results useful to human life."[13]

Curiously, the limits of scientific method to explain all of reality seem to be appreciated more readily in the philosophy of religion than in biblical studies. Views and methods that students in philosophy of religion recognize as "positivist," "reductionist," or even "materialist" are often embraced quite uncritically in issues of judgment about, for example, acts of God in biblical narrative. In place of the more rigorous and judicious exploration of these issues in philosophical theology, biblical studies seems too readily to become polarized. What one side regards as proper scholarly historical science, the other regards as secular rationalism or as prejudice drawn from a narrow Enlightenment worldview. The temptation then arises to stake everything on a "literary" approach to the Bible. Still less rationally, evangelicals who have felt excluded from much mainline debate find — or imagine that they find — a more level playing-field when "modernity" is excluded from biblical interpretation in favor of the radical pluralism of postmodernity. If each competing view is perceived as incommensurable with any criterion of evaluation, the "softer" literary paradigm seems more hospitable to "religious" meanings. But now the problem has taken a different form. Are we to say that anything goes? Are we committed to hermeneutical anarchy? All three main parts of this book seek to steer between the Scylla of mechanical replication and the Charybdis of radical polyvalency and unconstrained textual indeterminacy. We shall return to a further critique of autonomy below.

Between the Scylla of Mechanical Replication and the Charybdis of Orphaned Indeterminacy

Lundin's initial illustration from mass advertising formulates a major dilemma in hermeneutics.[14] No advertiser, no preacher, no teacher, no literary author will gain a hearing merely by saying "the same old thing." Even

---

13. Hans-Georg Gadamer, *Hans-Georg Gadamer on Education, Poetry and History: Applied Hermeneutics,* ed. Dieter Misgeld and Graeme Nicholson (Albany: State University of New York Press, 1992), vii.
14. Lundin, 1-2 above.

the most devout Christian congregation perceives a difference between reciting the creed or hearing a biblical reading and the aim of the preacher "to make it all come alive once again." But a discerning congregation does not want gimmicks, personal anecdotes, or the trivial banalities of a liturgical talk-show host if what is projected is mere novelty unrelated to the "text" of the gospel to be proclaimed. It does not want mere novelty or mere shock for its own sake. Both earlier in this book and in his recently published volume *Disciplining Hermeneutics,* Lundin cites the judicious observation of Joel Weinsheimer: there can indeed be "wrong interpretations"; nevertheless, a text invites "interpretations that are not just duplicates of it but genuinely other. . . . If a text had *but one right interpretation* and many wrong ones, or many right interpretations *and no wrong one,* there would not be a problem" (my italics).[15]

This is less complicated and less speculative than it may sound. To propose an analogy that offers a loose fit, I have almost completed a very extensive, detailed commentary on the Greek text of 1 Corinthians, making my own translation. Mostly, the NRSV, NJB, NIV, and REB are "right" translations in relation to achieving particular points. But they may serve to underline different aspects of the Greek, and certain translations (including those of certain undergraduate students) must certainly be excluded as "wrong" by almost any serious criterion of interpretation.

Lundin perceptively observes that the choppy waters which threaten shipwreck on either of two sides are made all the more treacherous by the post-Cartesian neglect of tradition and the history of traditions.[16] (This will become clear when we discuss Hans Robert Jauss.) Whereas traditions offer the possibility of "speaking creatively" while remaining faithful to the content of tradition, an "orphaned" self can choose only either tedious mechanical repetition or idiosyncratic novelty. (The term derived from the Greek *idios* — "belonging to an individual, one's own" — with *sygkrasis* — "brew, mixture" — was once a live metaphor.) The inexhaustible, multilayered, multifunctional polyphony of biblical texts transcends repeatedly any single way of saying it; but this does not, need not, and should not invite the disastrous hospitality to radical pluralism that brings anarchy. "Every classic text," David Tracy constructively writes, "comes to any reader

15. *Disciplining Hermeneutics: Interpretation in Christian Perspective,* ed. Roger Lundin (Grand Rapids: William B. Eerdmans; Leicester: Apollos, 1997), 13; cf. Joel Weinsheimer, *Philosophical Hermeneutics and Literary Theory* (New Haven: Yale University Press, 1991), 87.

16. Lundin, 11-12 above.

through the history of its effects (conscious and unconscious, enriching and ambiguous, emancipatory and distorted) upon the present horizon of the reader. The text can become a classic for the reader only if the reader is willing to allow that present horizon to be vexed, provoked, challenged by the claim to attention of the text itself."[17] We shall consider Tracy's approach in more detail when we come to consider Jauss's version of the aesthetics of reception. Jauss draws both upon Gadamer's attention to history and tradition in hermeneutics, and upon literary theory in Juril Lotman, Viktor Shklovsky, and Wolfgang Iser.[18] Thus our habituated modes of thinking can be challenged by reading. We can be surprised by the sudden, eventful disclosure of the genuinely new; yet this comes not from a new text or a new method, but springs from the impact of a classic text which, as Ernst Fuchs would say, "speaks anew" (*AI*, 107).[19]

Tracy shares with Walhout the belief that this "happening" depends on the impact of the whole or "total situation of any work of art," although not every aspect of the whole applies to every encounter with every text. This totality includes the following: (1) the act of creating the text or work of art (related to romanticist or authorial concerns); (2) the work itself (the formalist interplay of textual forces), (3) "the world the work creates or reveals (mimetic understandings ranging from Aristotle to hermeneutical understandings of the creative power of mimesis in Gadamer and Ricoeur)"; and (4) the audience the work affects; within Tracy's pragmatics, we should include reader-response theory and reception theory (*AI*, 113). Indeed, Tracy uses language closely akin to the way Jauss does when he continues: "Somehow the classics endure as provocations awaiting the risk of reading: to challenge our complacency, to break our conventions, to compel and concentrate our attention, to lure us out of a privacy masked as autonomy into the public realm" (*AI*, 115).[20] This last point is also Walhout's, while Tracy resonates with Lundin in refusing to hand over "the classics to the levelling

---

17. David Tracy, *The Analogical Imagination: Christian Theology and the Culture of Pluralism* (London: SCM; New York: Crossroad, 1981), 105; cf. 99-153. All further references are to this edition and will be cited in parentheses with the abbreviation *AI* within the body of the essay.

18. See below under "The Temporal and Historical Character of Jauss's Aesthetics of Reception," 191-99.

19. We may compare Tracy with Ernst Fuchs, *Hermeneutik*, 4th ed. (Tübingen: Mohr, 1970), 249-56, and *Studies of the Historical Jesus*, trans. Andrew Scobie (London: SCM; Naperville, Ill.: Allenson, 1964), 191-206; cf. 8, 30.

20. We discuss Jauss below.

power of a technical reason disguised as publicness, to consign them to a privacy of a merely entertaining ... realm.... Instead we need, I believe, a rehabilitation of the notions of the normative, the authoritative — in a word, the classical ... welcomed again as the communal and public heritage of our common human experience of the truth of the work of art" (*AI*, 115).

In his later work, Wittgenstein shares with Gadamer an antipathy toward "craving for generality" and "the contemptuous attitude towards the particular case," which both associate with "science," mathematics, and deductive logic.[21] Wittgenstein reacts against his own earlier captivity to a single generalizing method.[22] Gadamer speaks of his own attraction over a lifetime to issues of "artistic sensitivity ... interaction with poetry [and its] powerful formative effect on human beings."[23] His insistence that we cannot decide on the propriety of some prior "method" in advance of encountering the phenomenon which is "other" to us resonates with Karl Barth's insistence that God cannot be known through some "method" which stands independently of God's making himself known.[24]

Yet it would be a mistake to press too far this polarization between scientific "method" and hermeneutical understanding. It has led to unfortunate simplistic distortions in biblical interpretation, theology, and other areas of life. I argued above, following Tracy and Walhout, that each of at least four dimensions of communicative acts and/or performative acts produced by texts or instantiated in texts should be kept in view. To pit "historical" paradigms against "literary" paradigms as if these were necessarily *competing* hermeneutical endeavors in biblical interpretation constitutes a distracting polemical exercise that points away from the more important issue of *when and for what purposes* each approach might have some place. Tracy observes, "Explanation and understanding are not enemies, but uneasy, wary allies" (*AI*, 118). This seems to be overlooked when

21. Ludwig Wittgenstein, *The Blue and Brown Books: Preliminary Studies for the "Philosophical Investigations,"* 2nd ed. (Oxford: Blackwell, 1969), 18.

22. Ludwig Wittgenstein, *Philosophical Investigations,* trans. G. E. M. Anscombe, 2nd ed. (Oxford: Blackwell, 1958), §§97-115. All further references to this work indicate section numbers and will be cited in parentheses with the abbreviation *PI* within the body of the essay.

23. Gadamer, "Reflections on My Philosophical Journey," 5.

24. Karl Barth, *Church Dogmatics,* 4 vols., trans. G. T. Thomson et al., ed. G. W. Bromiley and T. F. Torrance (Edinburgh: T. & T. Clark, 1936-69), II/1.27, 179. All further references are to this edition and will be cited in parentheses with the abbreviation *CD* within the body of the essay.

various "paradigms" of biblical studies are pitted one against the other, as if, for example, the rise of historical interpretation in the eighteenth century excluded Patristic exegesis, or as if the rise of literary theory in biblical studies offered an exclusively different "worldview" from the "historical" paradigm and its so-called worldview.[25] This over-ready drive toward the disjunctive disruption of a long theological tradition, which Lundin judiciously identifies as the *"post-x," "post-y"* phenomenon, usually occurs in the context of an oversimplified search for the novel.

The via media for which this book argues, however, is no merely bland attempt at compromise and leveling down. It is the reverse. We seek, with Ricoeur and Tracy, to evaluate the contributions and the limitations, respectively, of "explanation" and "understanding." Even then, our approach will not simply apply comprehensively to all texts or to all kinds of texts. Lundin has exposed the peril of abstracting interpreters, texts, and acts of interpreting from history and tradition, or from the prior "world" in which these are situated. Walhout has shown that while issues about textual form, descriptive reference, narrative strategy or point of view, and anchorage in the actual world all play a part in engaging with texts as objects of action, the part played by each may become radically different when texts are understood as instruments of action.[26] We may approach fictional texts, for example, with a different hermeneutical agenda from those which claim to embody historical report.

I shall endeavor to take these arguments further in the pages that follow. Many examples emerge from the hermeneutics of biblical texts, but such "theological" fiction as George Eliot's *Adam Bede* and especially Dostoyevsky's *The Brothers Karamazov* instantiate the differences between (1) single meaning and replicated understanding; (2) radical indeterminacy of meaning and the dissolution of the author; and (3) the under-

25. This tendency seems overplayed in the otherwise helpful volume by Roy A. Harrisville and Walter Sundberg, *The Bible in Modern Culture: Theology and Historical-Critical Method from Spinoza to Käsemann* (Grand Rapids: William B. Eerdmans, 1995) — e.g., 29-31, 262-73 and throughout — where the "new" becomes in effect a "single issue" approach to a complex history of twists and turns, the complexity of which is recognized when the authors are not pressing their main thesis. I have spoken of "shifts" of this kind, but like Jauss (following Thomas Kuhn), I have used the term *paradigm* as *both transcending and including* an earlier paradigm: Thiselton, "New Testament Interpretation in Historical Perspective," in *Hearing the New Testament: Strategies for Interpretation,* ed. Joel B. Green (Grand Rapids: William B. Eerdmans; Carlisle: Paternoster, 1995), 10-36, 263-73.

26. Walhout, 84-99 above.

standing of texts as speaking with polyphonic voices and performing multiple speech-actions. As we argue below, to follow Camus in reducing *The Brothers Karamazov* to a philosophy of anti-theistic protest, or to follow Berdyaev in understanding it as Christian gospel, misses the more convincing readings of M. M. Bakhtin and Malcolm Jones as "unmerged voices" of polyphonic validity.[27] More than this, Camus and Berdyaev transparently subsume Dostoyevsky's speaking voices within their own horizons, assimilating them into their own beliefs and expectations *before* adequately identifying the otherness *of* Dostoyevsky and the otherness of other voices *within The Brothers Karamazov,* each from the other. Dostoyevsky's voice is no more easily to be reduced to the single voice of the brother Ivan, or to that of the brother Alesha (Alyosha), than the plural voices within the Book of Job are to be reduced simply to the divine "reply," to the editor's appendix, or to any other single character. Yet, while "right" understandings remain dynamic, polyphonic, and irreducible to a single simplified concept, some "understandings" are clearly *wrong.* At the same time, it would be a mistake, as Gadamer warns us, to determine criteria for "right" or "wrong" in advance of engaging with the work. No biblical book or fictional work that wrestles with the problem of evil can take us forward unless we share in its wrestling and dialogue. Evil is too complex to permit any single packaged "answer," even if for the theist some answers are plainly wrong (e.g., that evil is illusory, or that God is not good). In these pages, then, we shall seek to avoid shipwreck by steering between Scylla and Charybdis.

Yet some biblical texts constitute apostolic or prophetic communications of warning, promise, teaching, or ethics. To claim that a reconstruction of the situation initially in view has no bearing on what it is to understand the text is, at minimum, doctrinaire. Here the contrasts between Wisdom literature, the hymnic mode of I-Thou address in the Psalms, the

---

27. On the sources of literature, see below under "Polyphonic Voices in Theological Fiction: Job, Eliot and Dostoyevsky on Evil," 172-82. Meanwhile, cf. Kevin Mills, *Justifying Language: Paul and Contemporary Literary Theory* (New York: St. Martin's, 1995), 155-69 ("'Dialogism' in Bakhtin and 'the Gravity of the Other'"); and esp. *New Essays on Dostoyevsky,* ed. Malcolm V. Jones and Garth M. Terry (Cambridge: Cambridge University Press, 1983), including S. Hackel, "The Religious Dimension: Vision or Evasion?" 139-68; and Harriet Murav, *Holy Foolishness: Dostoevsky's Novels and the Poetics of Cultural Critique* (Stanford: Stanford University Press, 1992). I am also indebted to Malcolm Jones, "Dostoevsky: Re-thinking Christianity," seminar paper presented in the Department of Theology, University of Nottingham, June 1997.

narrative of a corporate people, narrative fiction, and apostolic, prophetic, or dominical pronouncement call for a variety of hermeneutical models and emphases. Agency and action form the stuff of such texts. If they are to function as operative communicative action, we cannot bypass questions about the commitments, responsibilities, and appointments of extralinguistic authors or agents, or about the directionality of their address. This theme will emerge throughout this study, and especially in our consideration of speech action. Once again, it coheres with the arguments of Lundin and Walhout.

Lundin offers a critique of the Cartesian obsession with self-conscious *"thoughts,"* while Walhout explores the value of models in hermeneutics that focus on *"action."* In the context of noting certain logical paradoxes that arise from "private" language, the later Wittgenstein observes, "The paradox disappears only if we make a radical break with the idea that language always functions in one way, always serves the same purpose: *to convey thoughts"* (*PI* §304; my italics). As he states elsewhere in the same work, "Here the term 'language-*game*' is meant to bring into prominence the fact that the *speaking (Sprechen)* of language is part of an activity *(ein Teil einer Tätigkeit)* or a form of life *(oder einer Lebensform)"* (*PI* §23). Lundin and Walhout have already alluded to "the multiplicity" of these linguistic acts, like "the tools in a tool-box" (*PI* §§11, 24). "Commanding, questioning, recounting" are no less actions or activities than "walking, eating, drinking" (*PI* §25). By contrast, "giving names to things" would be no more than as it were to place pieces on a game-board before anyone can make a move with them (*PI* §49; cf. also 38, 26-30). Understanding comes through *watching* language *in action* (*PI* §54; cf. 31, 43).

From Wittgenstein and J. L. Austin through to John Searle and Jürgen Habermas, the most helpful term to describe the function of most utterances and most texts (although not all of them) is *communicative action* (*PI* §491).[28]

---

28. See J. L. Austin, *How to Do Things with Words* (Cambridge: Harvard University Press, 1962), 6-24; John R. Searle, *Speech Acts: An Essay in the Philosophy of Language* (London: Cambridge University Press, 1969), 54-71; and *Expression and Meaning: Studies in the Theory of Speech Acts* (Cambridge: Cambridge University Press, 1979), 1-57; Jürgen Habermas, *The Theory of Communicative Action,* 2 vols., trans. Thomas McCarthy (Cambridge: Polity, 1987-91; Boston: Beacon, 1984-87).

ANTHONY C. THISELTON

Some Presuppositions and Entailments
of Illocutionary Speech-Acts

The later Wittgenstein observes that the utterance "We mourn" at a funeral service is not to inform people of our thoughts but *to perform an act of mourning* (*PI*, II: ix, 189). In the Psalms and elsewhere in the biblical writings, we regularly find cries for help and cries of complaint. Wittgenstein notes, "A cry is not a description" (*PI*, II: ix, 189). In liturgy, to confess "I believe" is not only to convey a belief-content; it is also to stake one's commitment to that content, to nail one's colors to the mast (*PI*, II: x, 190-92).[29]

It might be unwise, however, to appear to lean too heavily here on Wittgenstein. To my surprise, one reviewer of my work appears to believe that my insistence on the major importance of speech acts stems from being seduced by the later Wittgenstein. The reverse is the case. Since 1970, if not earlier, I have produced a series of writings urging that a biblical and theological account of language gives weight and currency to the importance of speech acts, especially to *acts of declaring* (kerygma); *acts of worship* (hymns and psalms); *acts of pronouncement and legal direction* (laws and commissionings); and most especially *acts of promise* (for Paul, Hebrews, Luther, and Tyndale, the very heart of what constitutes the liberating gospel).[30] I have just completed a short commentary on the Epistle to the Hebrews in which it is noted how this epistle (or sermon) embodies *acts of worship* (Heb. 1:5-13); *acts of appointment* (1:1-4, 14); *acts of witness*

---

29. Cf. H. H. Price, *Belief* (London: Allen & Unwin, 1969), and in biblical studies, Vernon H. Neufeld, *The Earliest Christian Confessions* (Leiden, Netherlands: Brill, 1963), 13-68 and throughout.

30. Among the earliest are Anthony C. Thiselton, "The Parables as Language-Event," *Scottish Journal of Theology* 23 (1970): 437-68; "The Supposed Power of Words in the Biblical Writings," *Journal of Theological Studies* 25 (1974): 283-99; and *Language, Liturgy and Meaning* (Nottingham: Grove, 1975). Among the more recent are "Christology in Luke, Speech-Act Theory, and the Problem of Dualism in Christology after Kant," in *Jesus of Nazareth: Lord and Christ: Essays on the Historical Jesus and New Testament Christology*, ed. Joel B. Green and Max Turner (Grand Rapids: William B. Eerdmans; Carlisle: Paternoster, 1994), 453-72; *New Horizons in Hermeneutics*, 16-19, 283-311, 597-617; "Authority and Hermeneutics: Some Proposals for a New Agenda," in *A Pathway into the Holy Scripture*, ed. P. E. Satterthwaite and D. F. Wright (Grand Rapids: William B. Eerdmans, 1994), 107-42; and "The Logical Role of the Liar Paradox in Titus 1:12, 13: A Dissent from the Commentaries in the Light of Philosophical and Logical Analysis," *Biblical Interpretation* 2 (1994): 207-23.

(2:3, 4); *acts of proclamation and of trust* (e.g., 2:12-18); *acts of address* (3:7-15); and (to cut the list short), at the heart of the whole epistle, *acts of covenantal promise* (6:13–8:13; 10:16-18, 37-38; 11:8-13, 39-40).[31] In John and in 1 John, emphasis is put on "doing" the truth and on lifestyle.[32] It is not that Wittgenstein "invents" this view of language; he rescues it from its burial beneath an abstract Cartesian tradition that tends to equate language with argument or description alone. In Jesus Christ the Word was made *flesh;* Cartesian Protestantism threatens to turn flesh back into abstracted *word* again.

The importance of speech acts, especially illocutionary acts, for biblical hermeneutics and for theology has recently been placed on the agenda with compelling force by Nicholas Wolterstorff, primarily in his *Divine Discourse* (1995) but also in his essay "The Importance of Hermeneutics for a Christian Worldview," found in the volume edited by Roger Lundin to which we have already referred (1997).[33] Clare Walhout's work in the preceding section draws on the perspectives expounded by Wolterstorff, especially his notion of count-generation proposed in his earlier *Works and Worlds of Art.* Walhout's exposition of texts as *instruments of action* coheres well with Wolterstorff's essay. Walhout and Wolterstorff (like Austin, Searle, and developments in my own work) distinguish between locutionary and illocutionary acts. In using a locutionary act to perform an illocutionary act, Wolterstorff explains, "I have performed one action by performing another distinct action."[34] Thus a variety of locutionary acts capable of performance by or in texts may constitute instruments by means of which, for example, God or human agents may give commands, appoint to office, name or acquit, or most especially *make promises.* Hence, Wolterstorff argues, even the geocentric cosmology assumed in Psalm 93 may be used not as an instrument for mapping the cosmos but for other

---

31. Anthony C. Thiselton, "The Epistle to the Hebrews," in *Commentary 2000,* ed. J. D. G. Dunn and J. W. Rogerson (Grand Rapids: William B. Eerdmans, forthcoming). See also W. G. Übelacker, *Der Hebräerbrief als Appell* (Stockholm: Almqvist & Wiksell, 1989).

32. Dietmar Neufeld, *Reconceiving Texts as Speech Acts: An Analysis of 1 John* (Leiden: Brill, 1994); and Thiselton, "Truth," in *NIDNTT III,* ed. C. Brown (Exeter: Paternoster; Grand Rapids: Zondervan, 1978), 874-902, esp. "John," 889-94.

33. Nicholas Wolterstorff, *Divine Discourse: Philosophical Reflections on the Claim that God Speaks* (Cambridge: Cambridge University Press, 1995), 19-94 and throughout; and "The Importance of Hermeneutics for a Christian Worldview," in *Disciplining Hermeneutics,* ed. Roger Lundin, 25-47.

34. Wolterstorff, "The Importance of Hermeneutics," 30.

actions.[35] Historical reconstruction, if or when it is invited, is not to sustain a romanticist or expressionist hermeneutic, but to determine "what illocutionary action he or she [the author] performed. Call such interpretation *authorial discourse interpretation*" (Wolterstorff's italics).[36]

One effective test of Wolterstorff's thesis is invited by his assertion in *Divine Discourse* that "by way of a single locutionary act, one may say different things . . . several illocutionary acts."[37] It is generally agreed, to select a biblical case-study, that Hebrews 1–12 constitutes a sermon delivered in the form of a communication to addressees from whom the writer or speaker is unavoidably absent.[38] The opening verses (1:1-4) provide one of the most arresting beginnings possible, combining elegance, alliteration, rhythm, rhetorical artistry, and unstoppable force with probably the most sophisticated and stylish Greek in the entire New Testament. The very same words, however (as I have noted in my commentary), combine a number of functions — they perform several multilayered, multidirectional actions: "They are sermon, creed, confession, hymn, praise, acclamation, exposition, argument, celebration. Much of the poverty of some preaching today derives from exclusive attention *either* to 'teaching,' *or* 'exhortation,' *or* personal anecdote, in contrast to the richly multi-layered, multi-level model of preaching, teaching, and praise seen here."[39] Even if, as some claim, the "hymnic" material is supposedly borrowed from other (non-Christian?) sources, this would still cohere with Wolterstorff's comment on the cosmology of Psalm 93: a locutionary action that formerly operated in a different context is now utilized (in Walhout's terms, becomes "an instrument of action") to perform

---

35. Wolterstorff, "The Importance of Hermeneutics," 37.

36. Wolterstorff, "The Importance of Hermeneutics," 43.

37. Wolterstorff, *Divine Discourse*, 55.

38. William L. Lane, *Hebrews*, 2 vols. (Dallas: Word, 1991), 1:lxix-lxxxviii, 1-9; A. Vanhoye, *Homilie für halfbedürftige Christen* (Regensburg: Pustet, 1981), throughout; Übelacker, *Der Hebräerbrief als Appell*, although against Barnabas Lindars, *The Theology of the Letter to the Hebrews* (Cambridge: Cambridge University Press, 1991); but cf. Harold W. Attridge, "Paraenesis in a Homily," *Semeia* 50 (1990): 211-26, and *The Epistle to the Hebrews: A Commentary on the Epistle to the Hebrews* (Philadelphia: Fortress, 1989), 13-14.

39. Thiselton, "The Epistle to the Hebrews," 1:1-4, where I also allude to J. Frankowski, "Early Christian Hymns Recorded in the NT . . . in the Light of Heb 1:3," *Bib Zeit* 27 (1983): 183-94; R. Deichgräber, *Gotteshymnus und Christarhymnus in der frühen Christenheit* (Göttingen: Vandenhoeck & Ruprecht, 1967); cf. also Jack T. Sanders, *The New Testament Christological Hymns: Their Historical Religious Background* (Cambridge: Cambridge University Press, 1971), 19-20, 92-94.

illocutionary acts of ascription, doxology, and/or acclamation (*to* God *through* Christ) while simultaneously performing the illocutionary actions of proclamation and declaration (*from* God *through* Christ) and credal confession (*multidirectional* public witness). Multidirectional speech-action in the public domain is the operational model that opens understanding in this first test-case in biblical interpretation.

The interplay between linguistic action and states of affairs outside language, however, remains exceedingly subtle, complex, and diverse from case to case. A valuable resource for engaging this problem can be found in Searle's work *The Construction of Social Reality.* Predictably, he allows that, for example, acts of promising, appointing, and naming presuppose "institutional facts." But he also shows convincingly that "institutional" facts, in turn, presuppose "brute" facts. Thus, for instance, the utterance "I give and bequeath my watch to . . ." presupposes the *institutional* fact that if the text of the utterance has been duly signed and witnessed as a will, and has been proven at law, *it performs a legal act that transfers property ownership* from the deceased to the beneficiary. The Epistle to the Hebrews, we shall see, discusses such institutional facts in detail. Hebrews 9:16 deliberately uses the Greek *diathēkē* to mean both *covenantal* promise and legal *testament* of a deceased person. However, Searle insists that "the analysis of the structure of *institutional facts* reveals that they are logically dependent on *brute facts.* To suppose that all facts are institutional would produce an infinite regress or circularity in the account of institutional facts" (my italics).[40] For a printed piece of paper *to count as* a dollar bill or *as* a pound note logically depends on the brute fact that that certain piece of paper exists and carries certain printed words and designs. The piece of paper *qua paper* does not carry the promise for which a bank takes responsibility; but the social act of *counting it as* legal currency both transcends and presupposes the brute fact of its existence as a piece of paper. In Walhout's terms, a *text as an object of action* has become *a textual instrument of action* by the illocutionary (here, legal) act of *counting* the bill as operative currency. In law and commerce it *thereby constitutes* currency.

Wolterstorff's proposals about performing "one action by performing another distinct action" remain fundamental for speech-act theory, and Walhout has used this principle constructively.[41] Nevertheless, it

---

40. John R. Searle, *The Construction of Social Reality* (London: Allen Lane, 1995), 55-56; cf. 31-58 and throughout.

41. Wolterstorff, "The Importance of Hermeneutics," 30.

would be misleading to pretend that this principle as such has been over-looked in biblical hermeneutics. Rudolf Bultmann's entire program of demythologizing rests on the principle that pseudo-descriptive language about "objectified" states of affairs or events "should be interpreted not cosmologically but anthropologically or better existentially."[42] When he insists that "objectified" descriptive mythological language actually obstructs and impedes the intention, stance, or goal of New Testament writers, Bultmann is claiming quite simply that the locutionary acts which they use as instruments for the illocutions that they wish to perform direct attention to the wrong thing. Thus a locutionary act of asserting that Jesus rose into the air toward the stratosphere constitutes an instrument for an illocutionary act of acclaiming his glory and vindication. Yet, while Bultmann's program has been helpful in assisting us to "see the main point" about much biblical language that may distract us if we treat it as scientific description, Bultmann's proposals and program invite numerous criticisms. I have called attention to these extensively and in considerable detail elsewhere, and these criticisms need not be repeated here.[43]

Bultmann lapses into a generally noncognitive view of New Testament language. I have argued that by contrast Wolterstorff's speech-act theory does not rest on a polarization of this kind, and also elsewhere drawn a careful distinction between existential interpretation and speech-act theory.[44] Bultmann has an utterly polarized and simplistic view of how existential self-involvement and value relate to assertions about states of affairs. He believes that the former can operate virtually without reference to the latter, even correlating the Kantian fact-value duality with a supposed parallel between law and grace: to discover "facts" and to rest faith on this constitute an intellectual "work" as against bare trust and existential or volitional response

---

42. Rudolf Bultmann, "New Testament and Mythology," in *Kerygma and Myth: A Theological Debate*, 2 vols., ed. Hans-Werner Bartsch, trans. Reginald H. Fuller (London: SPCK, 1953-62), 1:10. The German edition is *Kerygma und Mythos*, 6 vols. (Hamburg: Reich & Heidrich, 1948-).

43. Anthony C. Thiselton, *The Two Horizons: New Testament Hermeneutics and Philosophical Description: With Special Reference to Heidegger, Bultmann, Gadamer, and Wittgenstein* (Grand Rapids: William B. Eerdmans, 1980), 205-92. In the Korean translation (Seoul: Chongshin, 1990), see 323-452.

44. Thiselton, "Speech-Act Theory and the Claim that God Speaks: Wolterstorff's *Divine Discourse*," *Scottish Journal of Theology* 50 (1997): 97-110; also Thiselton, *New Horizons in Hermeneutics*, 272-312.

to the kerygma.[45] Bultmann subsumes a simplified philosophy of language into a prior theological frame. Wolterstorff, like Searle, perceives that there is an irreducible and subtle relationship between extralinguistic states of affairs and the operation of illocutionary acts based on "institutional" (Searle) or "count-generating" (Wolterstorff) facts. Bultmann, like so many others, works with Karl Bühler's crude distinction between descriptive, expressive, and volitional utterances, as if these were virtually three self-contained, self-sufficient modes of discourse.

Even Wolterstorff's apparent readiness to speak of linguistic action at times, it seems, *in place of* "revelation" or "revealing" might be thought to come too close to drawing an over-sharp line between them, but he is too rigorous and subtle a philosopher to fail to offer some strongly qualifying comments that soften an initially over-robust distinction. He observes, "Perhaps the speech acts had what may be called a *revelational correlate,* consisting of God revealing that He was performing the act" (Wolterstorff's italics).[46] But he is not entirely happy with this. He tests various models, including that of "intransitive revelation."[47] As so often occurs, it is the paradigm case of *promising* that illuminates the issue best: "Acts of promising and commanding will always reveal something or other about the agent; [but] what they reveal about the agent is not that which the agent promised or commanded."[48] What is revealed is *the agent's right to make the promise and the agent's stance* toward constraining his own options for action.[49]

I shall expound these fundamental but complex issues later, especially in the final two sections of this essay. Meanwhile, I wish to call attention to the recent work of Francis Watson on this subject, together with some incisive comments by Kevin Vanhoozer, as well as to some hundred articles relating to the subject even before 1977.[50] All the same, can we genuinely propose that

---

45. Bultmann, *Kerygma and Myth,* 1:210-11, 2:182-83; *Essays Philosophical and Theological* (London: SCM, 1955), 133-50, esp. 135; and *Glauben und Verstehen: Gesemmelte Aufsatze,* 4 vols. (Tübingen: Mohr, 1964-65), 2:117-32, esp. 119-20.

46. Wolterstorff, *Divine Discourse,* 21.

47. Wolterstorff, *Divine Discourse,* 31.

48. Wolterstorff, *Divine Discourse,* 35.

49. It is impossible to exaggerate the importance of the commitments and ethical responsibilities of extra-linguistic *agents* here, as Walhout's work implies. Cf. Searle, "The Logical Status of Fictional Discourse," in *Expression and Meaning,* 58-75.

50. Francis Watson, *Text and Truth: Redefining Biblical Theology* (Edinburgh: T. & T. Clark, 1997), esp. 71-126; Kevin J. Vanhoozer, *Is There a Meaning in This Text?* (Grand Rapids: Zondervan, 1998), esp. 202-40 (cf. also 240-366); and R. B. Meyers and K. Hopkins, "A Speech-Act Theory Bibliography," *Centrum* 5 (1977): 73-108.

"counting" one locution *as* another speech act is other than volitional or noncognitive? Wittgenstein observes, "All confirmation and disconfirmation of a hypothesis takes place already within a system. . . . From a child up I learned to judge like this. *This is* judging. . . . The child learns by believing the adult. Doubt comes *after* belief" (Wittgenstein's italics).[51] Wittgenstein places such emphasis on "training" and on "customs," even to the point of saying what "counts as a mistake" is context-relative, that he acknowledges that an opponent might well exclaim, "Aren't you at bottom really saying that everything except human behaviour is a fiction?" (*PI* §307). But he rejects the criticism. He is not "a behaviourist in disguise"; he wants to show that what a linguistic or communicative act *counts as* doing depends on the intersubjective situation and public world of criteria that define the agenda in given cases (*PI* §307; cf. 281-349). Working, operative, communicative acts, however, are never self-contained, autonomous systems abstracted from tradition, training, and life. For understanding entails having "the right to say the words 'Now I know how to go on'" (*PI* §179). But this does not eliminate the possibility of criteria: "The application is still a criterion of understanding" (*PI* §146). The application, however, cannot be defined in the abstract; it entails "particular circumstances. . . . The difference lay in the difference of situation" (*PI* §§154, 166). When we speak of God as creator, or of the experience of feeling "safe in the hands of God" in ethical and religious language, "we seem constantly to be using similes. But a simile must be a simile for *something*" (Wittgenstein's italics).[52] But if we subtract the simile, it would be pointless to ask what the residual "facts" are; there is a subtle interweaving of utterance, stance, and intersubjective life in which language of this kind acquires currency only as it becomes *operational* from case to case, with sufficient regularity and patterned reiteration over time for it to make sense to ask what counts as "going on" or "following a rule" (*PI* §§138-242). To perceive "understanding" dynamically as "going on" or as in the context of agents, action, and the public world entirely matches Walhout's concerns about *acts and actions* in the first part of his essay, on texts as objects of actions; about *temporal narrative* in the sections on truth and fiction; and about *teleology and responsibility* in the final section on ethics and fiction. Four senses are emerging in which we may speak with validity of our *hermeneutics of promise:*

51. Ludwig Wittgenstein, *On Certainty,* ed. G. E. M. Anscombe and G. H. von Wright, trans. Denis Paul and G. E. M. Anscombe (Oxford: Blackwell, 1969), §§83, 105, 128, 160.

52. Ludwig Wittgenstein, *Philosophical Occasions, 1912-1951,* ed. James C. Klagge and Alfred Nordmann (Indianapolis: Hackett, 1993), 42-43.

(1) A hermeneutic of promise (simply in the sense of a promising hermeneutic) will steer between the Scylla of Cartesian individualism, which has *orphaned* itself from its parental history and tradition, and the Charybdis of an *intralinguistic indeterminacy* that has no anchorage within a public, intersubjective world. Lundin has addressed the issue of individualism, novelty, and tradition; Walhout has addressed the issue of action and agency in the intersubjective, extralinguistic world, which in turn generates textual "worlds," whether of refigured fact or fiction.

(2) We locate the *responsibility of hermeneutics* (which we considered in our earlier book) within a *teleological and temporal narrative frame*. *Accountability* in hermeneutics is part of the grammar of what this discipline properly demands. Responsible *attention* to the *present* task and *present* text, we argue, entails due recognition of the *past* history and the living tradition that has parented us, as well as an eye on appropriate *future directions and goals*. Lundin explored the former; Walhout, the latter. However, I explore this temporal dimension further in the third section of this essay.

(3) The biblical writings provide not only an especially illuminating workshop for hermeneutical theories and models but also one of very high personal stakes. In these texts, instantiations of various texts (or types of texts) and situations (or types of situations) may be found. According to the central traditions of the Old and New Testaments, *communicative acts of declaration, proclamation, call, appointment, command, worship, and most especially promise are constitutive of what it is for the word of God to become operative and effective.* The continuity (as well as some discontinuities) of these *actions* of calling, commanding, declaring, appointing, worshiping, and promising together contribute to a *narrative history of temporal actions* that in turn provides *the frame of reference within which* the hermeneutics of biblical texts and subsequent theological traditions operate with greatest promise. These issues will be developed in detail in the last two sections of this book when we consider *promise*.

(4) A closer examination of parallels between hermeneutical theory and the theology of the biblical writings (including historical and modern Christian theology) will serve to underline and to develop Lundin's critique of autonomy. From the standpoints of ethics, politics, hermeneutics, and theology, we shall see that respect for the other, especially respect for the otherness of the other, shifts the center of concern from the individual self to human relationality and responsibility. This will emerge as our arguments proceed, particularly in the last main part.

Reader-Response Theories and Biblical and Theological Fiction

It might seem more logical to expound the value of reader-response theories before exposing their limitations. This was the procedure followed in *The Responsibility of Hermeneutics*. However, since the publication of that work in 1985, my own thinking on reader-response models has undergone considerable development and modification, and in any case, this approach within biblical interpretation now has a status different from the one so popular in the late 1970s and earlier 1980s. It will prove less bland and more constructive first to take its impact for granted and to identify five specific reasons why it has ceased to command the attention which it once enjoyed, and then to explore what positive hermeneutical functions it may still perform in engaging with biblical texts, especially texts of fiction within the biblical writings.

Initially, however, a few brief comments on the nature of the approach and the issues that it raises are in order. Reader-response theories are of various kinds, but *all serve to underline and to encourage the active role of the reader (or of communities of readers) in engaging with texts*. Long before the terminology signified a particular model in literary theory, Socrates, parts of the biblical Wisdom literature, many (but not all) of the parables of Jesus, and the indirect communication of Søren Kierkegaard and the later Wittgenstein pioneered the approach. In all these cases the model of the reader as a passive recipient of knowledge or information was undermined by the perception that language achieves more than the communication of information — that it also, and often even more fundamentally, changes the reader's viewpoint.

Many of the parables of Jesus, and equally the communicative techniques of Kierkegaard and the later Wittgenstein, seduce readers into *making moves of their own*. Without such prompting into action, the text remains a closed book. Alternatively, a purely passive reader is led along by a particular logic only to discover that all that he or she had imagined to be the message is turned on its head and contradicted. All great "indirect communication" (in the sense presupposed in many utterances of Jesus, Kierkegaard, and Wittgenstein) serves to prevent superficial understanding by preventing prior understanding without inner change and active engagement with the issues. Parables of this kind simultaneously reveal and conceal. They stand a world away from the Cartesian categories of the certain, the self-evidential, or what is evident from purely deductive logic.

Reader-response dynamics thereby begin to indicate a price to pay for seducing or sometimes forcing readers into activity. They depend upon what I identify later in this section as "open" texts rather than "closed" texts. In general, the more "open" the text (or strictly, the semiotic code of the text), the more active the role of the reader becomes, but at the price of permitting less clarity and wider boundaries of possible meaning. Such texts achieve greater force and greater engagement, but often at the price of a degree of ambiguity or polyvalency. On the other hand, a "closed" text comes into its own as an instructional "handbook" where there must be no room for doubt, but the goal is replication rather than creative appropriation.

The implications when we view the biblical writings as scripture are clear. If we regard the Bible as a spiritual version of an engineering handbook — living the Christian life as a technology, praise and worship as techniques, and "right doctrine" as the central goal of revelation or divine speech — we shall expect "closed" texts that inform but ask nothing of the reader other than passive acceptance of information. At the other extreme, if we regard biblical texts as literary "productions" designed primarily to generate understanding of ourselves and to move us on (in virtually any direction as long as we move), we shall expect "open" texts that challenge, frustrate, surprise, or provoke us into active response, but leave it largely to us as readers or to our reading community to determine *how* we respond or *how* we act.

This sets the scene for the theme of this book. The biblical writings cannot be reduced to a Cartesian textbook of information that permits the response of only wooden replication of ideas or idiosyncratic novelty outside the clear boundaries of the text. Moreover, the biblical writings perform *acts* of declaration, proclamation, promise, verdict, pardon, liberation, commission, appointment, praise, confession, acclamation, and celebration that burst beyond the uniform model of flat "information." On the other hand, while many passages of the biblical writings operate with literary productivity that seduces, challenges, surprises, provokes, and transforms the expectations of readers, the biblical writings also contain creeds, doctrines, traditions, beliefs, and assertions that cannot be reduced without doing violence to the status of "literary" or "open" texts.

Reader-response theories are also of more than one kind. The progress of my own thinking since 1985 can be summed up by concluding that our assessment of reader-response theories depends on changing relationships between two sets of variables. From within the horizons of the biblical text, every degree of coding between fully "closed" and fully "open" texts can be found. From within the horizons of modern literary theory, a spectrum of models has emerged, from the more firmly based theories of Wolfgang Iser and Umberto Eco to the more precarious theories of David Bleich and Stanley Fish, at least within the terms of debate set by biblical interpretation and Christian theology. Furthermore, none of these theories takes genuinely adequate account of the histories of the reception of texts in terms of Gadamer's "history of effects" *(Wirkungsgeschichte)*. This will lead us to explore the resources of H. R. Jauss's aesthetics of reception below.

"Why Hasn't Reader-Response Criticism Caught on in New Testament Studies?" A Diagnosis Suggesting Five Reasons

The quotation marks signal that the phrasing of this question comes from someone else. One of my former doctoral candidates, Stanley Porter, now a chairholder and department head, contributed an article with this title to the *Journal of Literature and Theology* in 1990.[53] Porter found the work of Stanley Fish constructively suggestive, and complained that "Reader-response criticism . . . in New Testament Studies . . . is definitely lagging behind developments in the secular literary field."[54] He cited a string of biblical specialists who have tried to explore this area: N. Peterson is "disappointing," R. Fowler leans too heavily on the "historical" and becomes "formalistic," J. L. Resseguie "pulls back," and R. Culpepper is also "disappointing," showing lack of nerve in failing to follow Fish. Most have a "clear fixation with formalism."[55] I myself, Porter observed, began a bolder venture in *The Two Horizons* (1980), but drew back into a more cautiously "historical" approach in my joint work with Lundin and Walhout in *The Responsibility of Hermeneutics* (1985), the forerunner of this present volume. If Porter was right, what were the reasons for this "pull back"?

(1) I need not repeat the attack that I made in *New Horizons in Hermeneutics* (1992) on Fish's contextual pragmatism.[56] I concluded that the radical version of reader-response theory found in the later Fish

53. S. E. Porter, "Why Hasn't Reader-Response Criticism Caught on in New Testament Studies?" *Journal of Literature and Theology* 4 (1990): 278-92.
54. Porter, "Reader-Response Criticism," 290.
55. Porter, "Reader-Response Criticism," 280-85.
56. Thiselton, *New Horizons in Hermeneutics,* 537-55.

would, if used as a comprehensive biblical hermeneutic, transform biblical texts into "*potentially idolatrous* . . . instruments of self-affirmation . . . and *grace and revelation into a phenomenology of self-discovery*" (my italics).[57] This was not to deny that Fish allows for surprise and even for subversion of a reader's horizons in response to a text. But while this may do justice to a selected range of biblical texts (especially fictional parables), the interpretative background or communal pre-understanding needed itself to be reshaped in the light of the gospel and divine promise. I rejected Porter's contention that what a "right" interpretation of a biblical text might be said to amount to was largely determined by the power interests of the "biblical guild," and I asked whether the Reformers merely, in effect, substituted their own new power guild for that of the pope to determine their own new readings, rather than guiding their communities in undergoing reformation in the light of a transcendent "beyond" that they encountered through the texts themselves (even if mediated through interpretation).

We recall that Fish attacks Iser's more cautious version of reader-response theory by rejecting Iser's concession that there is something "there" in the texts to interpret.[58] Fish quite explicitly uses the words "reformed" and "from the outside." He writes, "The model in which a practice [i.e., of a way of reading] is altered or reformed by constraints brought in from the outside . . . never in fact operates."[59] All meaning (exhaustively and without remainder) is constructed by "the authority of interpretative communities."[60] "The reader's response is not to the meaning: it *is* the meaning" (Fish's italics): textual meaning is "readers performing acts."[61] While I agree that meaning depends on "performing acts," the question is whether only *readers* constitute exclusive agents of action, or whether authors and readers *collaborate* in communicative action.

In 1994, Porter responded to my arguments with a second round of

57. Thiselton, *New Horizons in Hermeneutics*, 550.

58. Stanley Fish, "Why No One's Afraid of Iser," in *Doing What Comes Naturally: Change, Rhetoric, and the Practice of Theory in Literary and Legal Studies* (Durham, N.C.: Duke University Press, 1989), 68-86, esp. 69-70.

59. Fish, "Introduction: Going Down the Anti-Formalist Road," in *Doing What Comes Naturally*, 2, 14.

60. Cf. Stanley Fish, *Is There a Text in This Class?: The Authority of Interpretive Communities* (Cambridge: Harvard University Press, 1980), 1-17.

61. Fish, *Is There a Text in This Class?* 1-17; "Introduction: Going Down the Anti-Formalist Road," 12.

observations and comments.[62] Generously, he made more of the points on which we agreed than of our possible disagreements, concluding that there was less disagreement than might earlier have appeared to be the case. Porter is helpful, provided that we do not lose sight of the radical difference between the reader-response theories propounded by Iser, Eco, and Jonathan Culler (which I in general treat positively in *New Horizons*) and those formulated by Bleich, Holland, and Fish (which, I argue, can be destructive for biblical studies if pressed too far).[63] In the light of the critique of fallen humanity implicit in the cross of Christ and his resurrection, we see the potentially destructive strategy invited by Norman Holland's words, "We use the literary work . . . to replicate ourselves."[64] This kind of hermeneutical model has more affinities with affirming the "autonomy" of individual readers, or the "autonomy" of the horizons of their own peer-group community, than with the fundamental principle discussed above: of seeking *to listen* to the "Other" with respect for the otherness of the giving and given Other. Even if Fish's reader belongs to a reading community, it has isolated itself, like an orphan, from an "Other" that addresses it "from outside."

(2) My arguments above concerning the need to steer between the Scylla of Cartesianism and the Charybdis of radical postmodern polyvalency confirm a claim I put forward in *New Horizons*. (This is the only point of overlap in the critique that I now offer.) I believe that there is a lack of integrity or, more probably, a profound mistake in the "set up" that Fish constructs between a full-blown systematic formalism and his own radical version of reader-response theory, in which the text is *constructed* rather than *construed or conditioned* by readers. "Going Down the Anti-Formalist Road," his key 1989 essay, "sets up" (my phrase in *New Horizons*) a formalist approach along the lines proposed by R. Kempson that is openly incompatible with any genuine sensitivity toward hermeneutics in any form akin to Gadamer, Ricoeur, or even Betti or Habermas.[65] Fish then asserts (rather than argues) that once you have "seen through" formalist systemic approaches to language and texts, his own contextual relativism or contextual pragmatism is all that remains as a live option.

62. S. E. Porter, "Reader-Response Criticism and New Testament Study: A Response to A. C. Thiselton's *New Horizons in Hermeneutics,*" *Journal of Literature and Theology* 8 (1994): 94-102.

63. Thiselton, *New Horizons in Hermeneutics,* esp. 515-55.

64. Norman Holland, "Transactive Criticism: Re-creation through Identity," *Criticism* 18 (1976): 342; cf. 334-52.

65. Fish, *Doing What Comes Naturally,* 1-33, esp. 1-6.

In *New Horizons* I appealed to the later Wittgenstein's experience of disillusionment with his own earlier systematic formalism expounded in his *Tractatus* to show that later observations about overlappings and criss-crossings between forms of life and language games, and Wittgenstein's later understanding of a philosopher as "not a citizen of any community of ideas," formed part of a far more subtle "middle way" than Fish considers still credible.[66] By his own account, his own rush down "the Anti-Formalist Road" is triggered by a series of supposed disillusionments in which he "sees through" what others propose. But hermeneutics, as Betti and Gadamer insist, is better served by patience than by extrovert iconoclasm. The purpose of this book is, among other things, to offer a patient course between a Scylla and a Charybdis in the light of a suspicion of both Cartesian certainty and the radical pluralism that postmodern perspectives encourage too rapidly.

(3) A crucial point that I think both Porter and I failed to identify is the *fundamentally a-historical viewpoint of reader-response theory,* in contrast to the genuine engagement with horizons of expectation located within an on-going historical tradition of textual effects, as this is explored in the reception theory of Gadamer's former pupil Hans Robert Jauss.[67] Lundin's critique of the price paid for Cartesian "certainty" — the abstraction of any "parent" tradition from the historical processes — helps to alert us to this problem. It achieves little for Fish to attack the Cartesian illusion of a "timeless" formalist system if he then replaces it only by "floating" self-contained readers or communities of readers who cannot be "reformed" or "corrected" from "outside." These have little temporally grounded critical engagement with the continuities and discontinuities in the historical tradition that shapes their horizons of expectation. Tradition mediates *judgments* concerning textual content. Even if Fish could claim that these are no more than reactive constructions by earlier reading-communities, at least these would constitute "something outside" Fish's self-sufficient reader or reading community. It is perhaps this embeddedness within a prior tradition that most clearly separates Fish's language about the decisive "authority" of interpreta-

---

66. Ludwig Wittgenstein, *Zettel,* ed. G. E. M. Anscombe and G. H. von Wright, trans. G. E. M. Anscombe, 2nd ed. (Oxford: Blackwell, 1981), sec. 455; cf. 452. Also see Thiselton, "What Fish's Counterarguments Overlook about Language: Fish and Wittgenstein," in *New Horizons in Hermeneutics,* 540-46.

67. The most widely known translated work is Hans R. Jauss, *Toward an Aesthetic of Reception,* trans. Timothy Bahti (Minneapolis: University of Minnesota Press, 1982). All further references are to this edition and will be cited in parentheses with the abbreviation *TAR* within the body of the essay.

tive community over textual effects from even medieval or pre–Vatican II accounts of the *magisterium* among some Roman Catholic thinkers.

These readers whom Fish posits are abstracted, bracketed out, or (in Lundin's terminology) "orphaned" from a classical heritage.[68] Even Bleich's communities of men and women, more educated elite and more ordinary masses, Afro-Caribbean and white, have horizontal relations but only marginal roots in traditions of textual interpretation.[69] Lundin distinguishes carefully between "taking history seriously" in Gordon Fee's sense of recovering a historical setting, and drawing on all the resources of "the history that stands between us and the text."[70] We shall explore how Jauss's reception theory offers an infinitely richer resource than reader-response theory as a hermeneutical resource for a variety of texts. Its shallow understanding of history (in the sense defined by Lundin here) offers another reason why reader-response criticism has not "caught on" in biblical interpretation.

(4) The *timing* of the brief period of welcome of reader-response criticism and the subsequent declining interest in it in biblical studies cast the movement into a fundamentally *reactive* role in relation to "historical" approaches especially to parables. In the 1970s and early 1980s, reader-response criticism provided a valuable hermeneutical model for correcting a tradition of interpreting especially the parables of Jesus, a tradition that was, in effect, dominated by concern about the historical reconstruction of an original setting (if possible) and subsequent settings in the ministry of Jesus and/or the life of the earliest Christian communities, and by concern for conceptual or propositional content that given parables were perceived to convey. The most influential figures in the early 1960s were still A. Jülicher, C. H. Dodd, and J. Jeremias. Jülicher is usually regarded as laying the foundations of parable interpretation for twentieth-century biblical criticism. In his view, the parables of Jesus served *to convey general truths* that could be expressed as propositions concerning the nature of the kingdom of God. A parable had a single general meaning.

Are not some parables, however, multilayered? Jülicher argued that the open-textured, multilayered interpretation of the parables of Jesus as *metaphor* belonged to the creative imagination and supposed allegorization of

---

68. Lundin, 54-55 above.

69. David Bleich, *The Double Perspective: Language, Literacy, and Social Relations* (New York: Oxford University Press, 1988).

70. Lundin, 36-37 above. Stephen E. Fowl similarly targets Ben Witherington, but his view of "history" is narrower than Lundin's. See Fowl, *Engaging Scripture* (Malden, Mass.: Blackwell Pubs., 1998), 34.

the evangelists or early believers, whereas Jesus himself used straightforward, single-meaning *comparison* or *simile (Vergleichung)*.[71] The German permits an understanding that encourages, or at least suggests, a word play here: *uneigentliche Rede* means both indirect or *nonliteral* (metaphorical) speech and *unauthentic* (not-one's-own) speech. *Eigentliche Rede* denotes both *literal or one-meaning speech* and *authentic speech* that is one's own. Whether or not the word play is intentional or merely suggestive, Jülicher formulated a theory of parable interpretation that allowed only for *clear, single-minded, didactic propositions*. Thereby they became tools for the "reconstruction" of a conceptual body of teaching that encapsulated "the message" of the historical Jesus. Hermeneutics became subsumed within historical reconstruction and conceptual theology.

Jülicher's theory compelled him to categorize a number of parables as later constructions that were not spoken by Jesus. These included certainly the interpretation of the parable of the sower (Mark 4:14-20) and most probably the quasi-metaphor on which it rested (Mark 4:3-9); the parable of the wicked husbandmen (Mark 12:1-9); and all others that were more nearly allegories with multiple codings rather than general comparisons that presented a single point capable of clear, succinct conceptualization: "We cannot stop half way.... Either the parables are wholly figurative speech or wholly literal *(eigentliche)*. The parable is there only to illuminate that one point ... an idea ... that is valid."[72] The hermeneutics of the parables aims at reconstructing their "chief thoughts."[73]

Although a "didactic" approach (linked in our present context with a Cartesian approach) to the parables would dominate biblical interpretation in effect from Jülicher (1st Germ. ed., 1899; 2nd Germ. ed., 1910) to Jeremias (1st Germ. ed., 1947; 8th Germ. ed., 1970; 3rd Eng. ed., 1972), voices of protest emerged from the beginning.[74] C. A. Bugge (1903) and more especially P. Fiebig (1904 and 1912) insisted that even if the Greek *para-bolē* denoted in purely linguistic terms "a placing beside," "juxtaposition," or "comparison" (at least in nonbiblical, classical Greek), the term translated the Hebrew *mâshâl* (e.g., Prov. 1:6; Ezek. 12:22), which (as Jeremias also concedes) denotes *proverb, riddle, dark saying, joke, fictional story, gnomic saying*, or almost any kind of indirect or double-meaning dis-

71. A. Jülicher, *Die Gleichnisreden Jesu*, 3rd ed. (Freiburg: Mohr, 1899), 1-148.
72. Jülicher, *Gleichnisreden Jesu*, 317.
73. Jülicher, *Gleichnisreden Jesu*, 580-81.
74. Joachim Jeremias, *The Parables of Jesus*, trans. S. H. Hooke, rev. ed. (New York: Scribner, 1972).

course.[75] Fiebig compares parables selected from rabbinic sources, including the Mishnah, the Jerusalem and Babylonian Talmuds, and the Tosefta. He notes that Jülicher is entirely ignorant of rabbinic uses of *mâshâl*, and places more emphasis on the alien meaning of *parabolē* found in Aristotle.[76] Simile, metaphor, allegory, fictional tale — all overlap and function in diverse ways.

Although he has historical and form-critical interests in multiple settings, C. H. Dodd anticipated a reader-response approach as early as 1935. He defines a parable in the Gospels as that which "arrests the hearer by its vividness or strangeness . . . *leaving the mind in sufficient doubt about its precise application to tease it into active thought*" (my italics).[77] Such a definition and approach entirely cohere with the versions of reader-response theory advocated respectively by Wolfgang Iser and Umberto Eco. For Iser, the role of the reader is active, not passive, and this activity is best aroused by those texts which are incomplete, in the sense of embodying "blanks" or "gaps" that must be "filled in" or "completed" by the reader to arrive at understanding.[78] Eco prefers to speak of the difference between texts that presuppose a "closed" coding, which in his view reflect the "handbook" model of tightly clear information or instructions, and more "literary" texts that utilize an "open" code, which generate multivalent or polyvalent meaning, inviting active decisions from the reader.[79] Through groundwork laid in biblical hermeneutics by Ernst Fuchs in the 1950s and early 1960s, Robert Funk gave further expression to this "open" coding or multiple meaning in the case of many metaphorical parables, as against the "discursive, non-figurative" language to which Jülicher had reduced them.[80]

---

75. Paul Fiebig, *Altjüdische Gleichnisse und die Gleichnisse Jesu* (Tübingen: Mohr, 1904), 14-73. Cf. Fiebig, *Die Gleichnisreden Jesu im Lichte der rabbinischen Gleichnissen der neutestamentlichen Zeitalters* (Tübingen: Mohr, 1912).

76. Fiebig, *Die Gleichnisreden Jesu*, esp. 6-132. The entries for *parabolē* in Liddell, Scott, and Jones, *A Greek-English Lexicon* (Oxford: Oxford University Press, 1968), and Bauer, Arndt, Gingrich, and Danker, *A Greek-English Lexicon of the New Testament*, 2nd ed., rev. and aug. (Chicago: University of Chicago Press, 1979), 612-13, are startlingly different.

77. C. H. Dodd, *The Parables of the Kingdom* (London: Nisbet, 1948), 16.

78. Wolfgang Iser, *The Act of Reading: A Theory of Aesthetic Response* (Baltimore: The Johns Hopkins University Press, 1978).

79. Umberto Eco, *The Role of the Reader* (London: Hutchinson, 1981); *A Theory of Semiotics* (Bloomington: Indiana University Press, 1976); *Semiotics and the Philosophy of Language* (Bloomington: Indiana University Press, 1984).

80. Robert Walter Funk, *Language, Hermeneutic, and Word of God* (New York:

Into this climate, reader-response theory was readily welcomed as a hermeneutical model that cohered with the emphasis of Jesus himself: "Let the person who has ears, hear" (Mark 4:9; 7:16; par. Matt. 13:9; Luke 14:35). Susan Wittig went on to develop Iser's approach and apply it to parables, and Eco and Culler offered further resources in the context of biblical fiction. (We shall trace these developments in the next section.) But once a multiplicity of hermeneutical models had been assured, these resources were perceived to be limited.

(5) Since we are dealing here not simply with mainly *fictional* parables but *also* with parables uttered by *Jesus,* those who approach the biblical writings as scripture cannot ignore the authorial dimension even if, with Wolterstorff, we prefer to speak of *authorial discourse* rather than authorial intention. I have argued elsewhere that it is too easy to become sidetracked by the so-called intentional fallacy. *Intention* generates problems when it is used as a noun, as if to apply a psychology of mental status. However, as Kevin Vanhoozer also recently argued, *intention* in adverbial form denotes *stance, responsibility, agency,* and *directedness.*[81] Although in broad terms I do not dissent from accounts of Schleiermacher put forward by Wolterstorff and discussed in similar terms by Lundin, we should give Schleiermacher credit for paying equal attention to the speech of the speaker and the intersubjective nature of the communicative act; to expression, content, and effect. He asserts, "The idea of the work can be understood only by the joint consideration of two factors: the content of the text and the range of *effects.*"[82] These effects can be determined only with reference to the contextual pre-understandings of addressees, not simply of authors.[83] Schleiermacher perceived that when or whether we place the emphasis on authors, readers, texts, or subject matter is largely a matter of

---

Harper & Row, 1966), 133; *Parables and Presence: Forms of the New Testament Tradition* (Philadelphia: Fortress, 1982), 30.

81. Thiselton, *New Horizons in Hermeneutics,* 558-62; cf. also 13, 37-38, 45, 597-600; Vanhoozer's book entitled *Is There a Meaning in This Text?* came into my hands at page-proof stage, after I had completed this present work. He argues vigorously for the importance of authorial agency.

82. Friedrich Schleiermacher, *Hermeneutics: The Handwritten Manuscripts,* trans. James Duke and Jack Forstman (Missoula, Mont.: Scholars Press, 1977), 151.

83. I described this as the beginnings of a theory of reader effects, as against populist notions of a purely "genetic" approach (*New Horizons in Hermeneutics,* 208); on Schleiermacher's complex and sophisticated hermeneutics, cf. 204-36 and elsewhere.

interpretative strategy, determined partly by biblical genre and textual directness, and partly by a specific hermeneutical goal and agenda.[84]

The relevance of this to interpreting the parables of Jesus and other New Testament material emerges particularly in David Demson's recent comparison of the hermeneutics of Hans Frei and the hermeneutics of Karl Barth.[85] Demson examines with special care their respective ways of understanding the identity and presence of Jesus Christ in New Testament narrative material, since both writers perceive this as the "point" of reading the church's scripture. Frei's use of the term "history-like" appears to allow him to speak intelligibly of "the public and communal form the indirect presence of Christ now takes."[86] It is important to Frei that the Jesus of the Gospels is perceived to have an "unsubstitutable individuality" that unites with "the presence of God."[87] Intratextually he commands, calls, and appoints on behalf of God. But in the end, Demson argues, the category of "history-like" without clear extralinguistic reference renders the establishing of the identity of Jesus through ecclesial interpretation "circular. . . . The factual question is pertinent and not irrelevant."[88] By contrast, Barth places weight upon the notion of *apostolic witness,* as attesting that Jesus' ministry is directed toward his death.[89] "What Frei says not only does not say enough, but, more specifically, does not say enough about how the texts are to be read"; Barth, by contrast, embraces the suspicions of mere historical reconstruction that concern Frei, but anchors the events of the history of Jesus as "events of the apostles . . . gathered, upheld and sent . . . denominated by the terms *appointment, calling, commissioning.*"[90]

These, we may note, constitute illocutionary acts that are interwoven in subtle and indirect ways and anchored in the public, extralinguistic world that finds a place in Barth, but evades Frei. Wolterstorff's critique of Frei reinforces this general point without particular reference to Barth. We

---

84. Schleiermacher, *Hermeneutics,* 97-99; cf. Thiselton, *New Horizons in Hermeneutics,* 218.

85. David E. Demson, *Hans Frei and Karl Barth: Different Ways of Reading Scripture* (Grand Rapids: William B. Eerdmans, 1997).

86. Hans Frei, *The Identity of Jesus Christ: The Hermeneutical Bases of Dogmatic Theology* (Philadelphia: Fortress, 1975), 157; cf. Demson, *Hans Frei and Karl Barth,* 43; and Frei, *The Eclipse of Biblical Narrative: A Study in Eighteenth- and Nineteenth-Century Hermeneutics* (New Haven: Yale University Press, 1974).

87. Frei, *The Identity of Jesus Christ,* 154.

88. Demson, *Hans Frei and Karl Barth,* 93, 94.

89. Demson, *Hans Frei and Karl Barth,* 97.

90. Demson, *Hans Frei and Karl Barth,* 97.

can be misled about Frei's aim unless we read his two major books together. But then we find a deep ambiguity about the sheer "thereness of the narrative." Since Frei confuses "the point" of a text with its "meaning," we sink into "total bewilderment."[91] The *meaning* of a narrative seems, for Frei, to lie *within* it, but its "point" must lie beyond and outside it. According to Wolterstorff, "Frei never succeeded . . . in explaining what he had in mind by *sensus literalis*."[92] For both Frei and George Lindbeck this becomes, in effect, the *sensus fidelium* of the church. Yet even such Roman Catholic writers as George Tavard would be dissatisfied with a recount of the relation between scripture and tradition.

The multifunctional nature of the parables of Jesus requires logical priority over the issue of polyvalent meaning and exclusive orientation toward the hearer. As instruments *designed to subvert the prior "worlds" of hearers or readers* (who may live within their own mundane, self-sufficient, perhaps even complacent secure horizons), reader-response explorations and even deconstructionist hermeneutics offer an invaluable and rich hermeneutical resource. J. D. Crossan well represents this model of "subversion" in his work of 1975.[93] But the parables, ironically, perform more functions than advocates of deconstructionism or radical indeterminacy usually recognize. They are also part of the *kerygma* of Jesus. This necessitates issues of agency and authorial discourse that radical reader-response theories tend to bracket out as irrelevant. Hence the role of reader-response theory does have real limits.

Moreover, the political and ideological agenda often associated with reader-response sits ill with *gospel* or *kerygma*. A political literary theory that establishes egalitarianism by making everyone (apostle and unbeliever, elder and inquirer) co-authors of a biblical text stands as a contradiction in terms. We shall return to the political implications of "autonomy" and egalitarian "rights" later. Meanwhile, we have established that reader-response theory admirably addresses the responsibility of readers to be active ("let the one who has ears to hear, hear . . ."). However, as part of a multi-action *kerygma*, this invitation does not mean simply "make whatever you like of it."

---

91. Wolterstorff, *Divine Discourse*, 231-32; cf. 219-22, 229-36.
92. Wolterstorff, *Divine Discourse*, 219.
93. John D. Crossan, *The Dark Interval: Towards a Theology of Story* (Niles, Ill.: Argus, 1975), 59.

ANTHONY C. THISELTON

The Value of Some Specific Reader-Response Models for Reading Biblical Fiction and the Role of Imagination in Interpreting Plot

The hermeneutical dynamics of a fictional biblical parable (in the strict sense of the term) can be seen in the classic example of the fictional story composed by Nathan the prophet when he was called to the sensitive and potentially dangerous task of confronting King David with an accusation and a rebuke concerning his adulterous conduct with Bathsheba and his manipulation of the death of her husband, Uriah (2 Sam. 12:1-15). The conscious choice to tell a fictional story to project a "possible world" for David's imagination accomplished several things: (1) it avoided initial confrontation by approaching the issue "from behind" by indirect discourse; (2) it operated not simply at the cognitive and conceptual level, but harnessed resources of deeper sympathy, indignation, and righteous anger; (3) it provoked David into an active response that simultaneously evoked self-knowledge, understanding, and proposal for action; and (4) it achieved a transformation of stance and deconstruction of prior attitudes, as well as a renewed re-appropriation of a moral tradition.

Nathan begins, "There were two men in a certain city, the one rich and the other poor. The rich man had very many flocks and herds; but the poor man had nothing but one little ewe lamb" (2 Sam. 12:1-3). The fictional "world" (which David construes as factual and into which he fully enters) raises the stakes: the poor man treated his one ewe as a prized part of his own household, cherishing it "like a daughter" (v. 3). However, when a traveler arrived at the house of the rich man who had flocks and herds in abundance, the man who had everything was reluctant to use any of his own vast resources as food for the wayfaring guest, "but he took the poor man's lamb, and prepared it for the man who had come to him" (v. 4). David is aghast at the willful selfishness of the rich man and his unjust use of his power and privilege: "As the Lord lives, the man who has done this deserves to die" (v. 5). Now comes the moment of confrontation: "Nathan said to David, 'You are the man. . . . You have smitten Uriah . . . and have taken his wife.'" As anointed king, David had many wives and much property, and God would have added "as much more" (12:7, 8, 9). David has actively *lived through* the experience of the fictional world, and his own expression of indignation and contempt at injustice has become transparent both to him and to Nathan. He cannot now change his stance without loss of face and transparent hypocrisy, but in any case the parable has *hit him* so hard (a phrase often used by Ernst Fuchs) that he has no desire to pretend.[94] As Fuchs would comment on such a use of fiction, it has grasped him "deep down," far more profoundly than any "pallid message" or packaged set of "concepts."[95]

Fuchs consciously sets such a hermeneutic in opposition and contrast to "an increasingly tyrannical positivism [in interpretation] . . . under the influence of Cartesian presuppositions. . . . From Descartes' *cogito me cogitare* one arrives at an ego-consciousness rather than a self-consciousness."[96] For within such a narrative world, Fuchs observes as early as 1963, the self unfolds *temporally* and in *relational* terms. On the other hand, a Cartesian "ego-consciousness is notably constant," that is, timeless or atemporal.[97] Fuchs not only makes points parallel with those of Lundin on Cartesianism and with Walhout's work on fictional worlds, but also anticipates Lundin's contrast between the fallaciousness of searching for verbal novelty and the authentic goal of re-appropriating a tradition.[98] In the end, David stands alongside Nathan, not over against him, just as in the parables, by the use of fictional narrative-worlds of possibility, "Jesus draws the hearer to his side . . . , so that the hearer may think together with Jesus. Is not this the way of love? Love does not just blurt out. Instead it provides in advance the sphere [possible world] in which meeting takes place."[99] The hearer or reader is "drawn over . . . to see everything with God's eyes."[100]

Nevertheless, as Walhout has argued, this kind of action on the part of the text often (not necessarily always) entails the projection of a *fictional world of possibility.* "Possibility" does not threaten, but sets up a workshop of scenarios in which the one who enters its world tries out, and discovers the impact of, various ways of acting and evaluating life. Even the physiological experience of the rush of adrenalin serves to indicate when our passions are aroused; we experience no such "rush" when we remain coolly untouched. This is why Jülicher was so profoundly wrong about a supposed lack of

---

94. Ernst Fuchs, *Zur Frage nach dem historischen Jesus* (Tübingen: Mohr, 1960), 411-18; cf. part translation, *Studies of the Historical Jesus,* 196-98.

95. Fuchs, *Studies of the Historical Jesus,* 35.

96. Ernst Fuchs, "The Hermeneutical Problem," in *The Future of Our Religious Past: Essays in Honour of Rudolf Bultmann,* trans. Charles E. Carlston and Robert P. Scharlemann (London: SCM, 1971), 271-73; cf. 267-78. The essay can be found in German in *Zeit und Geschichte,* ed. Erich Dinkler (Tübingen: Mohr, 1964), 361-63.

97. Fuchs, "The Hermeneutical Problem," 273; *Zeit und Geschichte,* 363.

98. Fuchs, "The Hermeneutical Problem," 267; *Zeit und Geschichte,* 357.

99. Fuchs, *Studies of the Historical Jesus,* 129.

100. Fuchs, *Studies of the Historical Jesus,* 155.

hiddenness in the authentic parables of Jesus. Often, as P. S. Hawkins comments, "The parables of Jesus are the utterance but not the unveiling of what has been hidden; a proclamation . . . rather than an explanation."[101] Like indirect communication in Kierkegaard and Wittgenstein, the parables are designed *to prevent premature take-it-or-leave-it confrontation prior to an active engagement that entails change of attitude on the part of the reader.* Hans-Josef Klauck and Madeleine Boucher merit attention among those New Testament specialists who perceive this dimension of designed hiddenness — double meaning and metaphor in the artistic structure of the parables of Jesus.[102] Boucher observes, "Those who do not understand are those who will not allow [parables] . . . to impinge on their own existence."[103]

In our earlier work, *The Responsibility of Hermeneutics,* I selected Susan Wittig's view of the parables of Jesus as "a duplex connotative system in which the precise significance is left unstated" as an example of the application of Iser's reader-response theory to biblical interpretation.[104] Wittig examines in particular the parable of the prodigal son (Luke 15:11-32). Within the terms of reference in the projected fictional world, the opening sentence and the following narrative ("There was a man who had two sons" [v. 11]) constitutes a "first-order signifier," the reference of which is plain. But as the story unfolds, the original unit of signify-and-signified comes also to designate "some unstated signified" that invites construal or "filling in" by the reader. "The second-order signifier . . . is linked . . . to its unstated, implicit signified," and it is up to the hearer or reader to make the link. The reader is compelled "to complete the signification."[105] The model closely reflects the approach of Iser, in that the reader must be active in "completing" an "unstated" signified, yet the first-order *denotatum* imposes certain constraints that frame the sign system and allow multiple meanings without degenerating into readings where anything and everything goes.

101. P. S. Hawkins, "Parables as Metaphor," *Christian Scholar's Review* 12 (1983): 226; cf. 226-36.

102. Hans-Josef Klauck, *Allegorie und Allegorese in synoptischen Gleichnistexten* (Münster: Aschendorff, 1978), 29-31, 132-47, 354-60; Madeleine Boucher, *The Mysterious Parable: A Literary Study* (Washington, D.C.: Catholic Biblical Association of America, 1977).

103. Boucher, *The Mysterious Parable,* 84.

104. Susan Wittig, "A Theory of Multiple Meanings," *Semeia* 9 (1977): 84; cf. 75-103; discussed in Lundin, Thiselton, and Walhout, *The Responsibility of Hermeneutics* (Grand Rapids: William B. Eerdmans, 1985), 102-3.

105. Wittig, "A Theory of Multiple Meanings," 86, 87.

As I have argued more fully elsewhere, Iser, Eco, and Culler offer models of reader-response that are more rigorously grounded respectively in the philosophy of perception, philosophical semiotics, and semiotic theories than the less well-grounded speculations of Bleich, Holland, and Fish.[106] Iser draws on a philosophy of the perception of aspects formulated by Roman Ingarden, who in turn is informed by Edmund Husserl.[107] When we "see" a computer or any three-dimensional object, we do not literally "see" all six sides, faces, or aspects. It would be pedantic to require that we inspect all six sides before agreeing that an object of perception is a computer or a cube. Hollywood, of course, relies on such perspectival construal in using two-dimensional constructs to serve as three-dimensional objects in films. For Ingarden and Iser, filling in what we cannot see is part of a necessary process of *actualization*. This "actualization" results from "interaction" between text and reader, or object and perceiver.[108] The interactive dimension provides the very constraints on an intelligent range of options that Fish ridicules as arbitrary. Yet in the theory of knowledge the issue is as old as the difference between Kant and Fichte: the mind may well construe, as Kant argued, but it does not also exhaustively provide the datum, as Fichte may be understood to argue (followed by Nietzsche).

Nevertheless, the value of reader-response theory is not unqualified, even for fiction. The very same issue of *Semeia* to which Wittig contributed her theory of polyvalent meanings contains other "experimental" readings of the parable of the prodigal son in which congruence with the constraints of the first-order level of the text becomes more problematic. B. B. Scott believes that the identification of the elder son with Jesus' pharisaic critics blocks a more adequate "reading" in terms of a typological mythology of elder and younger sons.[109] Mary Ann Tolbert offers a Freudian "reading" in which the elder son is analogous to the superego, while the younger son breaks societal taboos by seeking sexual

---

106. Thiselton, *New Horizons in Hermeneutics*, 515-55.

107. Iser, *The Act of Reading*, ix, x; cf. Roman Ingarden, *The Literary Work of Art: An Investigation of the Borderlines of Ontology, Logic, and Theory of Literature*, trans. George G. Grabowicz (Evanston, Ill.: Northwestern University Press, 1973); *The Cognition of the Literary Work of Art*, trans. Ruth Ann Crowley and Kenneth R. Olson (Evanston, Ill.: Northwestern University Press, 1973).

108. Iser, *The Act of Reading*, 21.

109. B. B. Scott, "The Prodigal Son: A Structuralist Interpretation," *Semeia* 9 (1977): 45-73.

hedonism after the manner of Freud's id. The father in the story is portrayed as the self who attempts to satisfy the demands of the superego and the id, thereby offering as much partial unity and imperfect integration as is possible in this part-resolution.[110] As Tolbert explains in her book entitled *Perspectives on the Parables*, "These three elements are present in the psyche of every individual."[111] The superego "is the seat of morality, religion, law, and judgment."[112] The father is "the unifying centre" who values both sons, but is also "its [the parable's] most vacillating figure."[113] Dan Otto Via then tries out a Jungian reading.[114] Here the elder brother symbolizes the "shadow side" of the self, while the younger brother is the preconscious self in search of self-discovery in consciousness. The Jungian themes of departure from home and return to celebration, of *Urzeit-Endzeit* in symbolic, mythic form, also figure in the therapeutic tale of alienation and reintegration.

It is beyond dispute that Tolbert allows the imagery to function within a Freudian understanding of the self, Via within a Jungian understanding of the self. Does it matter that even the most generous critic will see little even of "congruence" (Tolbert's word) with what Wolterstorff termed "authorial discourse"? We need to explore further what is at issue in reading fictional or "literary" texts. However, first we must explore reasons that underlie the limitations of reader-response criticism.

Via earlier made a convincing attack on Jülicher's over-doctrinaire insistence that *all* authentic parables can have only one point.[115] The hermeneutical value of the "one point" principle is not that all parables can say only one thing, but that they operate with a different hermeneutic from that of allegory. Via rightly observes that whereas allegorical narratives depend upon a series of quasi-independent codings between the alle-

---

110. Mary Ann Tolbert, "The Prodigal Son: An Essay in Literary Criticism from a Psychoanalytic Perspective," *Semeia* 9 (1977): 1-20; subsequently repeated in substance in Tolbert, *Perspectives on the Parables: An Approach to Multiple Interpretations* (Philadelphia: Fortress, 1979).

111. Tolbert, *Perspectives on the Parables*, 106.

112. Tolbert, *Perspectives on the Parables*, 104.

113. Tolbert, *Perspectives on the Parables*, 106.

114. Dan Otto Via, "The Prodigal Son: A Jungian Reading," *Semeia* 9 (1977): 21-43.

115. Dan Otto Via, *The Parables: Their Literary and Existential Dimension* (Philadelphia: Fortress, 1967), 2-17, 21-25. All further references are to this edition and will be cited in parentheses with the abbreviation *Par* within the body of the essay.

gory and the extralinguistic world (e.g., in John Bunyan's *Pilgrim's Progress,* the house of the interpreter is code for the human heart; the oil, for the Holy Spirit; Mr. Worldly Wiseman, for people who are streetwise but without conscience or soul), distinctions within the narrative world of a parable are "secondary to their fusion into the internal coherence of the parable story. Neither one nor many of the *elements* [my italics] point directly and individually out of the story. That is why the one-point approach is only less allegorizing in degree than the old pre-critical allegorizing" (*Par,* 25). The parable *as a whole* has "aesthetic function . . . aesthetic quality" (*Par,* 24).

Via's earliest work on the parables offers a hermeneutic which superbly exemplifies how certain specific parables function as comic or tragic plot. Thus in the parable of the ten wise and foolish maidens (Matt. 25:1-13), the plot spirals down to tragedy for the foolish because "they supposed that the world would take care of them, that someone else would pay the bill: if we run out of oil, our friends will help us, or the merchants will still be up, or even if we are late the groom will not lock us out. . . . The foolish maidens too presumptuously believed that their well-being was guaranteed to them no matter what they did" (*Par,* 126). Within the narrative there is a temporal dimension: expectation gives purpose and tests responsibility for action (*Par,* 128). Another tragic character is the "loser" in the parable of the talents (Matt. 25:14-30; *Par,* 113-28). The one-talent man was crippled by anxiety over self-security and refused to venture. "He will not risk trying to fulfil his own possibilities. . . . Action is paralysed by anxiety. . . . He understood himself as a victim and in understanding himself as a victim he *was* a victim" (*Par,* 118-19). In the unfolding of the fictional narrative to the climax of the employer's verdict that he cannot, like the others, exercise stewardship on a larger scale, the plot moves "*from* refusal to take a risk, *through* repressed guilt which is projected onto someone else, *to* the loss of opportunity for meaningful existence" (*Par,* 119, Via's italics). His "punishment," as regularly happens in the biblical writings, is one of "internal grammar" (in Wittgenstein's sense): he rejects responsibility; thereby he loses positive opportunity.

This rich reading, which exploits positively the "possible worlds" or life scenarios of dramatic biblical fiction, coheres more with Eco's exposition of the multilayered coding of "open" or "literary" texts (as against flat, one-point, "closed" or "handbook" texts of, for example, engineering and building construction) than with Iser's model of filling in gaps or completing schemata. As long as a parable remains coherent as a parable world of possibility, readings may explore its multilayered possibilities. Thus in his unduly neglected work *The Art and Truth of the Parables,* G. V. Jones expounds not simply, initially, the repentance of the prodigal son, but his sheer remorse (Luke 15:17-18; "How many of my father's hired hands have bread enough and to spare, but here I am dying of hunger! I will get up and go to my father, and I will say to him, 'Father, I have sinned against heaven and before you'").[116] He has left his father's house in a confident, defiant mood. He enjoys the temporal phase of spending money, but as time moves on he discovers that in destitution he has lost his superficial friends and his personal dignity. He recollects his home in the solitude of abandonment, self-pity, and despair. The recollection (Jones compares such parallels as, for example, the smell of heather and the freshness of a mountainside) brings home the wretchedness of his alienated state. He resolves to return simply as a hired servant. But his father welcomes him not as a commodity to work and to earn, but as a fully personal human member of the family, whose dignity as a family member is restored by the gift of shoes on his feet, a ring on his finger, "the best robe" (Luke 15:22), and festal celebration in eating at the family table.

Jones offers "a broader interpretation" because he shares the view of *the importance of imagination for hermeneutics,* which Walhout also expounds above. Such themes as freedom and responsibility; estrangement; the personal nature of life and dignity; longing, anguish, and return; grace and reconciliation — all find their place in imaginative scenarios projected in life worlds "transfigured and given meaning by vision" with a dynamic power that sets in motion a dramatic living-through of a genuine possibility.[117] This principle receives a sharp theoretical focus in Umberto Eco's *A Theory of Semiotics* and his later works, *The Role of the Reader* and *Semiotics and the Philosophy of Language* (cited above). The great strength of Eco's work in relation to the different field of discourse of biblical hermeneutics lies in his valid recognition that "transmissive" or "handbook" texts may function with an encoding and decoding hermeneutic different from that which may be presupposed in "productive" or "literary" texts. Indeed, diverse "subcodes" may operate within each category, especially those that Eco and Wittgenstein call a "training," and Eco "a professional training."[118] This closely resembles what Jonathan Culler terms "competency," and John Searle

---

116. G. V. Jones, *The Art and Truth of the Parables: A Study in Their Literary Form and Modern Interpretation* (London: SPCK, 1964), 135-66.

117. Cf. Jones, *The Art and Truth of the Parables,* 167-205.

118. Eco, *A Theory of Semiotics,* 56.

discusses in terms of engaging with a "background."[119] Eco's distinction between "transmissive" and "productive" codes goes back to Juril Lotman.[120]

"Transmissive" texts reflect the interests of an information-driven culture, of which engineering is regarded as a paradigm. The contrast between a technological model and "productive" texts recalls our initial discussion of sciences and arts in the context of Gadamer's reflections and the spell of the Cartesian paradigm. *To reread a "handbook" text* is simply to seek greater *clarity* concerning a *single, fully determinate meaning*. "Productive" texts reflect the interests of literary cultures, of those whom Gadamer's father called "those chattering professors" in the humanities and arts. *To reread a "literary" text* is to seek not clarity but *resonances, intertextual allusions, new perspectives, transformed horizons*. Here the greatest contribution of biblical criticism, frequently too readily dismissed by conservatives as wholly destructive, is to force us into an appreciation of the *diversity of biblical texts and genres*. When the Reformers insisted on a meaning that was "single" or "plain," the context most regularly concerned issues of *transmission*. When medieval mystics contemplated distinctions between locutionary acts performed by biblical writers and further acts (of which these texts were instruments) that pertained to modes of living or to God's larger eschatological purposes, the focus of meditative contemplation was often *generative, productive, or poetic texts* such as those of the wisdom literature or apocalyptic literature. Yet even the four canonical Gospels are not all of a piece. Very often texts operate in multifunctional, mixed modes.

Biblical *fiction* deserves special consideration because beyond question it has explicitly entered a domain foreign to the culture of the "engineer" *qua* engineer. Conservative writers are now far more open than was the case twenty years ago to recognize this distinction and even to identify as "literary" or "productive" texts those which an earlier generation insisted on reading as historical report. Thus Tremper Longman III writes in the Westminster Theological Seminary Symposium of 1988 entitled *Inerrancy and Hermeneutic* that the Book of Job contains "literary artifice," and

---

119. Cf. Jonathan Culler, *Structuralist Poetics: Structuralism, Linguistics, and the Study of Literature* (London: Routledge; Ithaca: Cornell University Press, 1975); and *The Pursuit of Signs — Semiotics, Literature, Deconstruction* (London: Routledge; Ithaca: Cornell University Press, 1981); John R. Searle, *Intentionality: An Essay in the Philosophy of Mind* (Cambridge: Cambridge University Press, 1983), 141-59.

120. Juril Lotman, *The Structure of the Artistic Text,* trans. Ronald Vroon (Ann Arbor: University of Michigan Press, 1977).

that the scriptures are "multi-functional." Standard conventions of literary production (for example, that "human" time may not correspond to astronomical or "natural" time, and that multiple "points of view" may underline different aspects of a narrative) are accepted as part and parcel of biblical narrative.[121] Sidney Greidanus rightly urges that in Job and in Jonah "the historical referent is *hermeneutically* inconsequential" (his italics), but that the historical referent of the Exodus narrative remains "indispensable."[122] These distinctions are not, as Frei might claim, mere social constructs of the eighteenth and nineteenth centuries; they are integral to issues of "authorial discourse" (Wolterstorff) or to what I call the "directedness" of the text.

The most striking examples of a "directed" generation of multiple reader-responses that cohere with authorial discourse can be found in those texts which beyond question embody several "voices." In biblical hermeneutics we may suggest the example of the Book of Job, while in the context of "theological" fictional texts in the modern era, we may return first to the text — cited both by Lundin and by me earlier in this section — of Dostoyevsky's *The Brothers Karamazov,* and then to George Eliot's *Adam Bede.* It is no accident that all three address the problem of intense human suffering and the nature of evil.

Polyphonic Voices in Theological Fiction: Job, Eliot, and Dostoyevsky on Evil

An important hermeneutical resource has been provided in more general terms by Terrence Tilley, who argues that the problem of evil cannot be addressed adequately or appropriately by any neatly packaged system of propositions designed merely to argue or to inform. Hence he entitles his book *The Evils of Theodicy.*[123] Tilley devotes the first part of his book (more than eighty pages) to an exposition of speech-act theory, including illocutionary acts of declaring, preaching, swearing, praying, and confessing. He concludes that the great Christian literature which addresses the issues of evil and suffering does

121. Tremper Longman in *Inerrancy and Hermeneutic: A Tradition, a Challenge, a Debate* (Grand Rapids: Baker, 1988), 137-49, esp. 140, 148, 149.

122. Sidney Greidanus, *The Modern Preacher and the Ancient Text: Interpreting and Preaching Biblical Literature* (Grand Rapids: William B. Eerdmans, 1988), 194-95.

123. Terrence W. Tilley, *The Evils of Theodicy* (Washington, D.C.: Georgetown University Press, 1991).

not function primarily as "assertives"; this is "read back" into the texts in the light of "Enlightenment theism."[124] Indeed, such reading *obscures* the writings. "Job . . . cannot be taken as an assertive which conveys doctrines."[125]

Tilley further maintains that "Augustine did not write a theodicy. He wrote numerous works to various audiences, for various purposes, and with various illocutionary forces which touch on God and evils . . . in various ways."[126] Typically, his *Confessions* perform confessional acts; while his early *On Free Will* and his later *The City of God* and anti-Pelagian writings perform a variety of defensive and polemical communicative acts. Against the Manichees, he defended the freedom of the will; against the Donatists, he called attention to habituated patterns in constraining human will and choice; against the Pelagians, he urged that only grace could liberate a will under bondage.[127] But our concern at present is with fictional discourse. Tilley applies his speech-act theory not only to Job and to Augustine, but also to George Eliot's *Adam Bede*. I agree with Tilley that *Adam Bede* performs multiple communicative actions and deliberately speaks with polyphonic voices. The same is to be said, following especially Malcolm Jones, about *The Brothers Karamazov*.

Amos Wilder notably urges that biblical speech performs a variety of linguistic acts. These include dialogue, narration, fictional parable, poetic discourse, exhortation, instruction, testimony, hymnic praise, confession, promise, letter-writing, and many others.[128] However, where *dialogue* is involved, this need not be the artificial dialogue between questions and prepared "answer." Gadamer repeatedly insists that in true dialogue something emerges which transcends the sum of the two individual standpoints initially represented, as the horizons of each expand to take respectful and listening account of the other.[129] Gadamer declares, "Conversation does

124. Tilley, *The Evils of Theodicy*, 86.
125. Tilley, *The Evils of Theodicy*, 86.
126. Tilley, *The Evils of Theodicy*, 115.
127. Tilley convincingly points out that the *Enchiridion* comes nearest to an open "assertive" or didactic mode of communicative action. Nevertheless, many of the standard textbooks on the problem of evil abstract "doctrines" of freedom and of the nature of evil from situations in Augustine's works, and not surprisingly identify inconsistencies; cf. John Hick, *Evil and the God of Love,* rev. ed. (New York: Harper & Row, 1978).
128. A. N. Wilder, *Early Christian Rhetoric: The Language of the Gospel* (Cambridge: Harvard University Press, 1971).
129. Gadamer, *Truth and Method*, 362-80; "Reflections on My Philosophical Journey," 50-55.

not advance the view of one interlocutor against the view of another. Nor does conversation simply add the view of one to the view of another. The conversation alters both."[130] This Gadamerian theme is discussed and illuminated in detail by Hans-Herbert Kögler.[131] If this is so, then it suggests that it may be a mistake to ask whether the Book of Job speaks through the "omniscient" narrator, or through one of the "friends," or through Job, or with or without a "happy-ending" postscript. As typical wisdom literature, the Book of Job, like Kierkegaard's interplay with his own pseudonymous texts, constitutes a *productive* text that "speaks" *not through any one character or even narrator but in and through reading processes of wrestling with its plurality of voices.*

Admittedly, as David Clines argues, this text, probably above all other biblical texts, lends itself to deconstruction. The "doctrine" that God rewards the righteous is undermined by Job's experience. But, as Clines expresses it, here it does not help to "cure the problem of a dogma with another dogma."[132] Ricoeur, too, observes that the questions which Job asks in Job 42:1-6 are never "answered." The themes of wisdom literature emerge in "the limit-situations spoken of by Karl Jaspers . . . solitude . . . suffering and death."[133] But by definition a "limit-situation" unveils truth only to the person who experiences it. Thus any perspective that is more than individual can be produced only by many voices in dialogue, whether in harmony or dissonance. Deconstruction suggests a *seriation* undermining of each voice by another. Hence, deconstruction would end not by multiple voices but in silence. But, as we shall see from *The Brothers Karamazov* and *Adam Bede,* those who suffer need at very least *a voice.* Deconstruction may serve to knock away the corners of any otherwise complacent, overconfident, dogmatic voice; but in the end, the Book of Job invites readers' active, agonized responses to multiple voices that refuse to package the problem into neat concepts. *Conversation with the voices (plu-*

---

130. Hans-Georg Gadamer, *Gesammelte Werke,* vol. 2 (Tübingen: Mohr, 1986), 188.

131. Hans-Herbert Kögler, *The Power of Dialogue: Critical Hermeneutics after Gadamer and Foucault* (Cambridge, Mass.: MIT Press, 1996), esp. 1-56, 113-158.

132. D. J. A. Clines, "Deconstructing the Book of Job," in *The Bible as Rhetoric: Studies in Biblical Persuasion and Credibility,* ed. M. Warner (London: Routledge, 1990), 79; cf. 65-80. See also Clines, *What Does Eve Do to Help?: And Other Readerly Questions to the Old Testament* (Sheffield: JSOT, 1990).

133. Paul Ricoeur, "Toward a Hermeneutic of the Idea of Revelation," in *Essays on Biblical Interpretation,* ed. Lewis S. Mudge (Philadelphia: Fortress, 1980), 89.

ral) of Job carries us forward, even if inch by inch; it does not leave us in silence, even if wrestling with the voices is hard.

Tilley's contribution to the hermeneutics of Job is mainly of a negative nature: no single perspective or speech action, whether of Job or of the "framework" perspective, will be adequate for the performance of the book: "closure of the meanings of [the] texts . . . may not be possible."[134] His exposition of a reading of George Eliot's *Adam Bede* offers a more distinctive example of how "multiple voices" address suffering and evil, and of how "giving a voice to the victim" also stands at the heart of Eliot's book.[135] Tilley engages with major interpreters and critics of George Eliot's novels.[136]

One of the four central characters is Hetty Sorrel, a farm girl or dairy maid, who daydreams of marrying to become "a lady," kept in luxury and style. She sets her cap for the heir to the estate, Arthur Donnithorne, and later the reader learns that she bears his child. The second main character is the devout Dinah Morris, a sincere, believing "Methody" whose goodness and piety is beyond question. The third (even if less prominent) major character is Donnithorne. The fourth major character is Adam Bede, the master carpenter, who, after discovering that Arthur is toying with Hetty, beats him and secures his exile from the estate. The centerpiece emerges when we discover Hetty, having left home to search for Arthur, in prison, convicted of murdering her own baby. Dinah visits her and seeks to pray with her and speak with her, but Hetty cannot speak: she cannot find a voice to express her grief, shame, and anger at Adam and Arthur. Eventually Hetty inches a little way forward: "Help me," she implores Dinah; "I can't feel anything. . . . My heart is hard." In response, Dinah performs the speech act of prayer, in which "all her soul [goes] forth in her voice."[137] At last the speech acts of prayer and expressed co-suffering enable Hetty to acknowledge, accept, and confess the reality of her actions. But George Eliot is too much of a realist to imply that this "resolves" it all. She speaks through the voice of Adam, who points out that "the blackness of it" is that whatever is said, "it cannot be undone."[138] Evil is irrevocably evil,

---

134. Tilley, *The Evils of Theodicy*, 109.

135. Tilley, *The Evils of Theodicy*, 189-216.

136. For example, Robert Liddell, *The Novels of George Eliot* (New York: St. Martin's, 1977); Janice Carlisle, *The Sense of an Audience: Dickens, Thackeray, and George Eliot at Mid-Century* (Brighton, Sussex: Harvester, 1982); Mary Wilson Carpenter, *George Eliot and the Landscape of Time: Narrative Form and Protestant Apocalyptic History* (Chapel Hill: University of North Carolina Press, 1986).

137. George Eliot, *Adam Bede* (1859), New American Library ed. 1981, 422-31.

138. Eliot, *Adam Bede*, 434.

even if it can also generate certain redemptive effects. Moreover, Eliot adds a final twist typical of her critique of institutional religion: ironically, Dinah, who has "given Hetty a voice," loses her own voice within the church when the Methodist Conference forbids women to preach. This was Dinah's vocation.

Multiple voices, again, *together* address the evil and partial redemption. No single character expresses any "answer"; but in the intersubjective interplay of three or four distinct voices, the dynamic of the "possible world" that enlarges our imagination develops. The tortured price of confession and acknowledgment can be paid only in co-suffering dialogue in a plurality of speech acts. Adam's declarative "it cannot be undone" resists a "solution" that transforms evil simply into an instrument for good. Even the act of speaking cannot be taken for granted: within the narrative world, the Methodist Conference withdraws it from Dinah. No single packaged statement by any single voice can adequately address the existential anguish and complexities of suffering and evil in human life. Both the Book of Job and *Adam Bede* address the issues through multiple voices, and through conversations that readers may take up and continue, albeit with struggle and wrestling. As Kierkegaard and Gadamer would urge within their own contexts of thought, this continuing *process* of *conversation* with a *plurality* of voices permits further discovery and decisions on the part of readers, as they wrestle with possibilities in *possible* worlds.

Fyodor Dostoyevsky (1821-1881) pursues the same kind of imaginative strategy in his magisterial work *The Brothers Karamazov*. As I observe at the end of this example, it is Mikhail Bakhtin who first identified his polyphonic voices in 1929.[139] We cannot doubt the theological nature of much of Dostoyevsky's fiction. Even his first novel, *Poor Folk* (1846), constitutes a social critique on behalf of the oppressed. From the period of *Notes from the Underground* (1864) and *Crime and Punishment* (1866), he produced a series of writings that reflect disenchantment with the influential positivism of Feuerbach and with the merely utilitarian ethics of J. S. Mill. In *The Idiot* (1868), he portrays a "saintly fool," Prince Myshkin, the embodiment of childlike compassion and beauty of soul, who combines Russian traditions of the saintly fool with quasi-allegorical resonances drawn from the narratives of the Gospels.[140] Like Jesus, Prince Myshkin embodies a "goodness" that entails a "powerlessness" in the world's sense

139. Mikhail M. Bakhtin, *Problems of Dostoevsky's Poetics*, trans. R. W. Rotsel (Ann Arbor, Mich.: Ardis, 1973).

140. See Murav, *Holy Foolishness.*

of power. The reader must find his or her way through the paradox, the ambivalence, or the "voices" that are presented.

All the same, the novel of greatest power is *The Brothers Karamazov* (1880), at least if this is to be judged in terms of its "effective history" or history of effects on various readers. Albert Camus identifies its central "voice" as that of Ivan Karamazov, who takes the part of the metaphysical rebel. He identifies Ivan with Dostoyevsky. However, the novel also speaks through the Christian brother Alesha (or Alyosha) and the Orthodox church elder Zosima. Here N. Berdyaev identifies the major "voice" that articulates Berdyaev's own Christian philosophy of freedom. Yet neither of these interpretations does justice to the subtlety and multivalency of the work. It is worth noting, in passing, that Dostoyevsky's own life was complex and marked by suffering. His father was murdered by serfs when he was a child, and his mother died when he was fifteen. In 1849 he was imprisoned for supposed subversion, condemned to death, and reprieved only moments before his scheduled death. He endured solitary confinement, forced labor in Siberia, and compulsory military service. The experiences of a sensitive man of letters forced to live in close physical contact with brutal prisoners are reflected in *The House of the Dead* (1861), even if the hero of *Crime and Punishment* (1866) finds rebirth and renewal.

Two chapters in *The Brothers Karamazov* leave an indelible mark on the history of the effects of fictional texts or literary history — namely, "Rebellion" and "The Legend of the Grand Inquisitor."[141] In "Rebellion" Ivan tells a series of tales about cruelty inflicted upon innocent children. A person rarely, if ever, grasps and understands the suffering of another: not the real suffering that degrades, humiliates, and takes away the spirit of the other. Ivan compares the ways in which different cultural conditionings can obscure what counts as cruelty. The very "defenselessness" of a victim can tempt the tormentor. The high point of the tales is the little girl, brutally beaten and locked away in an outhouse, who prays to "Dear, kind God" in her misery. Why is this permitted? Ivan is aware of the "answers" of his pious brother Alesha and other Orthodox Christians about a *"higher harmony"* for which freedom and suffering are necessary conditions. But Ivan is a rebel against Orthodox theism and against metaphysical argument: "I renounce the higher harmony. It's not worth the tears of that one tortured child who

---

141. Fyodor Dostoyevsky, *The Brothers Karamazov*, the Constance Garnett translation, rev. ed. by Ralph E. Matlaw (New York: Norton, 1976), esp. 216-26 in "Rebellion" and 232-42 in "The Grand Inquisitor."

beat itself on the breast with its little fist and prayed in its stinking outhouse with an unexpiated tear to 'dear kind God.' It's not worth it." Ivan would not give his consent "to make men happy in the end, giving peace and rest" at the price of needing "to torture one tiny creature."

Yet this is not a denial of God's existence. Ivan wishes to opt out of a debate that he believes transcends any *logical* solution. "It isn't God I don't accept, Alesha," he says, "only I most respectfully give him back his ticket [i.e., ticket of admission to the metaphysical enterprise]."[142] Moreover, the narrative (the polyphonic voices of the novel) has not yet reached closure. There are hints from the devout Alesha and from the mystic Zosima that whether or not Ivan "keeps his ticket," the suffering of the child has at least had the effect of inviting from this "hard" man the deepest compassion. How could such compassion arise if all is forever well with the world? Further, the next chapter recounts Ivan's long poem of the Legend of the Grand Inquisitor. The elderly Grand Inquisitor has presided over the burning of nearly a hundred "heretics" in the Spanish Inquisition, set here in Seville. Suddenly Jesus appears in Seville and mingles with the crowd, healing the sick, until he encounters the Grand Inquisitor, who has him arrested and places him under sentence of death.

The Inquisitor's charge is that Jesus gave to his disciples a *freedom* that is too great a burden for ordinary people to bear. The Inquisitor's accusations resonate with the Messianic temptations of Jesus as the Christ: the masses need to be fed with bread, confronted by an unambiguous object of worship, and persuaded by openly miraculous power (cf. Matt. 4:1-11; Luke 4:1-13). The Grand Inquisitor turns out to be the atheist, rejecting the responsibility of faith and freedom in favor of "religion." It is the seductions of the devil that define the Grand Inquisitor's religion, while in the Legend the figure of Jesus silently kisses him. Yet it would be too simple to reduce this to a narrative "message" of a critique of institutional religion. For, paradox of paradoxes, it is Ivan the rebel through whose "voice" the Grand Inquisitor is unmasked. Furthermore, Ivan's voice hardly represents "the message" of the novel, whether this is construed, with Camus, as a "message" of metaphysical rebellion, or with Berdyaev, as a "message" or "gospel" of freedom.

As my university colleague and Dostoyevsky specialist Malcolm V. Jones convincingly argues, the clue lies neither with the reading of Camus nor with that of Berdyaev, but with the polyphony of voices in which Dostoyevsky "placed the Testament of the Elder Zosima which set forth the

---

142. Dostoyevsky, *The Brothers Karamazov*, 226.

Elder's deviant but basically Orthodox religion credo, based upon the ideal of a life of *active love* which facilitates our sense of links with other worlds in which everyone accepts responsibility (i.e. guilt) for everything."[143] Dostoyevsky is not using one voice alone to "present Christianity in all its fullness in fictional form"; rather, he is seeking through several voices to present "its fragmentary expression in the lives of individuals."[144] The Eastern Orthodox conception of *sobornost,* in which each remains jointly responsible for the mutuality and reciprocity of the whole while retaining an individual freedom within the constraints of this frame, constitutes a distinctive Russian theme in Christian interpretation to which Dostoyevsky gives expression through possible worlds of fiction. This stands in contrast both to the Cartesian individualism of partially secularized Protestantism and to the authoritarianism of partially secularized Roman Catholicism.

Just as the *process* of hearing multiple voices in the Book of Job and perhaps in *Adam Bede* projects worlds of possibility that invite a variety of transformations and refigurations in the processes of reading, so *The Brothers Karamazov* offers not a "closed" message but a polyphonic chorus that presents variations on a theme and invites active participation in the choral conversation.[145] As Kierkegaard and the later Wittgenstein would agree, without such multivalency it would be difficult to maintain, as Dostoyevsky wishes to maintain, that the process of unraveling mysteries remains inseparable from action and from how readers live their lives. That in which "freedom" and responsibility for the Other consists can appear only in the context of living out active love. If love entails interaction, the "voices" also interact. We have traveled a thousand miles from the abstract individual

143. Quotation from Malcolm V. Jones, "Dostoevsky: Re-thinking Christianity," research seminar paper at the Dept. of Theology, University of Nottingham, June 1997, 3. Jones explores this more fully and in further detail in *Dostoyevsky after Bakhtin* (Cambridge: Cambridge University Press, 1990). For much of this section (but none of its faults) I am indebted to his specialist insights as Emeritus Professor of Slavonic Studies here.

144. Jones, "Dostoevsky," 3.

145. On *The Brothers Karamazov,* see especially Malcolm V. Jones, "The Brothers Karamazov: The Whisper of God," in his *Dostoyevsky after Bakhtin;* S. Hackel, "The Religious Dimension: Vision or Evasion?" in *New Essays on Dostoyevsky,* ed. M. V. Jones and G. M. Terry, 139-68; Stewart Sutherland, *Atheism and the Rejection of God: Contemporary Philosophy and "The Brothers Karamazov"* (Oxford: Blackwell, 1977); and A. B. Gibson, *The Religion of Dostoevsky* (London: SCM, 1973); Michael Stoeber, *Evil and the Mystics' God* (Toronto: University of Toronto Press, 1992), 21-49; and Robert Belknap, *The Structure of the Brothers Karamazov* (Paris and The Hague: Mouton, 1967), 9-16, for a brief survey of divergent views.

cogito of Descartes; but we have already entered the hermeneutical world of communicative action and of active respect for the otherness of the Other, not least through the "possible worlds" of narrative fiction.

Ultimately, however, the recovery of understanding Dostoyevsky as "the creator of the polyphonic novel" goes back to Mikhail Bakhtin in his work of 1929. Bakhtin asserts, *"The plurality of independent and unmerged voices and consciousnesses, and the genuine polyphony of full-valued voices, are in fact characteristics of Dostoevsky's novels"* (Bakhtin's italics).[146] In Walhout's terminology, the textual worlds projected by Dostoyevsky's main characters are more than merely *objects* of textual action; each becomes a cojoined, quasi-independent *instrument* of textual action. In Bakhtin's language, they are "not only objects of the author's word, but subjects of their own directly significant word as well. . . . Dostoevsky is the creator of *the polyphonic novel.* He originated an essentially new novelistic genre" (his italics).[147] Does this imply, then, that our "polyphonic" reading of the Book of Job was anachronistic? In *Dialogue of the Word,* Walter L. Reed explicitly reads Job "according to Bakhtin" and finds such multiple voices there.[148] Indeed, once philosophers of language and literary and hermeneutical theorists have identified the importance of understanding texts as communicative acts that perform diverse functions and that leave a "history of effects" in Jauss's sense of reception theory as literary "history," the perspective which we have identified in the context of Job, Dostoyevsky, Bakhtin, and perhaps also George Eliot becomes all the more convincing as a means of provoking responsible, thoughtful reader response and reader transformation.

Nevertheless, we must beware of understanding Bakhtin in the way in which many Marxist critics assimilated him into Marxist literary theory. Bakhtin is not interested in "de-privileging" an elite author under the principle of the reader's egalitarian co-authorship or in detaching the text as a system of self-generating forces. It may well be that the combination of Dostoyevsky's social critique of oppression in conjunction with this polyphonic strategy allowed his works to remain "permitted" texts in the era of Soviet Marxism, in spite of his own Christian faith. But neither Bakhtin's polyphony nor that of Dostoyevsky should be equated with the radical pluralism and indeterminacy that arise from Roland Barthes' multiple codes or Jacques

---

146. Bakhtin, *Problems of Dostoevsky's Poetics,* 4.

147. Bakhtin, *Problems of Dostoevsky's Poetics,* 4.

148. Walter L. Reed, *Dialogues of the Word: The Bible as Literature according to Bakhtin* (New York: Oxford University Press, 1993).

Derrida's deconstruction.[149] Permitting Dostoyevsky's text to speak through his "voices" allows us to hear the voice of "the other," on whom Dostoyevsky bestows his own ethical and Christian concern. Hence, as Kevin Vanhoozer declares in Lundin's collection of essays entitled *Disciplining Hermeneutics* (1997), "Deconstruction, far from protecting . . . an 'other,' licences interpretive violence. . . . Deconstruction claims to be ethically responsible for the 'other.' . . . I do not agree. Deconstruction does not serve the other."[150] This coheres with Lundin's own comment, expressed both briefly above and more fully in *Disciplining Hermeneutics,* that since interpretations are interpretations *of* the texts, "there can be wrong interpretation"; but also that since no single interpretation merely replicates another, we can hardly claim that there is "but one right interpretation."[151] Lundin is explicating the observations of Joel Weinsheimer, who is also an expositor and translator of Gadamer.[152]

In this respect it would be injudicious to try to claim that the readings of *The Brothers Karamazov* by Camus (in terms of protest) and by Berdyaev (as gospel of freedom) are as "good" or "right" as those of Bakhtin, Sutherland, or Malcolm Jones. Thus polyphony does not imply indeterminacy. We continue to steer between our Scylla and Charybdis: between the shallows of a Cartesian paradigm and the quicksands of radical postmodern relativism, which admits to no stable marker.

Walhout's advocacy of the importance of fiction, imagination, and "possible worlds" comes into its own here. We may recall that Gadamer drew a contrast between the abstract rationalism of Descartes and the more historical, full-blooded, "human" approach of Giambattista Vico (1668-1744). Vico simultaneously notes the creative importance of "imagination" and its seductive potential noted by Tacitus: people no sooner imagine than they believe *(fingunt simul creduntque).*[153] Samuel Taylor Coleridge (1772-1834) likewise perceives the limitations of "lifeless technical rules" and abstract rational reflection. In spite of the constraints of his romanticist expressivism, he begins to anticipate Gadamer and Ricoeur in urging the temporal dimension of imagination as that which relates to

---

149. On Barthes and Derrida, cf. Thiselton, *New Horizons in Hermeneutics,* 80-141.

150. Kevin Vanhoozer, "The Spirit of Understanding: Special Revelation and General Hermeneutics," in *Disciplining Hermeneutics,* 158, 161; cf. 131-65.

151. Lundin, "Introduction," in *Disciplining Hermeneutics,* 13.

152. Cf. Joel Weinsheimer, *Philosophical Hermeneutics and Literary Theory* (New Haven: Yale University Press, 1991), 87.

153. Giambattista Vico, *The New Science of Giambattista Vico,* trans. Thomas Goddard Bergin and Max Harold Fisch (Ithaca: Cornell University Press, 1968).

memory and hope, and like them, he perceives how imagination transcends mere replication: "If the artist copies the mere nature, the *natura naturata,* what idle rivalry!"[154] The artist "abandons" what he or she interprets and presents "for a time," but also returns to it, presenting not just replications but genuine *possibilities.* Walhout's claims about imagination and "possible worlds" do not mean abandoning "the discipline of hermeneutics" but steering between the Scylla of lifeless replication and the Charybdis of making what the reader wishes to make of the text. This principle remains true to life in the lecture room in biblical studies. A student who is requested "to interpret" a biblical text invites a zero grade if he or she offers *either* mere replication in the form of close paraphrase *or* a speculative construct that bears no relation to the "directedness" of the text (in Wolterstorff's terminology, to the text as authorial discourse) or to the history of the effects of the text in successive traditions of interpretation.

All this serves to throw into relief the gains and losses of so-called reader-response theory. Gain occurs in the active engagement of readers with texts, their entry into the text's projected world, and the participatory and potentially transforming effects especially of hearing more than one possible voice or comparing projections of more than one possible world. But reader-response theory, especially that of the American literary criticism of the late 1970s up to the 1980s, shares a certain abstraction from time and history with Cartesian traditions. As Lundin observed in connection with Gordon Fee, "history" entails not only a setting in the past but the effects of processes of reading between the past and the present. Hence we need now to examine further issues of temporality and time, and in this context the contributions of reception theory and speech acts.

---

154. The citation is from Coleridge, "On Poesy or Art" (1818). Cf. also his observation in *The Statesman's Manual* that "Faith is either buried in the dead letter or its name . . . usurped by a counterfeit product of the mechanical understanding which . . . confounds symbols with allegories. Allegory is but a translation of abstract notions in picture language."

Hermeneutics within the Horizon of Time:
Temporality, Reception, Action

Natural Time, Clock Time, and Human Time:
Temporality, Hermeneutics, and Theology

Paul Ricoeur's magisterial *Time and Narrative* draws on Aristotle, Augustine, Heidegger, and narrative theory to explore the indispensable status of the temporal dimension for understanding in hermeneutics, for issues of narrative identity, and for projecting worlds of "possibility" in Heidegger's sense of the term.[155] His crowning work *Oneself as Another* (published five years later) firmly and convincingly situates personal identity, humanness, personal agency, and action within a frame of temporal narrative history.[156]

In his fifty-page introduction to *Being and Time*, Heidegger observes that Descartes attempted to inquire about Being without reference to temporality, while in spite of attempts to the contrary, "Kant could never achieve an insight into the problematic of Temporality. . . . Instead of this, Kant took over Descartes' position quite dogmatically," even if he goes well beyond him in many other respects.[157] Descartes provided a "seemingly new beginning" that entailed "the implantation of a baleful prejudice" detrimental to "later generations," namely, in abstracting "the Present" in less historical, dynamic, and concrete terms than even Parmenides or Aristotle.[158] Descartes not only isolated the individual self in lone subjective reflection and consciousness but, as Lundin forcefully argues, in effect "orphaned" the self from the temporality that lends it identity, meaning, and the narrative history of the community to which the self concretely belongs. The turning point that re-united timeless "mind" and historical contingency came with Hegel's exploration of historical reason. Lundin has argued that Hegel perceived the problem and attempted a new direc-

---

155. Paul Ricoeur, *Time and Narrative*, 3 vols., trans. Kathleen McLaughlin and David Pellauer (Chicago: University of Chicago Press, 1984-88); the French edition is *Temps et Récit* (Paris: Editions du Seuil, 1983-85). See esp. 1:5-30 (Augustine); 31-51 (Aristotle); 3:60-98 (Heidegger); 1:95-230; 3:104-274 and throughout (on narrative theory).

156. Ricoeur, *Oneself as Another*.

157. Martin Heidegger, *Being and Time*, trans. John MacQuarrie and Edward Robinson (London: SCM, 1962), 45; cf. *Sein und Zeit*, 7th Germ. ed. (Tübingen: Niemeyer, 1953), 24.

158. Heidegger, *Being and Time*, 46, 48; Germ. 25, 26.

tion, but also that his work provided no more than a start in this more fruitful direction.

It is not difficult to understand why hermeneutics, even in Schleiermacher, still awaited proper attention to the temporal dimension that began to emerge in Hegel, Droysen, and Dilthey and then, implicitly as "life" and "life-worlds," assumed more prominence in Husserl and Yorck, and explicitly in Heidegger, Gadamer, and Ricoeur. For many centuries, hermeneutics was bound up with the interpretation of sacred (especially biblical) texts. The dynamic, temporal nature of the biblical writings first became submerged in the need to formulate Christian theology in the Hellenistic world, especially in the context of Alexandrian and Graeco-Roman thought, and then in the context of the legacy bequeathed by the commanding figure of Augustine. At first sight, Augustine appears to wrestle with issues of temporality. Nevertheless, by his insistence — partly under influence of neo-Platonism — that God created the world *cum tempore* rather than *in tempore,* Augustine may seem to deprive temporality, in Heidegger's sense of the term, of ontological seriousness.[159] The very context of reflection on time in *The Confessions* seems to presuppose the very "private subjectivity" that Gadamer perceives as excluded for the first time since Aristotle in Hegel's *Logic* and temporal dialectic.[160]

Augustine, however, achieved at the very least one lasting gain in his reflections on time. For him, time constitutes a fundamentally "human" phenomenon. Metaphysical speculation about time, he reflects, is difficult to formulate, but memory and hope are fundamentally *human* modes of being: *"Quid est ergo tempus? si nemo ex me quaerat scio; si quaerenti explicare velim, nescio."*[161] To be *human* is to live among day-to-day experiences of "before" and "after" even if Augustine cannot answer the question "What is time?" in purely abstract terms. His insistence that there is no "before" and "after" with God, since nothing can be "before" him or "after" him (i.e., past and future seem to become an eternal present) does not locate God in some "timeless" Platonic realm of ideas. Rather, it cancels out the applicability of *human* time to God. Augustine lays a foundation, in ef-

---

159. Augustine, *Confessions* 12.12.13.

160. Hans-Georg Gadamer, *Hegel's Dialectic: Five Hermeneutical Studies,* trans. P. Christopher Smith (New Haven: Yale University Press, 1976), 85; cf. 54-74 (dialectic), 75-99 (logic).

161. Augustine, *Confessions* 11.14.17; further, see 11.14-29. On his view of time, cf. Wittgenstein, *The Blue and Brown Books,* 26; and more indirectly in *Philosophical Investigations,* 89.

fect, for Heidegger's distinction between *time (Zeit)* and *temporality (Zeitlichkeit),* which provides *the ground for the possibility of modes of time.*[162] Since in the biblical writings God is the living God (Heb., *el chay;* Greek, *theos zōn*), God as embodying "temporality" (but not astronomical time, clock time, or human time, which all belong to the creaturely) remains capable of the experience of succession and can act purposively and in active faithfulness. But astronomical time depends on the stars and solar system; clock time depends on technical reason; and "human" time depends on every experience of human allocation, organization, periodicity, tempo, planning, and subjective perception. All these belong to the created order and form irreducible dimensions in the processes of human understanding and in the re-actualizations of texts, art, wisdom, traditions, and varieties of communicative acts.

Sociologists have explored "human time" in contrast to "natural" time in terms of the allocation of time for purposes of human organization and social planning. Literary theorists have demonstrated that narrative embodies a working distinction between "natural" and "human" time in terms of flashbacks, tempo, and so forth. Physicists have indirectly endorsed the notion of time (i.e., natural and human time) as "creaturely" by exploring equations that correlate time with space in theories of relativity. Thus, in accordance with dominant relativity theory, the pilot of a space capsule would spend one year of his life traveling at 260,000 kilometers per second, but two years of earth time, or Newtonian clock-time, would have elapsed during the same period.[163] To separate the divine creation of space and "creaturely" time would be as arbitrary as to abstract time or location from processes of contingent hermeneutical understanding.

Several theologians endorse this explicitly. Barth writes, "Time . . . is the form of existence of the creature. . . . God is temporal, precisely in so far as he is eternal. . . . But time as such, i.e. our time, relative time, itself created, is the form of existence of the creature . . . in that one-way sequence" (*CD,* III/1.41, 67, 68). "Human" time in contrast to natural time or clock time is seen in the model of "man as isolated from God" when

162. It is no accident that *Zeitlichkeit,* "temporality," is closely linked in Heidegger with *Möglichkeit,* or "possibility," which in turn invites authentic decision (*"existentiell eigentliche Ganzseinkönnen . . . als . . . Entschlossenheit") (Being and Time,* 351-52; *Sein und Zeit,* 304-5).

163. L. D. Landau and G. B. Rumer, *What Is Relativity?* (New York: Basic Books, 1960), 47-55.

time becomes "a flight" and in God's eyes is "lost time" or time with "no real past and future, no centre. . . . As the time of lost man it can only be lost time" (*CD*, III/1.72). In contrast to cyclical or timeless myth, which does not do justice to the biblical material, redeemed time moves toward what is symbolized in "the event of God's Sabbath freedom, Sabbath rest, Sabbath joy, in which man has been summoned to participate" (*CD*, III/1.98).[164] Human time for the self-sufficient individual remains "'our' time [i.e., human time], distorted and caricatured" (*CD*, III/1.73).

The contrast between natural time and human time in literary theory has been explored by Seymour Chatman, Gérard Genette, and Paul Ricoeur, and will already be familiar to many readers. The distinction is correlative with that between narrative and story, or between story and plot, or (in Russian formalism) between fable *(fabula)* and plot *(siuzhet)*. Where Chatman distinguishes between *story* and *discourse,* Emile Benveniste contrasts *histoire* and *discours,* while Genette uses the distinction between *historie* and *récit.*[165] As I observed in *New Horizons in Hermeneutics,* the plot of a detective story almost invariably holds back reports of earlier happenings that gradually come to light through flashbacks, conversations, and various other editorial devices. How could Charles Dickens write *Great Expectations* as a narrative plot if he chronologically placed the event of Pip's benefactor's making financial arrangements for Pip in the sequence of "natural time" as it unfolded through the story?[166] As Ricoeur insists, and as Walhout argues concerning fiction, mere replication of the events of natural time in the form of a report would have different effects from "the effects of fiction, revelation and transformation [which] are essentially the effects of reading."[167]

Wesley Kort is one of many who note that the Gospel of Mark uses devices of "narrative time" (as against strictly chronological or "natural" time), especially in terms of speed or tempo. The first eight chapters pro-

---

164. By contrast, cf. "myth," III/1.84-94.

165. Gérard Genette, *Narrative Discourse: An Essay in Method,* trans. Jane E. Lewin (Ithaca: Cornell University Press, 1980), and *Narrative Discourse Revisited,* trans. Jane E. Lewin (Ithaca: Cornell University Press, 1988), 13-16; Seymour Chatman, *Story and Discourse: Narrative Structure in Fiction and Film* (Ithaca: Cornell University Press, 1978), 19-21; and Ricoeur, *Time and Narrative.* For further details, see also M. Toolan, *Narrative: A Critical Linguistic Introduction* (London: Routledge, 1988), 12-14; and Thiselton, *New Horizons in Hermeneutics,* 354-58, 479-85.

166. Thiselton, *New Horizons in Hermeneutics,* 355, 479.

167. Ricoeur, *Time and Narrative,* 3:101.

ceed at a very fast pace, rushing through a diversity of actions, situations, and events.[168] The pace clearly slows, however, when serious questions begin to be raised about the identity of Jesus and the nature of his mission. Arguably the transition occurs in Mark 8:27-38, where Peter makes his confession of the Messiahship of Jesus, only to receive a rebuke from Jesus that he does not perceive this Messiahship as standing under the shadow of the cross. The middle, slower section concludes with warnings to be on the watch (13:33-37), and this leads to the final section, which from 14:1 onward portrays the Passion in detailed slow motion. Slow motion is a device widely used to highlight "this is what it is all about." Since the ancient world was aware of utilizations of the contrast between natural (chronological) time and human (narrative) time for the purposes of suspense or emphasis in emplotment, some of the supposed "discrepancies" in sequence or timing between parallel narratives in the Gospels need not cause disquiet about historical accuracy, unless "the point" of a specific episode in question has more to do with replicated report than proclamation. It would be a different matter, for example, if the crucifixion were depicted as occurring at different, incompatible times. A "narrative" reading should not become a "docetic" reading, since this would contradict the directionality (cf. Wolterstorff's "authorial discourse") of the Gospels themselves.

The present volume, however, is concerned with more than literary theory and its contribution to hermeneutics. Lundin and Walhout also raise issues that have ethical, social, and political import. Here the work of such sociologists as Robert Lauer and Alvin Toffler assumes a special importance. Lauer shows that the concern — some might say obsessional concern — with clock time constitutes the hallmark of the organizational, technological efficiency of the post-Enlightenment Industrial Revolution. Clock time assures not only punctuality but also periodicity: the strategic division of natural time into operational units for maximal efficiency.[169] A mid-morning coffee break and a midday lunch break enhance concentration and allocate measurable periods for work. However, executive management may have greater flexibility than those in the workforce to refigure or reshape a timetable around designated or necessary tasks. Moreover, a measure of social control is exercised in day-to-day social and

168. Wesley A. Kort, *Story, Text, and Scripture: Literary Interests in Biblical Narrative* (University Park: Pennsylvania State University Press, 1988), 44; cf. 14-42. On Mark, see further P. Grant, *Reading the New Testament* (London: Macmillan, 1989).

169. Robert H. Lauer, *Temporal Man: The Meaning and Uses of Social Time* (New York: Praeger, 1981), 1-28 and throughout.

professional politics in terms of who sets the timetable for whom, who waits for whose prior claims of timing, and who sets the pace of timing.

In practice, as Lauer argues, five markers differentiate "human" sociopolitical time from natural time through clock time. These turn on (1) the allocation of units of time — i.e., *periodicity* — for tasks, leisure, and rest; (2) the control of the speed with which tasks are to be completed, or the rapidity with which a series of tasks is to be handled — i.e., *tempo;* (3) the setting or "take up" of so-called windows of opportunity — i.e., *opportune timing* or *kairos*-determination; (4) the determination of appropriate lengths of time that define the units of time which are allocated for different tasks — i.e., *duration;* and finally (5) the specific ordering of tasks by a scale of temporal priority — i.e., *sequence.*[170] Clearly a hermeneutic of selfhood and the hermeneutics of the understanding of human institutions and the texts produced in the context of management interests or consumerist interests cannot pretend indifference toward these aspects of "human" time. It is to be noted, for example, that stability, rationality, and humanness come under threat when an unacceptable acceleration of tempo coincides with a clash of competing value systems.[171] In this respect, those versions of postmodernity that reflect irrational excess are symptoms of human breakdown. Stress disorders today derive not only from the acceleration of tempo imposed by "performance-related pay" but also from its coupling with huge bureaucratic monitoring systems that simultaneously bring disempowerment.

In few areas can the difference between Christian and secular values be discerned more clearly than in the deployment of these five axes of social time. They can be used to exercise control for self-interest, regardless of dehumanizing effects. The stress of the overworked and the unemployed stands in contrast to the common ground shared by hermeneutics and Christian theology, where patience, respect for the other, and responsibility in relation to periodicity, tempo, timing, duration, and sequence suggest that "results" can be "forced" only at serious risk, and that time is more than a commodity or an unlimited space for autonomous "play." Only Cartesian individualism could permit us to imagine that how one person spends his or her time has no repercussions on the "human time"

170. Lauer, *Temporal Man,* 28-51. See further W. E. Moore, *Scarce Resource: Man, Time, and Society* (New York: Wiley, 1963).

171. See Alvin Toffler, *Future Shock* (New York: Random House, 1970), on the disruption of "the human" in psychosocial breakdown.

of others. What is known as the intersubjectivity of understanding in hermeneutics — that is, respect for the subjectivity of the other as agent — becomes a matter of cooperative "teamwork" in the marketplace or factory. But just as in hermeneutics or theology we can unwittingly give privilege to "our" community as the norm or vantage point from which everything else is judged, so in the distribution or allocation of "human" time the values of management, company loyalty, or "tribalism" can become a social or political tool for manipulating others.

This profoundly illustrates a major principle expounded by Kevin Vanhoozer in Lundin's collection of essays entitled *Disciplining Hermeneutics.* Using italics, he states "the following thesis: *All hermeneutics, not simply the special hermeneutics of Scripture, is 'theological.'* . . . I am arguing that general hermeneutics is inescapably theological. . . . Interpretation ultimately depends upon the theological virtues of faith, hope and love . . . a mutual relation of self-giving." This also coheres with the emphases in Vanhoozer.[172]

The theologies of Barth, Jüngel, Moltmann, and Pannenberg confirm that, in Pannenberg's phrase, true humanness that bears the image of God entails "being with others as others."[173] It does not reside in "autonomous . . . life," but in an "openness" to the other, in contrast to a Cartesian or psychological "fixation on the self" (*SysT*, 2:183, 204, 229, 250). "Absolute self-willing . . . alienates us from God by putting the self in the place that is God's alone" (*SysT*, 2:261). In contrast to Cartesian isolation and Kantian autonomy, both of which give privilege to the self, "it is of the nature of our human form of life to be 'eccentric' relative to other . . . beings" (*SysT*, 2:229). Barth and Pannenberg both follow the New Testament witnesses in arguing that Jesus Christ, in his relation to others, to God, and to time, constitutes the paradigm of what it is to be truly human. Barth observes, "Jesus is man as God willed and created him. . . . The nature of the man Jesus is the key to the problem of the human. This man is *man*" (*CD*,

---

172. Kevin Vanhoozer, "The Spirit of Understanding: Special Revelation and General Hermeneutics," in *Disciplining Hermeneutics*, 160-61. Cf. also Vanhoozer, *Is There a Meaning in This Text?* 642-718.

173. Wolfhart Pannenberg, *Systematic Theology*, 3 vols., trans. Geoffrey W. Bromiley (Grand Rapids: William B. Eerdmans, 1991-98), 2:193. All further references are to this edition and will be cited in parentheses with the abbreviation *SysT* within the body of the essay. Cf. Jürgen Moltmann, *The Spirit of Life: A Universal Affirmation*, trans. Margaret Kohl (London: SCM, 1992), 83-143; and Eberhard Jüngel, *God as the Mystery of the World*, trans. Darrell L. Guder (Edinburgh: T. & T. Clark, 1983), 299-396.

III/2.43, 50; Barth's italics). Jesus, unlike fallen humanity, lived within the framework of what Barth terms "given time" and "allotted time" (*CD*, III/2.47, 511-72). In contrast to Lundin's critique of orphan imagery, which implies abstraction from due temporal processes, Jesus' "own time extends backwards and embraces all prior time . . . and extends forwards" (*CD*, III/2.511-12). He bases his trust on the pregiven promises of God and the history of God's saving acts, accepts the constraints of allotted time in the present, and understands the meaning of his life and work within the frame of past promise and future purpose and goal.

Hence humanity in relation to God is not "in time in such a way that it continually slips away into infinity and is therefore lost. . . . Human life means to have been, to be, and to be about to be," as is also my fellow human being, "the thou without whom I could not be a human" (*CD*, III/2.521, 522, 523). Even human finitude, which provides the boundary of death, thereby defines the allotted time that God bestows as a gift for the determination of periodicity, duration, moments of opportunity, sequence, and tempo. Opportunity comes as a gift of grace under his lordship; he is the one who assigns time and task, and thereby the meaning of the present (*CD*, III/2.47, 587-640). In Pannenberg's view, this provides the very stuff that makes promising an act of *promise*. A hermeneutic of promise brings together issues of personal identity, personal agency, action, and time. Pannenberg writes, "All action presupposes the identity of those who act, at least to the extent that this identity is needed to bridge the difference in time between the planning and execution of an act. . . . *Those who make a promise that they can keep only many years later, or over a whole life, have to retain their identity if they are to meet the promise* [my italics]. Actions owe their unity to the time-bridging identity of their subjects" (*SysT*, 2:202). Pannenberg adds that identity becomes what it will be not in some selected arbitrary moment, but over the full course of "our whole life-history." *Human and divine faithfulness* entails not only *accepting constraints* so that we *do not choose* to act unfaithfully, but also a *consistency and faithfulness of action and life which show themselves only by persistence and consistency over time or through duration in extended time.*

The Epistle to the Hebrews insists that the only instance of a visible display of humankind "crowned with glory and honor" as bearer of the image of God is Jesus Christ (Heb. 2:7-9; cf. Ps. 8:4-6). Yet this epistle speaks more movingly than any other passage in the New Testament of Jesus as the One who showed patience, endurance, and even "learning through suffering" in his determination to reach the *telos* appointed by

God (Heb. 5:2, 8, 9, and throughout).[174] A hermeneutics of promise, then, presupposes a hermeneutic within the horizon of time. Here, as Vanhoozer insists, hermeneutics and Christian theology converge, for respect for "the other" embraces the Other of past, present, and future, not merely the Other of spatial differentiation. This is the missing dimension of *otherness* that has emasculated and to some degree sidelined reader-response theory. To place reader effects within a temporal horizon, we might do well to explore the reception theory of H. R. Jauss. To this we now turn.

The Temporal and Historical Character of Jauss's Aesthetics of Reception

Hans Robert Jauss acknowledges Gadamer, who was his teacher at Heidelberg, as his determining influence.[175] However, from 1963 onward he worked in collaboration with a circle of literary theorists based at the University of Constance in southern Germany, whose approach is widely described as that of "aesthetics of reception" *(Rezeptionsästhetik)*, or more loosely and less precisely as "reception theory." Those aspects that find common ground with certain American literary theorists may be compared with aspects of reader-response theory; but the Constance group, and especially Jauss, deliberately and self-consciously describe their work as combining *both literary poetics and hermeneutical theory.* If one stream of influence comes from Gadamer and hermeneutics, the other comes from Lotman, Iser, and literary theory. Thus, hermeneutics is "historical" in the sense identified by Lundin above, when he calls into question the narrower use of "history" as historical reconstruction of a single situation (as in his allusion to Fee). Lundin notes that "historical" refers primarily not to some setting behind the original production of the text, but to a series of historical intervals between then and now; to intervals between successive generations of readers for whom their own situatedness within a given tradition of reading has generated successive horizons of expectation, and thereby successive horizons of understanding.

As in reader-response theory, the emphasis lies on the impact of the

174. I have expounded this theme elsewhere, partly in "Human Being, Relationality and Time," *Ex Auditu* 13 (1997); and more fully in Thiselton, "The Epistle to the Hebrews," in *Commentary 2000*, forthcoming from Eerdmans.

175. Hans Robert Jauss, *Toward an Aesthetic of Reception.* The comment is from Paul de Man, "Introduction," xi.

text on readers. As David Tracy urges in the context of the hermeneutics of religious texts and of "classics," hermeneutical inquiry entails attention, with varying degrees of emphasis, "upon any one of the four elements basic to the total situation of any work of art: the artist who creates the work (expressive theories . . .); the work itself (objective theories . . . often formalist); the world the work creates or reveals (mimetic theories . . .); and the audience the work affects (pragmatic theories from Philip Sidney to . . . Lukacs)" (*AI*, 113). Without appearing to mention Jauss, Tracy then declares, "The position defended here emphasizes, above all, the *reception* by the reader of the classic text" (*AI*, 118; Tracy's italics). Attention is given to the "personal questions, opinions, responses, expectations, even desires, fears and hopes" that readers already bring with them as the text addresses them (*AI*, 118). These make up their "pre-understanding" (Tracy uses the term drawn from Schleiermacher, Heidegger, and Bultmann), "Background" (Searle), or "competency" (Culler). Although he does not appear to locate the theoretical dialogue in the explicit contrast between Gadamer on one side and reader-response theory on the other, Tracy adopts a thoroughly Gadamerian perspective. He writes, "Every present moment is, in fact, formed by both the memories of the tradition and the hopes, desires, and critical demands for transformation for the future. The notion of the present moment as pure instant, an ever-receding image, is as mistaken as the allied notion of a pure — isolated, purely autonomous — subject" (*AI*, 119). This is precisely the point made by Lundin above about Cartesianism and the point subsequently made by Walhout and in the above arguments about time, possible worlds, and the otherness of the other. "No one," Tracy concludes, "escapes the reality of tradition" (*AI*, 119).

It is into this Gadamerian context of thought that Jauss transposes the notion of the directedness of texts as "address" or "appeal" to audiences or readers (*Appellstruktur*). This at once modifies any version of literary formalism into a speech event that addresses an extralinguistic readership. Jauss opposes any theory of hermeneutics or of literary reception that is either merely intralinguistic or "timeless."[176] Following Gadamer, he traces the legacy of "historical" hermeneutics through Droysen and Heidegger. He makes his key programmatic statement in "Literary History as a Challenge to Literary Theory" (originally entitled

---

176. Hans Robert Jauss, *Literaturgeschichte als Provokation* (Frankfurt: Suhrkamp, 1970), 231.

"Literaturgeschichte als Provokation der Literaturwissenschaft," his In-
augural Lecture of 1967 delivered at the University of Constance).[177] Before formulating seven major theses, Jauss urges that the past of history
is not a "closed" past; it remains open to renewed understanding as it remains open to fresh perceptions that are generated by subsequent events
and experiences. Similarly, every literary or artistic work is not "timeless" in the sense of being abstracted from processes of history and tradition, but *re-actualized as eventful* in each changing context of successive
processes of understanding. In Walhout's terminology, texts that were
once objects of action become also instruments of action in this process
of re-actualization.

Like Gadamer, therefore, Jauss perceives literary *history* as a *story* of
the literary work and its effects *in process (Literaturgeschichte)*. This in turn
constitutes an essential component of literary theory (*Literaturwissenschaft*), in which successive impacts or impressions (*stossen*) present discontinuities, differences, disturbances, or challenges (*Provokation*) that
"hit" readerships in such a way that the history of effects of texts
(*Wirkungsgeschichte*) moves beyond any bland descriptive collection of cumulative continuities of reading. Like Gadamer, Jauss perceives differences
and tensions between past and present, or between successive re-
actualizations, as essential for the process of understanding.

In his essay of 1969, Jauss draws a contrast between a bland, innocent assumption of developmental continuity in the appropriation of the
meaning of texts, and discontinuities and points of departure of the kind
that Lundin described above as creativity within the constraints of tradition, as over against the Cartesian choice between barren replication and
novelty for novelty's sake.[178] As Paul de Man notes, Jauss rejects literary
approaches that make too much of "play" in the Barthesian sense.[179]
Each new event of understanding and interpretation within the context
of the history of effects (*Wirkungsgeschichte*) of a text produces, in turn,
new effects (*Wirkungen*).[180] These are not, however, the merely "causal"
effects of a positivist view of history or of a "causal" or Marxist sociology
of literature, but a matter of more subtle "influences" that operate at an
aesthetic level and may even lead to paradigm shifts (*Paradigmawechsel*)

177. Printed as chapter 1 in Jauss, *Toward an Aesthetic of Reception*, 3-45.
178. Hans Robert Jauss, "Paradigmawechsel in der Literaturwissenschaft,"
Linguistische Berichte 3 (1969): 44-56.
179. "Introduction," *Toward an Aesthetic of Reception*, xix.
180. Jauss, "Paradigmawechsel in der Literaturwissenschaft," 55-56.

in the sense explored by Thomas Kuhn in his philosophy of science (*TAR*, 8).[181] This criticism lies behind Jauss's critique of so-called genetic models of hermeneutics. Even the emphasis on audience reception in much of Marxist literary theory suffers, in Jauss's view, from such a quasi-positivist reduction of more complex human agencies to mere socio-economic "forces." Metaphors of "production" and "consumption" of works of art take us only partly along the way. An intersubjective, reciprocal mutuality is entailed (as Gadamer's language about conversation implies; *TAR*, 15).

Earlier we noted that Jauss brings together two streams of influence: that of literary theory, which includes Russian formalism and the work of J. Lotman and W. Iser, and the hermeneutical and historical concerns of Droysen, Heidegger, and Gadamer. His emphasis on the discontinuities or disruptions within traditions of reading brings together "tension" or "distance" in Gadamer (and subsequently Ricoeur) and "defamiliarization" *(ostraneniye)* or "estrangement" in V. Shklovsky and Russian formalism (*TAR*, 16-17). "The gradual course of tradition (Überlieferung) [is] a procession with fracturing changes, the revolts of new schools, and the conflicts of competing genres" (*TAR*, 17). It is only through the critical recognition of these changes in the "paradigms" of historical eras (as in the sense associated with Thomas Kuhn and noted above, with reference to the history of the natural sciences) "that the work enters into the changing horizon-of-experiences of a continuity in which the perpetual inversion occurs from simple reception to critical understanding, from passive to active reception, from recognized aesthetic norms to a new production that surpasses them" (*TAR*, 19). The goal of "re-appropriation" of a text occurs only in the interaction of temporal processes of past and present (*TAR*, 20).

For the appropriation of the sacred text of the biblical writings, this brings us into a different world from that of a more "timeless" reader-response theory, which may allow the kind of "free play" that Jauss rejects. Jauss allows for the creativity of fresh appropriation, but within the witness of a tradition. Different eras do not merely replicate earlier understandings, but neither do they merely make what they like of the text. Our

---

181. Note the changes, however, in the second edition of Thomas Kuhn, *The Structure of Scientific Revolutions* (Chicago: University of Chicago Press, 1970), and *The Essential Tension: Selected Studies in Scientific Tradition and Change* (Chicago: University of Chicago Press, 1977).

exegesis, understanding, and appropriation of justification by grace in the Epistle to the Romans can never be the same again after the work of Luther, Calvin, Kierkegaard, Barth, Stendahl, and Sanders, but that does not thereby necessarily lead to a radical pluralism in interpretation. It means that present interpretation takes place on ground that has been made more fertile and yet also yields certain boundary markers. The post-history of the text has become an indispensable but unduly neglected area of biblical studies. We need to recover the hermeneutical insight of Gerhard Ebeling and Karlfried Froehlich, both of whom plead for an understanding of "church history as the history of the exposition of Holy Scripture."[182]

Froehlich speaks of "the extremely complicated history of a self-interpretation and interpreted Bible," and urges, "Understanding must take into account the text's post-history as the paradigm of the text's own historicity, i.e. as the way in which the text itself can function . . . in a variety of contexts . . . in the shaping of life."[183] Ebeling reminds us that "Implicit in the German word *'Geschichte'* is the dialogue between the objective event in the past and the subjective understanding of the past event in the present."[184] He adds, from a theological perspective, "The communication of the Word of God . . . is only given in the constantly renewed interpretation of Holy Scripture. This interpretation is not to be separated from its relation to the actual assembly of those who hear it, and . . . fulfil it. Herein lies . . . the historical character of the Word of God. . . . Church history as the history of the interpretation of Holy Scripture."[185] However, Ebeling seems less ready than such writers as Stanley Hauerwas, George Lindbeck, and Hans Frei to neglect the "objective event in the past," which he has identified as in "dialogue" as conversation partner with the present community or with successive communities in the re-actualization of the text.

---

182. "Church History as the History of the Exposition of Holy Scripture" is in fact the title of Ebeling's "Habilitation Lecture" (1947), in Gerhard Ebeling, *The Word of God and Tradition: Historical Studies Interpreting the Divisions of Christianity* (Philadelphia: Fortress, 1968), 11-31; and developed and endorsed by Karlfried Froehlich, "Church History and the Bible," in *Biblical Hermeneutics in Historical Perspective: Studies in Honor of Karlfried Froehlich*, ed. Mark Burrows and Paul Rorem (Grand Rapids: William B. Eerdmans, 1991), 1-18, esp. 7.

183. Froehlich, "Church History and the Bible," 8, 9.

184. Ebeling, *The Word of God and Tradition*, 17.

185. Ebeling, *The Word of God and Tradition*, 26.

Jauss takes a stance that does justice to the emphasis upon the active role of the reader in reader-response theories, but also locates changing horizons of readers within formative processes of historically constituted tradition. Thereby he places greater emphasis on the constraints and boundaries of a public, intersubjective world, and softens the problems of supposed potential incommensurability that the more subjective or pragmatic stances of Fish or R. Rorty may be thought to suggest. Like Ricoeur, Jauss envisages a surplus of meaning that may "surpass" previous interpretations in a "new production," but this need not imply distortion or subjectivism. If it were otherwise, the marketing, let alone the writing, of new biblical commentaries would be only for homiletical rather than exegetical and interpretative purposes. It would be a mistake, Jauss argues, to oversimplify the process as if to imply that each new interpretation merely takes an earlier one as its point of departure. The "first" effect combines with the text or with the work itself in "co-producing" a "second" effect interactively (*TAR*, esp. 15-20).

If he places as a first thesis a warning against an unduly positivist, causal, or objective view of historical processes of understanding, Jauss balances this with a second thesis that excludes reducing changing horizons of expectation to the merely psychological or subjective. Processes in which horizons of expectation are "varied, corrected, altered, or even just reproduced" enter the public domain as open to public and historical scrutiny (*TAR*, 22-24). The ways in which *texts perform actions* in the multiple effects of *both* projecting a content of meaning *and* satisfying, disappointing, frustrating, confirming, or refuting the expectations, or horizons of expectation, of readers therefore bring about the third action of effecting, disrupting, or transforming social formation (*TAR*, 25-28). This represents Jauss's third main thesis.

This process and approach yields a fourth thesis. It brings "to view the hermeneutic difference between the former and the current understanding of a work; it raises to consciousness . . . the potential for meaning that is embedded in a work and actualized in the stages of its historical reception" (*TAR*, 28, 30; see further 146-47). This reminds us at once of Gadamer's comment that if "horizon" denotes "the range of vision that includes everything that can be seen from a particular vantage point," it becomes possible to speak of narrowness or "expansion" of horizons, "of the opening up of new horizons," but conversely of "tensions" between horizons of differing historical epochs when "the hermeneutic task consists in not covering up this tension by attempting a naïve assimilation of the two but in consciously bringing it out."[186] However, Jauss construes the stable marker of a "classic" text itself in different terms from Gadamer's more Hegelian account. Certain texts or works retain a status as decisive markers for interpretative vision in the history of effects. In Jauss's view, the differential tension facilitates the unfolding of the text itself, rather than placing most or all of the emphasis on the multiple re-actualizations.[187] Paul Ricoeur finds himself in broad agreement with Jauss's greater readiness to combine both explanation and understanding, suspicion and surplus, in the effects that texts produce on acts of reception.[188]

Jauss's fifth main thesis amplifies the fourth. It expounds the historical unfolding of understanding. As Lundin, once again, urged at the beginning of this volume, once we have gained the kind of historical perspective that is here advocated, the "new," Jauss notes, "is not [merely] absorbed into factors of innovation, surprise . . . re-arrangement, to which Formalist theory assigned exclusive importance. The new also becomes a *historical* category" (*TAR*, 35; his italics).

In this programmatic essay, Jauss concludes with a sixth and a seventh thesis that jointly affirm the interrelation of synchronic and diachronic dimensions. Together these present a succession of engagements of reading and display "the creative capability" of literary or classic texts, most especially revealing their "socially formative function" (*TAR*, 36, 39, 41, 45). We should note, however, that it is precisely because he agrees with Marxist literary critics that "social formation" arises from the historicity of literary texts in *life* (not simply in thought) that Jauss is so careful to distance himself at the same time from the Marxist-positivist view that these effects are *causal* or linked in any way with historical determinism. Neither socio-economic causality nor any supposed quasi-mechanical causality linked with cruder versions of structuralism is acceptable to Jauss. Literary theory for him remains grounded in hermeneutics as against a mere sociology or psychology of literature.

Ricoeur helpfully distinguishes between Wolfgang Iser's reader-response theory as "a phenomenology of the individual act of reading" and Jauss's aesthetic of reception as "a hermeneutic of the public reception

186. Gadamer, *Truth and Method*, 302, 306.
187. Cf. Kögler, *The Power of Dialogue*, 137; Ricoeur, *Time and Narrative*, 3:172-73.
188. E.g., Ricoeur, *Time and Narrative*, 1:77, 3:171-79.

of a work."[189] Thus, after stating the seven programmatic major theses, which are designed to distance his program from mistaken forms (including Marxist forms) of assimilating aesthetic theory into literary history, Jauss proceeds to explore in more positive detail the key theme "that the meaning of a literary work rests upon the dialogical *(dialogisch)* relation established between the work and its public in each age."[190] Behind this approach lies a logic of question and answer explored previously by R. G. Collingwood and by Gadamer, except that, as we have observed, Jauss sees "recognition" and "innovation" as complementary, and uses the now-familiar model of the reader as one "who performs the 'score' of the text in the course of the reception" (*TAR*, 145; cf. 143).

This coheres with several arguments put forward by Lundin, Walhout, and our present discussion. Engagement with the text occurs as an event in the public world, which is an intersubjective world of action and human agency, not merely an intratextual or intralinguistic world. A text may speak with polyphonic voices; but this is not to say that the meaning of the text is radically indeterminate or without boundaries, unless we are considering a clearly "open" code or genre in a certain type of "productive" fiction (in the sense explained by Lotman and Eco). As Ricoeur observes, this places within the task of hermeneutics the task of discerning changes of horizons that yield changes of reader effects: "The critical factor for establishing a literary history is the identification of successive aesthetic distances between the pre-existing horizon of expectation and the new work, distances that mark out the work's reception. . . . [More precisely, this means] to discover the interplay of questions to which the work suggests an answer . . . following once again Collingwood and Gadamer. . . . We can understand a work only if we have understood that to which it responds."[191]

This links closely with our previous argument on temporality and time. Jauss refuses to abstract a "classic text" from temporal processes: *part of what the text is consists in its performance of the temporal action of opening up a new horizon.* A text makes an impact *(Stossen):* it invites new questions and sets a new agenda. Creativity and integration constitute positive features; but a text may also challenge, provoke, and provide change of direction. Jauss's argument runs very close to Walhout's work (above) on fiction and "possible worlds." In tracing a variety of ways in

189. Ricoeur, *Time and Narrative*, 3:171; see also 318n.44.
190. Ricoeur, *Time and Narrative*, 3:171.
191. Ricoeur, *Time and Narrative*, 3:172.

which different kinds of texts may make an impact on different kinds of readers, Jauss writes, "Through the opposition between fiction and reality, between the poetic and the practical function of the language" readers may find horizons of expectation reshaped, sometimes "within the wider horizon of the experience of life," sometimes within a more narrowly focused horizon of "literary expectations" (*TAR*, 24). Ricoeur comments, "The horizon of expectation peculiar to literature does not coincide with that of everyday life."[192] In accordance with his own belief (against Gadamer) that understanding *(Verstehen)* also needs to be checked against the explanatory or critical axis, Ricoeur approves of the threefold emphasis in hermeneutics that the work of Jauss invites. It does not ignore the dimension of critical exegesis, but it sees this as taking place independently of understanding. Neither of these processes (against Gadamer) is to be assimilated too readily into "application," but successive re-actualizations give rise to distinct issues of *subtilitas applicandi*: "What equivalent to a sermon in biblical exegesis and to a verdict in juridical exegesis does literature offer on the level of application?"[193] Again, in accordance with Walhout's observations above, Ricoeur adds, "In this triadic structure [understanding, reflective exegesis, application] application orients the entire process teleologically."[194] Issues of purpose and ethics cannot be excluded from hermeneutics; questions of understanding necessitate a historical and relational (as against Cartesian) frame; examination of and dialogue with the questions and answers to which the text provides an address demand exegetical rigor and critical reflection. Jauss's concern for aesthetic impact allows room for the acceptance and indeed positive evaluation of "pleasure" or "enjoyment" *(Genuss)*. This can creatively open a space for fresh perception. Nevertheless, against the "free" play of postmodern deconstruction, Jauss believes that "play" is bounded by the constraints of what is to perform the "score" of *this* text, as against another. Paul de Man observes, "He has always treated such Parisian extravagances with a measure of suspicion."[195]

192. This is Ricoeur's summary of Jauss's point: Ricoeur, *Time and Narrative*, 3:173.

193. Ricoeur, *Time and Narrative*, 3:174.

194. Ricoeur, *Time and Narrative*, 3:174.

195. Paul de Man, "Introduction" in Jauss, *Toward an Aesthetic of Reception*, xix.

ANTHONY C. THISELTON

Some Implications for Speech-Act Theory in Hermeneutics and for the Post-History of Biblical Texts

Although it was not Jauss's purpose to explore speech-act theory, the emphasis that arises from his work on successive re-actualizations of texts within traditions of transmission (together with his valid insistence on agency, action, and especially on the intersubjectivity of the public world) provides an appropriate framework within which to explore speech-act theory. More precisely, it allows not merely for fresh perspectives on texts as instruments of action (to use Walhout's phrase), but more specifically for the significance of speech-act theory as a contribution to *hermeneutics*. In this book we have consistently tried to steer between the Scylla of an Enlightenment "handbook" notion of interpretation as wooden replication and the Charybdis of radical pluralism, contextual pragmatism, or uncontrolled indeterminacy. An exploration of reception theory in terms of the performance of speech acts may perhaps take our case further.

We begin with the fundamental recognition, voiced by Tracy (among many others), that hermeneutical inquiry demands attention to not less than "four elements basic to the total situation of any work of art: the artist who creates the work . . . ; the work itself . . . ; the world which the work creates *or reveals* [my italics] . . . ; and the audience the work affects" (*AI*, 113).[196] (On this last point, it is perhaps worth noting the possibility of confusion over the term *pragmatic* or *pragmatics*. In the sense in which C. S. Peirce distinguished pragmatics [action of a text] from semiotics [relations between signs] and semantics [meaning currency generated by linguistic interaction between system and use], *pragmatic* denotes *action* and *audience impact*. In philosophical discourse, however, *pragmatic* theories of truth operate simply in terms of supposed instrumental success. In this sense, the contextual *pragmatism* of S. Fish and R. Rorty remains inadequate, even if when Fish, like Jauss, concerns himself *also* with *pragmatics*, certain insights may emerge.)[197]

It is arguable, as David Parris, one of my doctoral research candidates, has proposed, that each actualization and subsequent reactualization of a text constitutes successive concretions of meaning or instan-

196. The point is made, for example, by M. H. Abrams and Giles Gunn.
197. In Stanley Fish, the contrast emerges in the difference between "How to Do Things with Austin and Searle" (1977; on performance, action, and "counting as") and "How I Stopped Worrying" (1980) in *Is There a Text in This Class?*, 197-245, 1-20; and more especially in the contextual pragmatism of *Doing What Comes Naturally*.

tiations of speech acts generated by the text and also co-operatively by the text and by subsequent horizons of expectation generated by the text as traditions of reading unfold, or as paradigms of reading change. I will argue that if we explore this model, further light will be shed on the axiom cited by Lundin (quoting Weinsheimer) that to speak of more than one possible "right" meaning by no means excludes the possibility that certain other meanings may simply be "wrong."

In sum, at the risk of initial oversimplification for the purpose of introduction, I offer these distinctions: (1) At one end of a spectrum of stable "givens" and "variables," *the originating agent(s) of the text* (author, editor, speaker, even history of tradition within the biblical canon) retains a privileged, if not unique, identity, even granted that it may become mediated through successive interpretive voices *also*. Readers at least *aim* to hear Jesus, or the apostle Paul, or the prophet Amos, or the voice of God, whatever mediating or conditioning factors may shape subsequent horizons of understanding. However, at the opposite end of the spectrum of stable-givens-and-variables: (2) the *audience* clearly differs, whether or not it tries to discount the effects of intervening history and tradition. Today most readers do not read the parables as first-century Jews of multicultural Galilee, nor do they read 1 Corinthians with the very same agenda of pastoral concerns and theological misunderstanding as that which Paul addressed at Corinth. As Jauss perceives, and as Ebeling and Froehlich observe concerning the history of the Christian church, horizons of expectation and agenda shift in direction and focus. This does not exclude the goal of Schleiermacher and Dilthey that we should work toward recovering, as far as possible, the life-world or creative vision that gave rise to the text, as long as, with Gadamer, we recognize that the differences can never be exhaustively dissolved. It is a naive argument to suggest that if biblical scholarship can never reach an absolute or final goal, we should not travel as far as we can, while recognizing that we are still *en route*, and recognizing also the impact of horizons of understanding that come about over the centuries.

The most significant hermeneutical factors, however, arise from (3) the "mimetic" world, or content, which the text projects or *"creates or reveals"* (Tracy), and (4) the dynamics or forces generated *within the text or work itself. These occupy variable or intermediate positions on our sameness-difference spectrum.*

Arguably, the content disclosed by the text (3) retains a *stable core of content* and *performs a virtually replicated speech-act if and only if the genre and content are of certain kinds.* For example, the historical report that Jesus was crucified under Pontius Pilate (Matt. 27:26-35; Mark 15:15-24; Luke 23:23-33; John 19:15-18) is repeated in Christian creeds Sunday after Sunday and day after day with a replicated core of historical report, although also with moving horizons of confessional commitment and audience involvement. On the other hand, we noted above that if the content of Job or of Dostoyevsky's *The Brothers Karamazov* itself constitutes a dynamic, shifting dialogue of polyphonic voices, it would violate the dynamics of this textual world to reduce it to some replicable package, just as it would violate the prophetic-apocalyptic poetry of the Book of Revelation if some amateur exegete who was a horticultural expert offered a fixed, single designation for "the leaves of the tree were for the healing of the nations" (Rev. 22:2). In his commentary on Revelation, G. B. Caird warns us against a mechanistic, analytical replication that would seek to unweave the colors of the rainbow. Hence, as Umberto Eco and H. R. Jauss observe, the performance of textual action is closely linked with genre. Here both look back to J. Lotman's *The Structure of the Artistic Text*.[198]

What are we to say of the textual forces generated *within* the text or work (4) as a formal semiotic system? Here again, it seems, their place on the spectrum may vary. At the "stable" end of the spectrum, in *intra*textual terms it is difficult to see how such devices as metaphor, paradox, or change of narrative tempo can be regarded as other than relatively stable devices, almost analogous to logical operators but within the frame of temporal narrative. Hence, the account by Aristotle (384-322 B.C.) of such textual forces still rings true.[199] These devices undergo fine-tuning and sometimes cultural modification, but their use in ancient literature is hardly entirely foreign to their uses today. However, while *intra*textual forces in a formalist sense remain near the stable end of the spectrum, *inter*textual resonances occur at the "variable" or "difference" end. For, as Jonathan Culler argues, different readers and different audiences bring with them a different repertoire of reading. Resonances in the New Testament with the texts of Philo, Qumran, or the Targums may be foreign to many modern readers, while modern readers may read the story of the sacrifice of Isaac in Genesis 22 while supplying intertextual resonances from Kierkegaard's treatment of this passage in his *Fear and Trembling*.

Culler rightly perceives that what Julia Kristeva and others call

---

198. On Eco and Lotman, see Thiselton, *New Horizons in Hermeneutics*, 524-29.

199. Cf. Aristotle's *Poetics* on rhythm, pattern, length, form, embellishment, pretense, character, metaphor, unity of plot, and tragedy.

intertextuality in practice constitutes what hermeneutical theorists usually call *pre-understanding (Vorverständnis)*, or what he himself prefers to call "presuppositions." "The inter-textual nature of any verbal construct" amounts to "formulating presupposition" or "describing intertextuality."[200] In theory, intertextual resonances are usually explored as if these were properties generated only by texts. This occurs in several studies of biblical intertextuality.[201] However, Culler's claim that intertextuality differs little from presupposition, pre-understanding, and reader competency (cf. Searle's "Background") demonstrates that what *counts as* intertextual depends on *the experiences and decisions of human agents,* not on supposed "textual properties" alone. Hence it is misleading to confuse the *inter*textual with the *intra*textual. Strictly, this belongs to the point in the spectrum where successive audiences are located, and entails extralinguistic factors of human agency.

All the same, the introduction of the phrase "counts as" alerts us to one more variable factor in the total speech situation. This is the factor explicated by Wolterstorff (and also by Searle and Walhout) as *counting* a particular utterance, locution, or piece of writing *as performing a specific action in the speaking or writing of it.*[202] In the context of Jauss's aesthetics of reception, it becomes clear beyond doubt that the institutions, presuppositions, or, less directly, states of affairs on which "institutional" currencies depend constitute primary candidates for the exploration of continuity, variability, disruption, or restoration in the history of effects of texts. It depends on evaluations of institutional facts and interpretations of the states of affairs that lie behind them whether we can say (to borrow Wolterstorff's language), "I have performed one action by performing another distinct action."[203]

Can explorations of such criteria be undertaken adequately without reference to the post-history of the text? It is quite astonishing that few

---

200. Culler, *The Pursuit of Signs,* 102; cf. 101-17.

201. For example, *Intertextuality in Biblical Writings: Essays in Honour of Bas van Iersel,* ed. Sipke Draisma (Kampen: Kok, 1989).

202. Wolterstorff, *Divine Discourse,* esp. 75-94, 183-222. Cf. also "count generation" in Nicholas Wolterstorff, *Art in Action: Toward a Christian Aesthetic* (Grand Rapids: William B. Eerdmans, 1980), 122-55; and *Works and Worlds of Art* (Oxford: Clarendon Press, 1980), 202-31.

203. Wolterstorff, "The Importance of Hermeneutics for a Christian Worldview," in *Disciplining Hermeneutics,* 30. On "facts" of Searle, see *The Construction of Social Reality,* 31-57, esp. 55-56.

commentaries on the biblical text embody a post-history of the text under consideration, with the notable exception of the better volumes in the *Evangelisch-Katholischer Kommentar zum Neuen Testament* series.[204] At its broadest, for example, the most widely known example in the history of Christian thought may perhaps be Martin Luther's reappraisal of the impact of the texts that speak of God's righteousness. In 1519 Luther was working on the meaning of "deliver me in thy righteousness" in Psalm 31 in preparing his university lectures on the Psalms. The "obvious" meaning of "righteousness" lay in its disturbing legal and forensic horizon of understanding, which reflected a solid medieval tradition of interpretation. Scholasticism, we might say, provided an explanatory axis. Yet as Luther would later recount it in his *Autobiographical Fragment,* a new horizon of *understanding* dawned as he opened himself afresh to Paul's language in Romans 1:17. As he wrestled, prayed, and patiently awaited eventful communication, Luther came to perceive that Paul argued "another case." The whole of scripture "took on another look" as "the gates of paradise had been flung open and I had entered." What had been "counted as" a disturbing communicative act of potential condemnation now "counted as" a speech action of promise and assurance that the righteousness *of* God is the righteousness that comes *from* God as a gracious gift.[205] Indeed, for Luther it "constituted" such a speech act.

Without question, Luther's horizon of understanding has had a continuous impact on successive generations of interpreters. However, readers have remained free to return to the language of Paul and to try to wrestle anew with the agenda that Paul himself addressed. On this basis, Krister Stendahl and E. P. Sanders advocate "non-Lutheran" approaches to Paul, and interpreters may hear the text of Romans anew, with their own horizons enlarged by drawing on both Luther and Stendahl.[206]

204. Cf. esp. Wolfgang Schrage, *Der erste Brief an die Korinther,* 2 vols. (Zürich: Benziger; Neukirchener-Vluyn: Neukirchener, 1991-95); also Ulrich Wilckens, *Der Brief an die Römer,* 3 vols. (Zürich: Benziger; Neukirchen-Vluyn: Neukirchener, 1978-82); Erich Rässer, *An die Hebräer,* 3 vols. (Zürich: Benziger; Neukirchen-Vluyn: Neukirchener, 1990-97); Ulrich Luz, *Das Evangelium nach Matthäus,* 2 vols. (Zürich: Benziger; Neukirchen-Vluyn: Neukirchener, 1985-90).

205. The fullest account is provided by Martin Luther, *Autobiographical Fragment, 1545.* The text is conveniently to hand in *Martin Luther,* ed. E. Gordon Rupp and Benjamin Drewery (London: Arnold; New York: St. Martin's, 1970), 5-7.

206. Cf. Krister Stendahl, *Paul among Jews and Gentiles* (London: SCM, 1977; Philadelphia: Fortress, 1976), esp. 78-96; E. P. Sanders, *Paul and Palestinian Judaism: A Comparison of Patterns of Religion* (London: SCM, 1977), esp. 431-46.

We need not resort to well-known examples to underline the point. The post-history of 1 Corinthians 2:10-16 provides an illuminating case-study. To that passage Irenaeus brings a horizon of understanding to Paul's language about the Holy Spirit and "the spiritual person" colored by concern about a Valentinian-Gnostic appeal to support a Gnostic "category" of a spiritual elite. For Irenaeus (c. 120 to 140–c. 200 to 203 A.D.), Paul's language liberates the reader from a Gnostic understanding and exposes the irrational basis of Gnostic exegesis.[207] With Paul, Irenaeus sees that what "counts as" (declarative act) being "spiritual" is inseparable from the centrality of Christ in life and thought.[208] In the exegesis of Irenaeus, this entails a public lifestyle, whereas Clement of Alexandria interprets "being spiritual" in private, individualist, quasi-Gnostic terms, thereby violating Paul's agenda with Corinth.[209]

Tertullian (c. 155 or 160–after 220 A.D.) reads the verses in part as an illocutionary act of doxology, calling on intertextual resonances with the Wisdom traditions of the Old Testament. If Wisdom "daily rejoices" in God's presence (Prov. 8:27-31), and the Spirit alone knows God's mind, yet is pleased to dwell among believers, who can but rejoice?[210] Nevertheless, the act of rejoicing is one of a series of multiple acts. For, like Irenaeus, Tertullian perceives it also as a polemic against a Marcionite and Gnostic dualism between the Old and New Testaments, and an affirmation of divine transcendence.[211]

Origen (c. 185-254 A.D.) also understands Paul's criterion of what it is to be "spiritual" in Christological and ethical terms.[212] Nevertheless, for Origen the major action performed by the text is an act expressive of gratitude to God: "We cannot even sing a hymn to the Father in Christ with proper rhythm, melody and harmony unless the Spirit who searches all things, even the depths of God, first praise and hymn him whose depths he has searched."[213] An act of gratitude, however, now becomes an expression of awe that carries implications of doctrinal declaration: Father, Son, and Spirit are uncreated, and through the Spirit the hidden depths of God are disclosed each to the other.[214] Clearly a Trinitarian horizon of understanding is in steady process of formation.

---

207. Irenaeus, *Against Heresies* 1:9:1.
208. Irenaeus, *Against Heresies* 5:8:4.
209. Clement, *Stromata* 1:12, 17; 5:4; 6:18.
210. Tertullian, *Against Hermogenes* 18.
211. Tertullian, *Against Praxeas* 8; *Against Marcion* 1:2 and 4:22.
212. Origen, *de Principiis* 4:1:10.
213. Origen, *de Principiis* 4:4:8 (Greek: J.-P. Migne, *Patrologia Graeca* 11:409B-D).
214. Origen, *de Principiis* 4:4:8.

This becomes the explicit agenda of question and answer for Athanasius in his *Epistle to Serapion* (c. 358 A.D.): he urges against the Pneumatomachi (who argue that the Holy Spirit is a "creature," Greek *ktisa*) that 1 Corinthians 2:11-12 conclusively demonstrates that the Holy Spirit is uncreated. The Spirit's "coming forth from God" (Greek *to pneuma to ek tou Theou;* 1 Cor. 2:10) opens a horizon of understanding of the Holy Spirit as "proceeding from the Father," as the Nicene-Constantinople Creed will articulate it.[215] This Trinitarian horizon becomes explicit in the reading of 1 Corinthians 2:10-12 by Basil the Great in his treatise *On the Holy Spirit* (c. 374 A.D.). For him, 1 Corinthians 2:11-12 performs a declarative act: it declares the intimacy and mutuality of the Father, the Son, and the Holy Spirit in actions of self-giving Trinitarian divine grace.[216] Most emphatically the Holy Spirit is not a mere "force," "thing," "it," or creaturely agent external to God himself, as becomes clear especially in Basil's *Refutation of Eunomius* (c. 364 A.D.).[217] If space allowed, we could trace the role of text in relation to revelation in Chrysostom and a multiplicity of textual actions in Augustine.[218]

In the period from Anselm to Calvin, however, and most especially in Luther, textual action is focused most particularly on giving assurance of knowledge through the agency of the Holy Spirit, and (except for Thomas Aquinas) affirming boundaries of attempts to achieve "natural" knowledge of God. Indeed, for writers in this period, these verses address the issue of the very ground and basis of Christian truth-claims. Following Jauss's discussion of the relation between originating and subsequent horizons of expectation and understanding, I suggest that this places 1 Corinthians 2:10-16 more adequately within the Pauline framework defined by 1 Corinthians 1:18-25 (cf. Schrage's "the cross as ground and criterion"); 1:26–2:5 (the nature of the gospel as received and as proclaimed); and 2:6-9 (In what sense may the gospel be thought of as "wisdom"?).

Anselm provides a bridge. Like Basil, he links 1 Corinthians 2:11-14

---

215. Athanasius, *Epistle to Serapion* 1:15, 22 (Greek: Migne, *Patrol Graec* 26:532A, 581A). Much of the *Epistle to Serapion* 1:1–4:7 turns on 1 Cor. 2:11, 12; 6:11; 12:11, 13.

216. Basil, *On the Holy Spirit* 16:37-40.

217. Basil, *Refutation of Eunomius* 1:13, 14; 3:4.

218. Cf. Chrysostom, *Homilies on 1 Corinthians* 7:6-11; Augustine, *Letters* 130:3, 7; *City of God* 13:24; *On Baptism* 3:15, 18. (I develop this further in my forthcoming commentary on the Greek text, to be published by Eerdmans.)

with Matthew 11:25: "Thou hast hidden these things from the wise." Thus the "unspiritual" *(psychikos)* person does not perceive the things of God (2:14). Knowledge of God depends not on human "cleverness" but upon an obedient openness to God's Spirit.[219] Thomas Aquinas recognizes that these verses declare the nature of theology and the boundaries of human knowledge. "Theology," these verses declare, is "above human wisdom" *(utrum haec doctrina sit sapientia).*[220] Aquinas distinguishes two types of "wisdom": cognition, which plays its part within theology *(modum cognitionis),* and habituated stances or virtues, which are gifts of the Holy Spirit *(habitum virtutis recte judicat;* cf. 2:15).[221] Nevertheless, Aquinas too readily assimilates his discussion of knowledge into an Aristotelian agenda that he imposes onto the text, thereby enlarging the text's effects.

Luther restores the agenda to the problem of knowledge as formulated by Paul and Anselm, but with further reference to his own times. He asserts that Paul limits "a natural knowledge of the senses, harmful to those who do not understand it [knowledge of God]" as "insufficient to know God."[222] The Holy Spirit comes "to enlarge our vision"; but this transcends knowledge as philosophers use the term.[223] Calvin's main emphasis falls on the revelatory action taken up by Chrysostom, Anselm, and Luther, but he also takes up the doxological motif found in Tertullian, as well as an expression of divine accommodation or adaptation of divine truth by the Holy Spirit toward human capacities to understand and to receive it: thus he speaks of "adapting (Latin *aptare*) spiritual things to spiritual when he accommodates the words to the reality."[224] In terms of communicative action, these verses constitute multiple acts of assurance, warning, thankfulness, praise, and explanatory doctrine.

Lack of space precludes further examples. But we should note the importance of broader studies of the post-history of the interpretations

219. Anselm, *Letter to Pope Urban II on the Incarnation of the Word,* conveniently available in *A Scholastic Miscellany: Anselm to Ockham,* ed. and trans. Eugene R. Fairweather (London: SCM, 1956), 97.

220. Thomas Aquinas, *Summa Theologiae* 1a, Qu. 1, art. 6.

221. Aquinas, *Summa Theologiae* 1a, Qu. 1, art. 6; 22-24.

222. Martin Luther, *Epistle to the Hebrews* (1517), on Heb. 6:13, vol. 25 of *Luther's Works,* 55 vols. (St. Louis: Concordia, 1955-); *Early Theological Works,* 16 vols., ed. and trans. J. Atkinson (Philadelphia: Westminster, 1962), 126.

223. Luther, *Commentary on 1 Corinthians 15,* vol. 28 of *Luther's Works,* 137-38 (German: *Weimar Auf,* vol. 36, 587).

224. John Calvin, *First Epistle of Paul to the Corinthians* (Edinburgh: St. Andrew's, 57-61).

of a larger corpus of texts in the history of thought. On Paul, we may refer readers to the radically diverse understandings of the significance of Paul and the impact of Pauline texts found, for example, in Marcion, Tertullian, Augustine, Luther, F. C. Baur, Nietzsche, Harnack, Barth, Schweitzer, Schoeps, and Stendahl. Comparisons between the understandings of these thinkers have been collected by Wayne Meeks in an illuminating anthology.[225] John Godsey traces the respective interpretative emphases drawn from the Epistle to the Romans by Marcion, Augustine, Luther, Calvin, Wesley, and Barth. Thus Marcion overdrew the Pauline contrast between law and gospel or promise; Augustine drew out Paul's emphasis on election, justification, and the creative redirection of the human will by divine grace; Luther applied the free gift of divine promissory grace to justification and release from bondage; Wesley ensured that faith appropriation was complemented by holy living; and Barth opened up "the strange new world within the Bible" as transformative word of God.[226] Maurice Wiles's work *The Divine Apostle* and William Babcock's *Paul and the Legacies of Paul* stand among a number of other useful sources that offer case studies for Jauss's claims, although in some cases in terms of a corpus of texts rather than more specific textual actions.[227]

225. *The Writings of St. Paul,* ed. Wayne A. Meeks (New York: W. W. Norton, 1972), esp. 236-57; 268-95; 349-64; 387-94; 422-34.

226. John Godsey, "The Interpretation of Romans in the History of the Christian Faith," *Interpretation* 34 (1980): 3-16.

227. Maurice F. Wiles, *The Divine Apostle: The Interpretation of St. Paul's Epistles in the Early Church* (London: Cambridge University Press, 1967); *Paul and the Legacies of Paul,* ed. William S. Babcock (Dallas: Southern Methodist University Press, 1990); Albert E. Barnett, *Paul Becomes a Literary Influence* (Chicago: University of Chicago Press, 1941); Harold Smith, *Ante-Nicene Exegesis of the Gospels,* 6 vols. (London: SPCK, 1925-29); Robert Morgan, "The Impact of Romans," in *Romans* (Sheffield: Sheffield Academic Press, 1995), 128-51. An invaluable source is *Biblia Patristica: Index des citations et allusions Bibliques dans la litterature Patristique,* 5 vols., ed. J. Allenback, A. Benoit, et al. (Paris: Éditions du Centre de la Recerche scientifique, 1975-).

Further Implications and the Paradigmatic Status
of Promise as Communicative Action

Further Implications for Theories of Knowledge and Philosophy

Throughout most of the central sections of this third part of our volume, I have been pressing home further implications of Walhout's claims about texts as objects and as instruments of action, including the special examples of transformative fiction and the projection of possible worlds. I began, however, by drawing out some further implications from Lundin's critique of Cartesian perspectives and their implications for philosophy, literature, and hermeneutics. I now return to Lundin's critique to elaborate the disastrous consequences of Cartesian individualism for a variety of areas and disciplines with which hermeneutics is directly concerned.

I turn first to theories of knowledge. My arguments up to this point about history, time, and tradition (especially with reference to Gadamer, Ricoeur, and Jauss) substantiate Lundin's use of the powerful metaphor of *parent-slaying and orphaning* in his critique of Cartesian individualism. It would be a mistake, however, to regard our common emphasis in this book as investing our entire philosophical credibility or currency in a Heideggerian-Gadamerian tradition of a German or Hegelian philosophy of historical reason as such. Ricoeur and Jauss, I note, remain thoroughly aware of currents in the Anglo-American analytical tradition. Here the work of the later Wittgenstein — with his emphasis on the public world of intersubjective community and the dynamic character of language and forms of life *(Lebensform)* as ever on the move, and above all the role that he assigns to "training" in a form which offers parallels with "competency" in Culler, "Background" in Searle, and "pre-understanding" in hermeneutics — provides a cumulative case of irresistible force.

Wittgenstein invites us to picture the artificiality of the kind of attempt made by Descartes to abstract himself from the communicative legacy of his fellow human beings and traditions. He writes, "If you tried to doubt everything, you would not get as far as doubting anything. The game of doubting itself presupposes certainty."[228] Later in the same work he adds, "Doubt comes *after* belief [his italics]. . . . Every human being has

---

228. Wittgenstein, *On Certainty,* 115. For more on doubt and "the Cartesian self," see *The Blue and Brown Books,* 69.

parents."[229] I have discussed the implications of this perspective in Wittgenstein for hermeneutics more fully elsewhere.[230] As Allan Janik and Stephen Toulmin have shown, his dual engagement with the thought of Vienna and English philosophy contributes to his understanding of language as a living, growing process of history, like "an ancient city: a maze of little streets and houses . . . additions from various periods . . . surrounded by a multitude of new boroughs with straight regular streets and uniform houses. . . . To imagine a language means to imagine a form of life *(Lebensform)*" *(PI,* 18, 19).[231] *Speaking* and *writing* constitute not "designating" but making *moves* within a *prior* competency or training: "*speaking* . . . is part of an activity, or of a form of life" *(PI,* 23; cf. 30, 49; Wittgenstein's italics). "Commanding, questioning, recounting . . . are as much part of our natural history *(unserer Naturgeschichte)* as walking, eating . . . playing" *(PI,* 25).

Only in his earliest thought, this aspect of which he later rejected, could Wittgenstein equate serious linguistic inquiry with the Cartesian "logic for a vacuum" *(PI,* 81). The frame of reference that a person inherits from parents, teachers, and "life" forms part of "receiving a training" *(Abrichtung)* without which that person would not understand even what might *count* as "belief" or as "doubt" *(PI,* 86). The Cartesian *cogito* generates confusion because it is generated not by intersubjective activity and observations that relate to it but an "engine idling" in abstraction from the hurly-burly of the everyday world *(PI,* 88). "The common behaviour of mankind *(die gemeinsame menschliche Handlungsweise)* is the system of reference by means of which we interpret an unknown language" *(PI,* 206). With regard to "unteachable" or "non-social" concepts, he comments, "It is not possible to obey a [linguistic] rule privately" *(PI,* 202). We cannot do without "examples" and "practice" in community contexts *(PI,* 208).

As Wittgenstein emphasizes in his devastating critique of Sir James Frazer's *The Golden Bough,* this lends different currency to the notion of "reasonable" belief from that which we find, for example, in Descartes, Hume, or Clifford.[232] A close parallel emerges here with Gadamer on tra-

229. Wittgenstein, *On Certainty,* 160, 211.

230. Thiselton, *The Two Horizons,* 174-75, 392-93 (in the Korean translation, 278-79, 600-602) and more broadly 370-85 (Korean, 566-90).

231. Cf. also Allan Janik and Stephen Toulmin, *Wittgenstein's Vienna* (London: Wiedenfeld & Nicolson; New York: Simon and Schuster, 1973).

232. Wittgenstein, "Bemerkungen über Frazers *The Golden Bough,*" *Synthese* 17 (1967): 233-53.

dition and authority. Gadamer observes, "Authority . . . is ultimately based not on . . . the abdication of reason, but on . . . reason itself, which, *aware of its own limitations, trusts the insights of others*" (my italics).[233]

This subtle relation between *reasonableness* or justification of belief and a historical approach that permits a version of *defeasibility* and gives up claims to *incorrigible* certainties raises an important terminological problem. The rejection of Descartes's reliance on *self-evident* or a priori propositions, together with a rejection of positivist reliance on propositions deemed to be *evident to the senses,* coupled with these comments about defeasibility and *incorrigibility,* correspond with what Alvin Plantinga, Nicholas Wolterstorff, and others would describe as a rejection of *"classical foundationalism."*[234] In classical foundationalism, Plantinga argues, the justification of a noetic structure (i.e., propositions believed to be true and the epistemic relation between them within the structure) rests on either (1) self-evident propositions (e.g., the *cogito* of Descartes) or (2) propositions evident from the senses (e.g., W. K. Clifford's evidentialism), or (3) incorrigible or indefeasible propositions.[235] Hermeneutical theory as an interdisciplinary account of human understanding does not attempt to meet these criteria. It does not subscribe to *"classical* foundationalism."

At this point, however, an unintentional ambivalence is introduced because the term *foundationalism* comes to be used more loosely in *theology* than it does in *philosophy* (where the term is more clearly defined and specifically used). This extension of meaning may begin to generate confusion. Certain theories of understanding also engage with philosophical theories of knowledge in terms of the unfolding of temporal history. Habermas's collaborator, Karl-Otto Apel, offers a "transcendental-pragmatic" philosophy that suffers undue neglect in America and in Britain.[236] Perhaps surprisingly to

---

233. Gadamer, *Truth and Method,* 279.

234. *Faith and Rationality: Reason and Belief in God,* ed. Alvin Plantinga and Nicholas Wolterstorff (Notre Dame, Ind.: University of Notre Dame Press, 1983), esp. Plantinga, "Reason and Belief in God," 16-93; and Wolterstorff, "Can Belief in God Be Rational If It Has No Foundations?" 135-86.

235. Plantinga, "Reason and Belief in God," 24; cf. William K. Clifford, "The Ethics of Belief," in *Lectures and Essays by the Late William Kingdon Clifford* (London: Macmillan, 1879), 183-86.

236. Karl-Otto Apel, *Towards a Transformation of Philosophy,* trans. Glyn Adey and David Frisby (London: Routledge, 1980), and *Understanding and Explanation: A Transcendental-Pragmatic Perspective,* trans. Georgia Warnke (Cambridge, Mass.: MIT Press, 1984).

Europeans, the application of "historical" approaches from within the philosophy of science tends to win a wider hearing than hermeneutical-historical approaches in some American theology. Nancey Murphy, for example, draws on the "historical" philosophy of science formulated by Imre Lakatos.[237] This turns on a contrast (partly parallel with Apel's but perhaps more pragmatic and less transcendental) between "degenerative" and "progressive" research programs that allows for disconfirmation. Hermeneutical theory shares with Murphy, as against Descartes, the perspective of knowledge or (better) understanding as that which historically "grows and develops"; but Murphy insists on calling this "a nonfoundationalist approach."[238] By parity of argument, our rejection of Cartesianism and defense of community, tradition, and a history of effects are likely to be perceived by many American philosophical theologians as "non-foundationalist," or worse, as "anti-foundationalist."

This would be a mistake. For just as Plantinga has shown that classical foundationalism is self-contradictory (because its identification of self-evident propositions or propositions evident to the senses is itself neither self-evident nor evident to the senses), even so the doctrine (and doctrine it is) that hermeneutical theology necessarily *excludes* any belief as "basic" is equally indemonstrable on the basis of hermeneutics.[239] *Hermeneutics simply does not address the question* of whether it is "nonfoundational," although it does remain incompatible with *classical* Cartesian or Thomist foundationalism. It is unfortunate that too often some kinds of American theology tend to map and to categorize in over-general terms, in contrast to the ongoing hermeneutical task of respecting particularity and contingency and refusing to subsume "the Other" into "my" or "our" *prior* agenda. Philosophical hermeneutics resists being misrepresented by being netted within the *prior* agenda of a "meth-

237. Nancey Murphy, *Theology in the Age of Scientific Reasoning* (Ithaca: Cornell University Press, 1990).

238. Murphy, *Theology in the Age of Scientific Reasoning*, 206. Examples of the "looser" meaning in theology can be found in Francis Schüssler Fiorenza, *Foundational Theology: Jesus and the Church* (New York: Crossroad, 1984), and William C. Placher, *Unapologetic Theology* (Louisville: Westminster/Knox, 1989). In her doctoral dissertation my Nottingham colleague Karen Kilby argues that the link between the theological and philosophical uses is "based on analogy" ("*Vorgriff auf esse*: A Study in the Relation of Philosophy to Theology in the Thought of Karl Rahner," Ph.D. diss., Yale University, 1994, 11n.10).

239. Plantinga, "Reason and Belief in God," 55-63.

od" dominated by the question, Is this approach foundationalist *or* anti-foundationalist? For, as Wolterstorff and Plantinga have so clearly shown, not only do intermediate approaches deserve respect, but also conditions for proper "basicality" become a key if complex issue concerning "entitlement to believe."[240] Belief in God is neither "groundless" nor "fideist" nor Cartesian.

A genuinely *"historical"* hermeneutic of *promise* will distinguish between at least two kinds of *possible* "basicality" in biblical theology. In terms of the founding of Christian traditions, some privilege must be accorded to the earliest pre-Pauline creed, "Jesus is Lord" (1 Cor. 12:3), and to the earliest *kerygma* concerning the death and resurrection of Christ, understood in terms of the fulfillment of divine promise and as a cosmic turning-point of "the last days" (Acts 2:16-39). Yet *promise* also looks ahead to the consummation of all things, when the Apel-Lakatos criteria of "unsurpassability" (Lakatos) or of a comprehensive horizon of understanding (Apel) will be reached in the indefeasible and incorrigible verdicts of God at the last judgment, of which the cross and the resurrection of Christ are the foretaste. To say that these are in no sense "basic" or "foundational" would mislead; but it would mislead even more seriously to perceive hermeneutics as cohering with *classical* foundationalism. Ideally, if all confusion is to be avoided, the term *foundationalism* should be reserved strictly for the agenda concerning "basicality" and *justified* belief addressed by Plantinga and Wolterstorff.

The recognition that certain articles of belief may be deemed to count as "basic" in the context of catechetical instruction, evangelistic preaching, or within a horizon of promise, however, does not militate, or need not militate, against Wittgenstein's picture of a structure of belief as a "nest" of interlocking, intertwining twigs, grasses, branches, or whatever. It is not of such a nature that to remove or to add twigs here and there either destroys the nest or utterly changes its character. Nevertheless, a sufficiently radical removal or addition could lead to destruction or total change. In attacking the generality and timelessness of Cartesianism, we leave no more room for sweeping generalizations about "non-foundational" or "anti-foundational" belief than we do for classical foundationalism. The use of either label risks imposing some prior *Tendenz* or interest which manipulates the agenda in place of pa-

240. Plantinga, "Reason and Belief in God," 71-78. See Plantinga's "Great Pumpkin" argument, 77.

tient, step-by-step inquiry that fully respects the relationality of the other as "other."

Our attempt to steer between the Scylla and the Charybdis identified above leaves room for questions about "entitlement" and "justification," but this agenda does not and cannot control every issue in hermeneutical theory. Wolterstorff's recent book on the ethics of belief with reference to John Locke's *Essay Concerning Human Understanding* (especially Book IV) reveals the subtleties of the relation between "modernity" and issues in the theory of knowledge.[241] This entirely coheres with our earlier book, *The Responsibility of Hermeneutics*, and with Walhout's arguments about ethics and teleology above. Richard Niebuhr makes this point in his well-known work *The Responsible Self*, and it is expounded in the volume edited by James Gustafson and James Laney on this subject.[242] Niebuhr grounds ethical responsibility not merely in "choice" but more especially in human *purposiveness*. This, in turn, presupposes a temporality in which past history and future goals shape a certain "basicality" for responsible agency and action. It is this, Niebuhr affirms, that links the ethics of responsibility with beliefs, attitudes, and actions which are deemed to be "fitting" in the light of the past, present, and future.[243]

Socio-Ethical and Political Individualism and a Theological Critique of Autonomy

The first half of this section remains tentative; our theological critique of "autonomy" is made without reserve. This tentative political critique takes up Lundin's allusion to Richter's quotation "We are all orphans. . . ."[244] Lundin also quotes from Nathan Hatch's illuminating book of 1989, *The Democratization of American Christianity*. In the wake of the Cartesian legacy of individualism and of Cartesian method, Hatch notes that "no less than Tom Paine or Thomas Jefferson, populist Christians of the early republic, sought

241. Nicholas Wolterstorff, *John Locke and the Ethics of Belief* (Cambridge: Cambridge University Press, 1996), esp. chap. 4, "Locke and the Making of Modern Philosophy," 227-46.

242. H. Richard Niebuhr, *The Responsible Self: An Essay in Christian Moral Philosophy* (New York: Harper & Row, 1963), and *On Being Responsible: Issues in Personal Ethics*, ed. James M. Gustafson and James T. Laney (London: SCM, 1969; New York: Harper & Row, 1968).

243. Niebuhr, "The Meaning of Responsibility," in *The Responsible Self*, 47-68.

244. Lundin, 26 above.

to start the world over again."[245] Arguably the link between religion and egalitarian individualism appeared earlier in the new beginnings of the Reformation. Martin Luther perceived both divine grace and the ordinance of law as administered by "godly princes" in terms of protection for the vulnerable, weak, and oppressed. James Atkinson writes of Luther, "In Martin there is nothing of the rebel. He hated revolution and revolt, enthusiasm and excitement."[246] Nevertheless, in the radical "left wing" Reformers, especially in Carlstadt and Müntzer, the encouragement of egalitarian individualism was bound up with declericalization and with the Peasants' War. Where Müntzer encouraged attack on those whom Luther regarded as due authorities, Luther defended the God-given power of secular rulers in their rule as guarantors of "order."[247] The charter of the Peasants' Revolt listed Christian "claims" to individual "rights." Luther saw grace as calling "claims" into question, and justice within an ordered corporate frame as a firmer protection of the weak than self-generated individual "rights."[248] Later, however, the two great revolutions of America and France would formulate, respectively, the Bill of Rights and the Declaration of the Rights of Man. *"Rights"* may indeed protect the weak, but they may also elevate the status of the "I" as a self-centered individual for whom *responsibilities* come second.

Yet it was Immanuel Kant who sharpened the issue toward the close of "the Age of Reason" by arguing for the centrality of the *autonomy* of the human self. I have argued elsewhere that secular postmodernity joins with Christian theology in questioning whether this notion of autonomy is not an illusory basis for ethics, politics, and hope.[249] Kant's three *Critiques* and his defining of "Enlightenment" as "man's emergence from his self-incurred immaturity [and] courage to use it [knowledge] without the guidance of another" (1784) led to the beginnings of a new era of modern theology with Schleiermacher (1799), for while Schleiermacher accepted Kant's challenge concerning the limits of human reason, against Kant's "autonomy" Schleiermacher urged that "the sense of *utter dependence* on God" *(das Gefühl schlechthiniger Abhängigkeit)* lay at the heart of all au-

---

245. Lundin, quoting Hatch, 35 above.

246. Atkinson, ed., *Early Theological Works,* 262.

247. Cf. Martin Luther, *On the Secular Power* (1523), and the evaluation in James Atkinson, *Luther and the Birth of Protestantism* (Baltimore: Penguin, 1968), 221-39.

248. Cf. Atkinson, ed., *Early Theological Works,* 239-41.

249. Anthony C. Thiselton, *Interpreting God and the Postmodern Self: On Meaning, Manipulation, and Promise* (Grand Rapids: William B. Eerdmans, 1995), 11-19, 93-99, 121-64.

thentic religion.[250] In Kant and in the Enlightenment, "autonomy" no longer carried the *corporate* meaning that it held for politics in Aristotle's city-state. There it denoted the self-government of a community free from external interference by other powers, and thereby constituted a virtue compatible with concern for others.

Susan Parsons, a Nottingham colleague, has recently written on feminism in a way that demonstrates some of the ambivalent consequences for ethics of Enlightenment individualism.[251] She observes, "The ripples of the Enlightenment ideal were beginning to be felt in the lives of women" in the late eighteenth and early nineteenth centuries. Whether we consider the secular "universal" rationalism of Voltaire, individual feeling in Rousseau, or the evangelical Second Awakening in the United States, in each case "women welcomed their acceptance *as individuals* in these structures. . . . Church life confirmed their *egalitarian* understanding" (my italics).[252] This egalitarian individualism promoted claims for a politics and an ethics based on *human rights*.[253] Hence in our own times the heated debate about abortion focuses on the opposition between "the right to choose" and "the right to life." One "side" seeks to monopolize "rights" to women as individuals at the cost of reducing the status of the human fetus to nothing more than part of a woman's own private body. Thereby she can exercise her autonomy without "interference" from the state, the medical guild, the church, or a husband.[254] The other "side" designates the undeveloped fetus as a full "individual human person" who owns "rights" equal to those of other individuals, regardless of issues about possible transmissions of genetic diseases or a possible context of rape. The *rights* argument presupposes Cartesian individualism on both sides, in contrast to *responsibility*,

---

250. Immanuel Kant, "An Answer to the Question: What Is Enlightenment?" in *From Modernism to Postmodernism: An Anthology,* ed. Lawrence Calhoune (Cambridge, Mass.: Blackwell, 1996), 51; and Friedrich Schleiermacher, *The Christian Faith,* ed. H. R. Mackintosh and J. S. Stewart (Edinburgh: T. & T. Clark, 1928), sec. 4, 12-18; and *On Religion: Speeches to Its Cultured Despisers,* trans. John Oman (New York: Harper, 1958), 26-101. It is now accepted that the older English translations which stressed *Gefühl* as feeling in a psychological sense missed the point that Schleiermacher stresses the *immediate awareness* of being *dependent* on an *Other.*

251. Susan F. Parsons, *Feminism and Christian Ethics* (Cambridge: Cambridge University Press, 1996).

252. Parsons, *Feminism and Christian Ethics,* 18.

253. Parsons, *Feminism and Christian Ethics,* 36.

254. Cf. Beverly W. Harrison, *Our Right to Choose: Toward a New Ethic of Abortion* (Boston: Beacon, 1983).

which at once transposes the key into that of *relationality* and respect for the Other. Carol Gilligan declares, "The attempt to set up the dilemma [of abortion] as a conflict of rights, turned it into a conflict of selfishness, precluding the possibility of moral decision."[255]

Admittedly, another side of the argument deserves attention. Language about *rights* does also resonate with biblical affirmations of the worth of the human individual, and the oppressed are invited to bring *claims* to entitlements before just judges. Naboth is perceived to have a "right" to his family property that Jezebel and Ahab violate (1 Kings 21:1-19; cf. the parable of the judge wearied by the widow in Luke 18:2-6). The widow and the fatherless have "rights" to be protected. Nevertheless, in the biblical tradition these rights derive from a different context from that of the status of an isolated individual who stands at the center of the stage. They belong to a framework of history and society, a framework such as the humanitarian laws of the Deuteronomist presuppose, which includes *the responsibilities of others* toward the Other. The language derives entirely from the recognition of *responsibilities toward them* that others bear. In particular, *covenantal* obligations presuppose a network of *relationality* which has a different basis from that of "rights" for an isolated, orphaned self who is not even "the sojourner-guest within the gates." The importance of *covenant* will emerge in the final part of this section, which focuses on the speech action of *promising*. In the Aristotelian context of political autonomy, each city-state may show respect for another by treaty, not by unrestrained self-affirmation. Protests on behalf of individuals and freedom become valid where the ideal relationality of humankind becomes distorted into structures of oppression and corporate evil. It is in this context that Gadamer stresses the importance of dialogue and conversation as against the manipulative propaganda of "closed" assertions, while Reinhold Niebuhr, as I have argued elsewhere, attacks the insidiousness of corporate structures of evil.[256] Neither individualism nor oppression is God's will for humanity.

255. Carol Gilligan, *In a Different Voice: Psychological Theory and Women's Development* (Cambridge: Harvard University Press, 1982), 35. On the wider issue of "rights," see also, for example, Ronald Dworkin, *Taking Rights Seriously* (London: Duckworth, 1977).

256. The attitude of Gadamer is incisively expounded by Robert R. Sullivan in *Political Hermeneutics: The Early Thinking of Hans-Georg Gadamer* (University Park: Pennsylvania State University Press, 1989), esp. 1-16, 165-92. Cf. Reinhold Niebuhr, *Moral Man and Immoral Society: A Study in Ethics and Politics* (New York: Scribner, 1932; London: SCM, 1963); Thiselton, *Interpreting God and the Postmodern Self*, 135-43; and Wolterstorff, *John Locke and the Ethics of Belief*, 240-46.

These social, ethical, and political issues are closely related to *implications about claims to "autonomy" and ways in which the biblical writings and Christian theology address these issues.* As Wolterstorff convincingly shows, Locke's concern with reasonableness coincides with social roles that are "more and more the consequence of choice," in contrast to the emphasis of the Reformers that as *fallen* humans we need to "look outside ourselves, to the Word of God."[257] In the New Testament, issues in 1 Corinthians provide a paradigm case. It is widely agreed that, in Margaret Mitchell's words, "Slogans calling for freedom also play a major role in party politics.... Paul in 1 Corinthians must re-define freedom ... for the sake of the whole."[258] The Greek slogan used at Corinth, translated in the NRSV as "All things are lawful for me" (1 Cor. 6:12; Greek *panta moi exestin,* repeated in 10:23), has the force of "I have the right to do anything," since *exestin* is cognate with *exousia* (right, power, or authority), which also becomes a catchword in this epistle. The Corinthian notion of "gospel freedom" is a thinly disguised politics of autonomy, and Paul subjects it to the critique of the cross, to community relationality, and to respect for the Other (Greek *agapē,* love that sets value on the other as shown in a corresponding attitude, stance, and action).

The background is convincingly painted in recent research by a number of specialists, including Stephen Pogoloff (1992), Andrew Clarke (1993), Duane Litfin (1994), Ben Witherington (1995), and Timothy Savage (1996).[259] Social and political values were imported into the church from non-Christian Corinth. Many at Corinth were "status-hungry people.... This new religion gave them status in their own eyes that they had been unable to obtain in the larger society." They expected a style of rheto-

257. Wolterstorff, *John Locke and the Ethics of Belief,* 243-45.

258. Margaret M. Mitchell, *Paul and the Rhetoric of Reconciliation: An Exegetical Investigation of the Language and Composition of 1 Corinthians* (Louisville: Westminster/Knox, 1992), 118-19.

259. Stephen M. Pogoloff, *Logos and Sophia: The Rhetorical Situation of 1 Corinthians* (Atlanta: Scholars Press, 1992), 97-236; Andrew D. Clarke, *Secular and Christian Leadership in Corinth: A Socio-Historical and Exegetical Study of 1 Corinthians 1–6* (Leiden: Brill, 1993), 23-134; Duane Litfin, *St. Paul's Theology of Proclamation: 1 Corinthians 1–4 and Greco-Roman Rhetoric* (Cambridge: Cambridge University Press, 1994), 137-262; Ben Witherington, *Conflict and Community in Corinth: A Socio-Rhetorical Commentary on 1 and 2 Corinthians* (Grand Rapids: William B. Eerdmans; Carlisle: Paternoster, 1995), 19-48 and throughout; and Timothy B. Savage, *Power through Weakness: Paul's Understanding of the Christian Ministry in 2 Corinthians* (New York: Cambridge University Press, 1996), 19-53, 130-63.

ric that would not "'encroach upon their independence.'"[260] In a culture
that prized individualistic competitiveness, they enjoyed "assessing" and
"applauding" rhetorical "performances." Many hoped and indeed expected that Paul would present the gospel in this competitive, applause-
oriented, "democratic" way: the hearers would grade its quality and "success" in the free market of rhetorical performance. Competition of this
kind would inevitably attract group followings. Paul points out, however,
that given their own democratic pluralism, the Corinthian addressees have
no value-neutral ground on which to offer such assessments. "For the
proclamation of the cross is folly [Greek *mōria*] to those who are on their
way to ruin" (1:18). If it is "cleverness" that wins the day, God will destroy
"the wise" (1:19); while for those who go on asking for signs, the gospel
proclamation is a sheer affront (Greek *skandalon*). The "affront" is to
present a status-obsessed, competitive, aspiring community who craved
social acceptance and social power "a crucified Christ."[261] From one side,
the proclamation is an *affront*. From the other side, the cross constitutes
"the *ground and criterion of Church and Apostle*" (Schrage's italics).[262]
Alexandra Brown understands the declarative proclamation of the cross in
1 Corinthians 1:18-25 as a transformative speech-act. It performs a declarative illocution resting on apostolic authenticity and its entailments (an
example of "institutional" facts, which in turn presuppose "brute" facts, as
Searle argues). Paul's words, as he explicitly asserts, are not mere perlocutionary acts of persuasive rhetoric (1 Cor. 2:1-5).[263]

In the face of this, there are still those who would consciously associate themselves sympathetically with Corinthian demands for autonomy.
Antoinette Wire endorses the view that "all things are lawful" means "I
have the right to do anything."[264] She interprets this, however, as the joy-
ous exclamation of the Corinthian women prophets that they have become empowered. These Corinthians, Wire writes, "see themselves called
out of lowliness, not into it," whereas Paul insists "that each live as the Lord

---

260. Witherington, *Conflict and Community in Corinth*, 24, 45.

261. See Schrage, *Der erste Brief an die Korinther*, 1:127-52; cf. 165-203.

262. Schrage, *Der erste Brief an die Korinther*, 1:165. (The phrase is also used by
E. Käsemann.) And see Alexandra R. Brown, *The Cross and Human Transformation:
Paul's Apocalyptic Word in 1 Corinthians* (Minneapolis: Fortress, 1995), 12-30, 65-83.
Cf. also Searle, *The Construction of Social Reality*, 55-57.

263. Brown, *Cross and Human Transformation*, 83-114, 133-39, 146-69.

264. Antoinette C. Wire, *The Corinthian Women Prophets: A Reconstruction of
Paul's Rhetoric* (Minneapolis: Fortress, 1990), 13.

has portioned out . . . (7:15-17)."[265] At Corinth, Wire writes, "Women are as active as men, in making choices. . . . There are women prophets in Corinth claiming that they have authority to do all things."[266] In response, Paul tells "the wise" to become "fools to become wise" (3:18); to "do as the churches of God" (11:16); to "recognize" or to lose "recognition" (14:37-38).[267]

Elizabeth Castelli also questions whether Paul seeks to suppress a healthy freedom by a repressive directive to be "imitators of me" (1 Cor. 11:1).[268] Although her approach is more tentative and exploratory than that of Wire, Castelli calls into play the critical-ideological hermeneutics of Michel Foucault, whose politics and philosophy are such as to question all claims to knowledge as such, and for whom established "norms" are understood to be no more than bids for power and control in the form of regimentation.[269] However, the first part of verse 1, "follow my example," leads on to the second part, "as I follow Christ." Paul makes it clear that "following Christ" is not a claim to election: quite the reverse, it entails sharing the "weakness" and shame of the cross. Hence witnessing to Christ as apostle entails, for Paul, not accepting the professional status of a rhetorician maintained by a wealthy patron, but laboring in the booth of a leather-worker and salesman in the scorching heat of the commercial *agora* (cf. 1 Cor. 4:6-13: "We are the scum, the dregs, the trash. . . . You are successful"; 9:1-27; and the research of R. F. Hock, John Chow, Peter Marshall, Timothy Savage, and others).[270]

265. Wire, *Corinthian Women Prophets*, 31.

266. Wire, *Corinthian Women Prophets*, 14.

267. Wire, *Corinthian Women Prophets*, 14.

268. Elizabeth A. Castelli, *Imitating Paul: A Discourse of Power* (Louisville: Westminster/Knox, 1991), 89-135.

269. Castelli, *Imitating Paul*, 35-38, 119-24. Cf. esp. Michel Foucault, *Discipline and Punish: The Birth of the Prison*, trans. Alan Sheridan (New York: Pantheon, 1977); and *The History of Sexuality*, 3 vols., trans. Robert Hurley (New York: Vintage, 1988-90). For a brief critique, see Thiselton, *Interpreting God and the Postmodern Self*, 12-21, 105-7, 125, 131-34, 140-44. Foucault's simultaneous approval of an anti-authoritarian, Kantian autonomy and his critique of Kant's naive innocence and optimism are well expounded by C. Norris, "What Is Enlightenment? Kant and Foucault," in *The Cambridge Companion to Foucault*, ed. Gary Gutting (Cambridge: Cambridge University Press, 1994), 159-96, esp. 190-92.

270. R. F. Hock, "The Workshop as a Social Setting for Paul's Missionary Preaching," *Catholic Biblical Quarterly* 41 (1979): 438-50; *The Social Context of Paul's Ministry* (Philadelphia: Fortress, 1980); John K. Chow, *Patronage and Power: A Study of*

Furthermore, as Paul Gardner has well shown, the issue of "autonomy" over the matter of eating "food offered to idols" in 1 Corinthians 8:1–11:1 is closely parallel to the issues concerning the use of "spiritual gifts" in 12:1–14:40. Respect for a positive self-awareness and assurance on the part of other believers that they "belonged" *take precedence over "the right"* to eat meat or *the ability* to use tongues in the public assembly. *Christ-like love for others, as the One who gave himself for the Other, constitutes the key criterion of what it is to be "spiritual" or "influenced by the Holy Spirit."*[271] The view that "respect for the otherness of the other," which lies at the heart of hermeneutics, especially in Gadamer, Ricoeur, and Betti, offers a close parallel to *love (agapē)* in the New Testament and in Christian theology is a valid claim. Again, Kevin Vanhoozer expounds this parallel in his own way.[272]

In the work of David Tracy, this issue stands at the interface between biblical hermeneutics and systematic theology. In his book *The Analogical Imagination,* much of Chapter 3, simply entitled "the Classic," reflects both Gadamer's insistence on respect for the Other in the process of listening and "conversation," and (although he never appears to allude to him) Jauss on the aesthetics of reception. Biblical exegesis begins to merge into theology when interpreters allow "their own history" to converse with "the history of the effects of those very classic texts" (*AI,* 102). Readers must "allow that present horizon to be vexed, provoked, challenged by the claim to attention of the text itself" (*AI,* 105). Only thereby can we be "surprised by the sudden, event-like disclosure of the genuinely new" that constitutes "contemporary systematic theology as interpretation of tradition" (*AI,* 107). If we follow Wolterstorff in accepting the intelligibility of recognizing textual action as also divine communicative action, we arrive finally at the contrast between being "open" to God and "closed" in the isolation of a self that discovers the sheer torment of hell in being totally wrapped up in a centered selfhood which has no ear to hear, no eye to see, but only eternal, timeless self-reflexity. In philosophical terms, there is a link of "inter-

---

Social Networks in Corinth (Sheffield: JSOT Press, 1992); Peter Marshall, *Enmity in Corinth: Social Conventions in Paul's Relations with the Corinthians* (Tübingen: Mohr, 1987); and Savage, *Power through Weakness.*

271. Paul D. Gardner, *The Gifts of God and the Authentication of a Christian: An Exegetical Study of 1 Corinthians 8:1–11:1* (Lanham, Md.: University Press of America, 1994).

272. Vanhoozer in *Disciplining Hermeneutics* and *Is There a Meaning in This Text?*, 642-718.

nal grammar" between the urge for self-sufficient autonomy by means of which I know and control everything else in my own way and on my own terms, and sheer "timeless" torment from which the self can never move on. Against Sartre's "hell is other people," a more "theological" notion of hell would be total self-absorption. The stance of hermeneutics is the exact reverse. In respect for and concern for the Other, I discover myself as a relational creature capable of communication, understanding, giving and receiving, loving and being loved.

Yet the social constructs of secular postmodernity offer no salvation from such a hell. As Zygmunt Bauman expresses it, whatever its illusions, modernity at least offered a sense of "rightness," even of "mission," whereas postmodern disintegration offers "no horizontal or vertical order, either in actuality or in potency . . . rarely conscious of its own responsibility."[273] Anthony Giddens sums up the ethical issue in terms of trust. In premodern societies, kinship, religion, the local community, and tradition provided solid ground for trust.[274] The era of modernity followed Descartes and the rise of technology in placing confidence in general "systems" and "experts"; Giddens refers to "mechanisms of trust in abstract systems, especially trust in expert systems."[275] Pastors and congregations who still view the Bible through the lenses of a technological "engineering" culture may still reflect this broad stance toward "biblical interpretation." Nevertheless, the questioning associated with a hermeneutic of suspicion and with postmodern exposés of "power" and "interest" has undermined trust even in "systems" and "experts," where macro-economics and bureaucratic planning can no longer master the complexities and fragmentations of our age. Christian theology offers a distinctive hermeneutic that steers between the Scylla of modernity and the Charybdis of postmodern skepticism to seek to establish a hermeneutic of *trust* — or, more precisely, *a hermeneutic of promise.*

273. Zygmunt Bauman, *Intimations of Postmodernity* (London: Routledge, 1992), 35, 187.

274. Anthony Giddens, *The Consequences of Modernity* (Cambridge: Polity; Oxford: Blackwell, 1990), 100-105.

275. Giddens, *The Consequences of Modernity*, 83.

The Paradigm of Biblical Promise as Trustworthy, Temporal, Transformative Speech-Action

The paradigmatic speech-act of promise may be explored from two different sides. In Christian theology the understanding of the proclamation of the grace of God in Christ occurs frequently under the mode of promise of divine action. This theme receives special prominence in Paul, in the author of Hebrews, in Luther, in Tyndale, and in Barth, Rahner, Moltmann, and Pannenberg (among many others) in modern theology. In the philosophy of language, speech-act theorists have identified promise as one of the clearest models of illocutionary action. It meets so many criteria for illocutions that it becomes virtually a paradigm case of illocutionary speech-acts.

We should note at the outset that a variety of genres and locutionary acts of utterance in biblical texts and elsewhere do not necessarily correspond with the illocutions that these forms of language may be used to perform. This constitutes a widely recognized principle in speech-act theory from J. L. Austin and John Searle to Steven Davis and others.[276] Although elsewhere in my own work I have cited biblical Hebrew or Greek verbs that frequently signal the occurrence of illocutionary acts in the biblical writings, these provide no more than available rough indicators: the occurrence of the word *promise* does not necessarily signal or constitute an illocutionary *act of promising*, while the use of the future tense of another verb in an appropriate context of utterance (of situation, speaker, and addressee) may in fact constitute a promissory act. Austin observes that "I'll be there" may constitute an illocutionary act of promise in appropriate circumstances, whereas an embarrassed mother's attempt to reassure an injured neighbor by insisting "He promises; don't you, Willie?" is not an illocutionary act at all.[277] Austin observes that we reach "an impasse over any *single, simple* criterion of grammar or vocabulary" (his italics).[278] Unless *the speaker has taken responsibility for his or her own speech and actions*, the

---

276. J. L. Austin, *How to Do Things with Words* (Cambridge: Harvard University Press, 1962), 4-7, 58-78; John Searle, *Expression and Meaning*, 8-29; D. Vanderveken, "A Complete Formulation of a Simple Logic of Elementary Illocutionary Acts," in *Foundations of Speech Act Theory: Philosophical and Linguistic Perspectives*, ed. Savas L. Tsohatzidis (London: Routledge, 1994), 99-131; and Steven Davis, "Anti-Individualism and Speech Act Theory," in *Foundations of Speech Act Theory*, 208-19.

277. Austin, *How to Do Things with Words*, 63, 69.

278. Austin, *How to Do Things with Words*, 59.

utterance does not *count as an act* of making a promise. Searle adds, "Many of the verbs we call illocutionary verbs" are not always, or not necessarily, "markers" of completed illocutionary acts.[279]

Hence, while it remains undeniably true that the biblical writings perform multiple speech-*acts* (e.g., acts of praise, evaluation, acquittal, appointment, call, invitation, proclamation, declaration, thanksgiving, warning, promise), these do not correspond in one-to-one ways with the multiple speech-*forms* that writers such as A. N. Wilder identify as the "New Utterance" of the gospel with multiple "modes and genres."[280] Hymns, stories, reports, parables, letters, greetings, poems, allegories, sermons, dialogues, polemics, doxologies, and other modes of utterance abound. Nevertheless, a hymn of praise may also enact or embody a promise in the context of worship; a sermon may embody acts of acclamation in the course of teaching or warning; parables may project worlds that both demand and promise, or both seduce and warn. I noted above that Hebrews 1:1-4 offers an outstanding example of multiple speech-acts as a dynamic model for the opening of a forceful and effective sermon.

Steven Davis insists that all illocutionary acts presuppose an intersubjective public world. Or, as he explicitly argues in negative terms, Cartesian individualism predisposes us to fail to notice illocutions. Yet if the biblical writings witness above all to a relationship or relationships between God and Israel, between God and Christian believers, between believers and believers, or between the church and the world, language that presupposes intersubjectivity may be expected. Moreover, given the biblical concern with the ethics of speech as faithful and true speech, it causes no surprise if the linchpin of "institutional facts" that underlie such illocutions as promise and appointment rests on relations of *covenant*. While Paul and especially the Epistle to the Hebrews base promissory speech-acts on covenant, including divine covenant faithfulness, the Epistle of James pays attention to the ethics of speech both in terms of the causal perlocutionary effects of the tongue and the need for trustworthy, responsible speech that can provide a condition for illocutionary acts.[281] If a performative is to constitute an illocution rather than merely a perlocutionary act of persuasion, it is fundamental that the agent or

---

279. Searle, *Expression and Meaning*, 27.

280. Amos N. Wilder, *Early Christian Rhetoric*, 9-47 and throughout.

281. The most recent extended study is that of William R. Baker, *Personal Speech-Ethics in the Epistle of James* (Tübingen: Mohr, 1995).

speaker of the utterance makes a self-involving commitment, or at least takes an appropriate expressive stance, in relation to the utterance. The ethics of speech provides a pivotal criterion for differences between illocutionary and perlocutionary acts. We shall return to speech ethics in James when we have clarified this point.

Alexandra Brown's recent study *The Cross and Human Transformation* rightly understands 1 Corinthians 1:18–2:16 as a "real world speech act" in which Paul serves as "*'speech-act'ivist*."[282] Paul's initial proclamatory acts led to the "founding of the church," but because the church at Corinth subsequently misinterprets what it is to live under the verdictive act of the cross, in effect (here Brown reflects Austin's terminology) "a prior speech act . . . has misfired."[283] Brown perceives the word of the gospel as transformative and trustworthy, and as temporally contingent on the circumstances of Paul's utterances, oral or written.[284] Nevertheless, with Pogoloff, Clarke, Witherington, and many others, she also perceives that Paul rejects the merely instrumental rhetoric of perlocution, since for Paul the "power" of the cross does not lie in rhetorical or psychological persuasion (Greek *ouk en sophiā logou;* 1:17). This *empties* the cross of its power (1:17; 2:1; 2:5).[285]

Pogoloff convincingly shows that the combination of Greek *sophia* and *logos* in 1:17–2:5 signifies "far more than just technical skill in language. Rather, they imply a whole world of social status related to speech."[286] "Clever speech" and "high-sounding language" are the tools of the professional, competitive rhetorician. As we have already observed, this stands in contrast to Paul's chosen status as menial leather-worker in the commercial *agora,* whose status as speaker derives from his apostolic life-commitment to the verdict of the cross and the transformative power of the resurrection of Christ. Pointing to this and living it out constitute the vocation of apostleship. To write *as apostle* is to point away from the self and to disengage from the *causal* power of rhetoric in order to allow the

---

282. Alexandra Brown, *The Cross and Human Transformation,* 19.

283. Brown, *The Cross and Human Transformation,* 30; cf. Austin, *How to Do Things with Words,* 16. Austin comments that in a "misfire" the performative act "goes through the motions" but becomes "void" or is "botched." Clearly Austin's term only approximates to Brown's point, since Paul does not doubt the genuineness of his converts' faith.

284. Brown, *The Cross and Human Transformation,* 13-35, 65-169.

285. Brown, *The Cross and Human Transformation,* 73.

286. Pogoloff, *Logos and Sophia,* 113.

kerygma of the gospel of the cross to perform the *illocutionary* act of transformation and promise in which both divine agent and apostolic agent pledge themselves to constraints that make possible its operative performance. Greco-Roman rhetoricians, by contrast, usually committed themselves to nothing. To try to convince an audience of an unjust case or untrue claim was a regular training routine in rhetorical competitions in performing *perlocutions*. Front-rank Roman rhetoricians such as Quintilian and reflective writers such as Plutarch disapproved of this scramble to be "greeted with a storm of ready-made applause," at the price of twisting truth: "the result is variety and empty self-sufficiency . . . intoxicated by the wild enthusiasm of their fellow pupils."[287]

In this light, the promissory proclamation of the cross becomes perceived and (mis)understood as "folly" (Greek *mōria*), even if those who allow themselves to be transformed by the proclamation of Christ discover its operative effect (Greek *dynamis tou Theou;* 1 Cor. 1:18). Brown rightly notes the ambivalence of Jewish "wisdom" traditions; Jewish "wisdom" is used both of divine wisdom and of that which nourishes a sense of "achievement."[288] The "wisdom" of the cross, however, "turns things upside down": those without influence, status, or learning (1:26) receive God's power, God's righteousness, God's wisdom through Christ, and the subverting action of the cross (1:30-31). Hence Paul adopts a style and mode of performing the declarative, proclamatory, promissory act of the *kerygma* "in weakness . . . in trepidation . . . that your faith might be built not on human wisdom but on the power of God" (1 Cor. 2:2-5), that is, on illocutionary promise, not on perlocutionary persuasion.

This does not preclude the use of rhetoric and persuasive power in other contexts. The Pauline Epistles and the Epistle to the Hebrews abound in rhetorical devices where persuasion by argument often constitutes the goal at hand. Once an addressee has accepted and understood the

287. Quintilian, *Institutio Oratoria* 2:2:9-12; cf. Pogoloff, *Logos and Sophia*, 173-78 and throughout, and Plutarch *Moralia*, 801e, 802e. Cf. especially Donald L. Clark, *Rhetoric in Greco-Roman Education* (New York: Columbia University Press, 1957), 67-262, for numerous examples and the reservations of Quintilian and Cicero about Provincial Schools and their techniques.

288. Brown, *The Cross and Human Transformation*, 3-63, 77-89. The strongest case can be found in a rewritten Nottingham Ph.D. thesis by James A. Davis, *Wisdom and Spirit: An Investigation of 1 Corinthians 1:18–3:20: Against the Background of Jewish Sapiential Traditions in the Greco-Roman Period* (Lanham, Md.: University Press of America, 1984). The stress on eloquence could lead to elitism (143).

verdictive and promissory frame of the cross and resurrection of Christ, Paul does not hesitate to use every kind of speech act, including rhetoric and assertion. Even in 1 Corinthians he uses the rhetoric of irony and the well-known device of the "rhetoric of affliction" (1 Cor. 4:7-13).[289] However, in such examples the illocutionary act whereby identification with the suffering and promissory power of Christ has been set in motion provides the larger frame of reference that is presupposed.[290] Brown comments, "The God of the cross . . . made weakness into power . . . folly into wisdom."[291] Yet this also carries entailments about "knowing," with the provision that "knowing" is grounded in the cruciform life. Luther makes this clear in his Pauline *theologia crucis*. Against the Corinthian *theologia gloriae*, "he deserves to be called a theologian . . . who comprehends . . . the things of God seen through suffering and the cross."[292]

The nature of declaration or proclamation more explicitly as promise occurs where proclamation is enacted in the context of covenant, as happens in the act of "solemnly proclaiming [Greek *kataggellete*] the Lord's death" (1 Cor. 11:26) by sharing in "the cup" as "the new covenant [ratified] in my blood" (Greek *to potērioon hē kainē diathēkn . . . en tō emō haimati*; v. 25). This pre-Pauline tradition goes back to the earliest time as an apostolic tradition traced back to Jesus, while the link between promise (Greek noun *epaggelia*, verb *epaggellomai*) and covenant *(diathēkē)* abounds in the Epistle to the Hebrews. Even God is understood as binding his future choices not only by a promise but by a promise endorsed (logically, redundantly) by an oath (Heb. 6:13, 16; 7:21; also 4:3, citing Ps. 95:11; 110:4). The first-century Jewish writer Philo expresses puzzlement over how the Psalms could speak of an oath on the part of One who already stands by his Word, and assumes that this is mere anthropomorphic accommodation to human doubt.[293] However, Hebrews has a *temporal*

---

289. Karl A. Plank, *Paul and the Irony of Affliction* (Atlanta: Scholars Press, 1987), esp. 33-70; S. M. Ferrari, *Die Sprache des Leids in den paulinischen Peristasenkatalogen* (Stuttgart: Katholisches Bibelwerk, 1991). More broadly, see Duane F. Watson and Alan J. Hauser, *Rhetorical Criticism of the Bible: A Comprehensive Bibliography with Notes on History and Method* (Leiden: Brill, 1994).

290. Cf. Karl Theodore Kleinknecht, *Der Leidende Gerechtfertigte* (Tübingen: Mohr, 1984), 208-304; and Schrage, *Der erste Brief an die Korinther*, 1:330-50.

291. Brown, *The Cross and Human Transformation*, 147.

292. Luther, *Luther's Works*, vol. 31, 40; *The Heidelberg Disputation*, in *Early Theological Works*, ed. Atkinson, 291-94.

293. Philo, *Legum alleg.* 3:203-7; *de sacrif. Abelis et Caini* 91:4.

view of divine action that Philo's Hellenistic-Jewish thought lacks, and is concerned to make the point that in the series of pledges which God makes to Melchizedek, to Abraham, to Moses, to Israel in the old covenant, and finally through Christ in the auguration of the new covenant (Jer. 31:31-34; Heb. 8:10-13) and Christ's priesthood and sacrifice, the latter remains irrevocable and unsurpassable. This sworn promise opens "the new and living way" through the mediation of Jesus Christ's own body and sacrificial death (Heb. 10:20), but if this is rejected, there is no further fallback on some further divine commitment (10:26-31).

Hebrews 9:15-18 shows in the clearest terms that the basis of this promissory act lies in the covenant *(diathēkē)* ratified by the blood of Christ, and (through conscious wordplay) that this promissory covenant has the active force of a promissory testament or will (also Greek *diathēkē*). Both *covenant (diathēkē)* and legal will or *testament* (also *diathēkē*) commit the covenant partner and the testator: "Where there is a testament it is necessary for the death of the testator to be established; for a testament takes effect [*bebaia*, becomes valid] only when a death has occurred; it has no force [*mēpote ischuei*] while the testator is still alive" (Heb. 9:16-17). Both Greek words have precisely the force that denotes operative speech-acts.[294] *Diathēkē, bebaios, epaggelia,* and *ischuei* denote aspects or attributes of "institutional facts" in the first-century Greco-Roman world. Contexts of "legally guaranteed security" relating to leases on property, terms of trade or employment, freehold sales, political transactions and compacts, decrees of magistrates, and valid action abound in nonliterary sources in the papyri of the Greco-Roman world of the first and second centuries.[295]

Hebrews looks both back to the promissory divine acts of the Hebrew scriptures (e.g., "You are a priest for ever after the order of Melchizedek," Ps. 110:4 [cf. Gen. 14:18]; Heb. 5:6; 6:20; 7:17; or "I will make a new covenant," Jer. 31:31; Heb. 8:8; 10:16), and ahead to promised divine action yet to be

---

294. In legal contexts, documents such as wills become *bebaios* — "valid," "proven," "in force" — when the necessary conditions are operative; cf. Bauer et al., *A Greek-English Lexicon of the New Testament,* 138. In other interpersonal contexts, *bebaios* denotes a reliable, dependable word that takes hold and has force (e.g., prophetic word in 2 Pet. 1:19). Similarly, *ischuō* denotes "having valid force," "holding its power"; Bauer et al., *A Greek-English Lexicon of the New Testament,* 383-84.

295. See James H. Moulton and George Milligan, *The Vocabulary of the Greek Testament: Illustrated from the Papyri and Other Non-Literary Sources* (London: Hodder and Stoughton, 1930), 107-8, 148-49, 226-27, 308.

performed (4:1; 11:13, 39). The word *promise* (both in noun and verb form) occurs at least eighteen times in Hebrews, where the emphasis that we discussed above on *temporality* assumes many of its nuances: entry into God's promises is possible only at the opportune *kairos* of "today" (Heb. 3:7; 4:7), "while the promise of entering is still open" (Heb. 4:1). However, *tempo* plays its part. Jesus accepts the constraints of temporal human existence; the addressees were disillusioned that everything had not come right quickly, and "need patience" (10:36); "let us run with patience" (12:1), for *allotted* time defines "the race that is set before us" (12:1). Faith embraces what is "not seen" because it has not yet occurred (11:1). Nevertheless, the history of Israel presents many examples of those who acted in the present on the basis of future promise, even if Noah's building an ark on dry land under a blue sky or Joshua's solemnly leading a procession around Jericho seven times appeared foolish and groundless before the world (Heb. 11:7, 30). The givenness of *allotted time* and *periodicity* not only defines the eras of the old and new covenants, but means that even Jesus, who alone represents being human as God intended humans to be (Heb. 2:6-9; drawing on Psalm 8), experiences the need to trust in God (2:13; cf. v. 18), and in costly obedience and trust remains faithful (3:2). Temporality means that in assuming genuine humanness, Jesus as pioneer of the new humanity accepts the constraints of time and even weakness, rather than seeking the shortcuts presented in the Messianic temptations that would supposedly offer an "easier" and less painful way to achieve the work.

Yet Austin, Searle, and more recent writers remind us that vocabulary and grammar are not in themselves reliable criteria to identify speech acts. The vocabulary of promise, covenant, testament, valid force, and their related temporal correlates do indeed signify a promissory context. Nevertheless, even where such vocabulary is absent, such language of address and invitation as "let us boldly approach the throne of grace, that we may receive mercy" (Heb. 4:16) receives its dynamic by embodying an implicit promissory dimension, as we shall note in more detail. The address to Christ which says "You are a priest for ever" (5:6) is an act of appointment that in turn rests in promise. Acts of promise may lie embedded in statement: "We have that hope as an anchor for our lives, safe and secure" (6:19); "the blood of Jesus makes us free to enter the sanctuary" (10:19). Some promises, however, are explicit without using the word *promise*: "I shall pardon their wicked deeds. . . . Their sins . . . I will remember no more" (8:12; 10:17); "He who is to come will come" (10:37); "I will never leave you or desert you" (13:5).

Other New Testament writings share these characteristics, but lack of space prevents our exploring them. The earliest Christian preaching, according to Luke, represented "the promise . . . to you and to your children" (Acts 2:39). The gospel fulfills promises made to Israel (Acts 13:23, 32; Rom. 9:9; 18:8). Justification by grace entails appropriating in the present a promise that in strict logic is eschatological (cf. Rom. 4:13-20; Gal. 3:14-29). For Karl Barth, the promissory and covenantal dimensions arise because every act of divine speech is both an *act* and an act of *self-giving* in which *God in sovereign freedom chooses to be constrained* by covenant promise. Since Jesus Christ, rather than the scripture that witnesses to Christ, stands pre-eminently as the Word of God, Jesus Christ constitutes the supreme model or paradigm case of "the Word of God in the humiliation of its majesty" in power, freedom, faithfulness, and action (*CD*, I/2.21, 675). This Word is temporal, eventful, promissory, and active. God exercises his sovereignty by "choosing to love humanity," which entails constraint and "cost" to guarantee the fulfillment of "promise": God refuses to deal with the ungodly as the ungodly deserve because this would countermand his promise to be gracious (*CD*, II/2.32, 318, 319).

Moltmann similarly urges that *promise* assumes a primary mode of divine speech when a description of the present stands in tension with that which should be and will be.[296] To assert the future as if it were present is presumption; to deny it is despair; to proclaim the gospel is promise and hope.[297] "Christian eschatology as the language of promise will then be an essential key to the unlocking of Christian truth."[298] Moltmann explicitly alludes to the enlargement of horizons in Gadamer and to temporal actualizations of traditions of expectation.[299] Like Jauss, Moltmann perceives that the process of hope and fulfillment throughout the biblical traditions and beyond into the history of the church leads to the reshaping of ever-new horizons of expectation as God fulfills his promise, yet also does so in often surprising ways that creatively transcend human expectations.[300] The resurrection of Jesus Christ provides an example of faithful fulfillment side by side with the radically new which, within the estab-

296. Jürgen Moltmann, *Theology of Hope: On the Ground and the Implications of a Christian Eschatology,* trans. James W. Leitch (London: SCM, 1967), 95-154.

297. Moltmann, *Theology of Hope,* 23; cf. 16-36.

298. Moltmann, *Theology of Hope,* 41.

299. Moltmann, *Theology of Hope,* 106-12.

300. Moltmann, *Theology of Hope,* 105-12. Moltmann draws on Gerhard von Rad and W. Zimmerli as well as Gadamer.

lished tradition of hope, opens far-reaching new horizons[301] As Dietrich Bonhoeffer urges (in parallel with Jauss on hermeneutics), the cross exhibits disruption and discontinuity as well as making possible the continuity of promise.[302] Thus, against Nietzsche, God's Spirit, for Moltmann, signals an "unreserved 'yes' to life."[303]

I do not have space here to trace these themes further in modern Christian theology. I should note, however, that Wolfhart Pannenberg also develops the importance of promise, holding together continuity of action by the faithful God with the possibility of novelty and surprise in the context of the re-actualization of traditions. He also observes, "Perhaps the most important service Luther rendered as a biblical exegete was to discover in the biblical texts the temporal structure of faith and therefore its nature as an act of trust, corresponding to God's Word of promise" (*SysT,* 3:138). "The truth of God must prove itself anew."[304] "The promises put the human present, with all the pain of its incompleteness and failure, in the light of God that comes to us as our salvation. . . . The concept of promise links our present . . . to God's future" (*SysT,* 3:545). Hence for Pannenberg, while the history of tradition and its effects is constituted by promise to Abraham, promise to David, promises of postexilic prophecy, and then to apocalyptic, acts of promise alone cannot be isolated from complex relations to truth and to states of affairs (*SysT,* 3:540-45).

Promise as a Key Example of Understanding Illocutions in Speech-Act Theory

We are now in a position to see why *promise* comes to constitute a key example for an examination of the nature and currency of speech acts in the biblical writings and in Christian theology. We may lay out the following proposals.

(1) The nature of promise in the biblical writings *presupposes institu-*

---

301. Moltmann, *Theology of Hope,* 165-229.

302. Moltmann cites Bonhoeffer, *Theology of Hope,* 198-99, and develops this theme in *The Crucified God: The Cross of Christ as the Foundation and Criticism of Christian Theology,* trans. R. A. Wilson and John Bowden (New York: Harper & Row, 1974).

303. Moltmann, *The Spirit of Life,* 97.

304. Wolfhart Pannenberg, *Basic Questions in Theology,* 3 vols. (London: SCM, 1970-73), 2:8.

tional facts, such as *covenant,* ratification by the blood of Christ, embodiments in such promissory signs of covenant as baptism and the Lord's Supper. *Yet these institutional facts cannot simply be absorbed into the intralinguistic world,* not even into Frei's "history-like" linguistic world.[305] Recent powerful advocates of this emphasis are Francis Watson in *Text and Truth* and Kevin Vanhoozer in *Is There a Meaning in This Text?,* as well as Searle in his "General Theory of Institutional Facts," which we have discussed above.[306] Searle concedes that "perceiving as" or "Background" plays a part in mediating, conditioning, and construing extralinguistic states of affairs *as* institutional facts.[307] Nevertheless, just as there could be no "institutional" facts of dollars or pounds sterling in the bank without paper or electronic signals, so there could be, I argue, no covenant without the history of events surrounding Moses, Israel, David, and the Patriarchs; no Lord's Supper without the crucifixion and the Last Supper; no ratification by blood without a sacrificial system and the violent death of Jesus. *Promise* presupposes *institutional facts;* but institutional facts can count as a basis for operative illocutions of the type under discussion only if at the end of the line certain *"brute facts"* (Searle) or states of affairs have occurred or occur in the extralinguistic world. We may also note that the "historical" *(wirkungsgeschichtlich)* perspective of Gadamer, Jauss, and Pannenberg places "counting x as y" in a frame more closely related to intersubjective (re)cognition than to individual noncognitive perception. In a robust tradition that crosses contextual boundaries, *"counts as"* is too weak; *"constitutes"* becomes a more adequate term.

(2) *Promising* provides useful examples of the variability *between explicit and implicit speech-acts:* between instances when *vocabulary* may seem to signal an illocution and when an illocutionary act of promise occurs *without* the use of expected or hoped-for vocabulary. Probably most acts of promise in the biblical writings *do not use the word "promise"* — for example, "I will be with you always" (Matt. 28:20); "Whoever believes in me, as scripture says, 'Streams of living water shall flow from within him'" (John 7:38); "Whoever has faith in me shall live, even though he dies" (John 11:25);

---

305. Cf. Demson, *Hans Frei and Karl Barth,* 107, esp. in Barth's recognition (neglected by Frei) of "appointment, calling, commissioning" as extralinguistic acts.

306. Francis Watson, *Text and Truth: Redefining Biblical Theology* (Edinburgh: T. & T. Clark, 1997), esp. 95-178; Vanhoozer, *Is There a Meaning in This Text?* and Searle, *The Construction of Social Reality,* 113-26; cf. 127-76.

307. For some examples from Searle, see *The Construction of Social Reality,* 131-34.

"Everyone who calls on the name of the Lord . . . shall be saved" (Acts 2:21). Furthermore, the word *promise* may occur without initiating an illocution, as when Paul discusses the respective roles of law and promise in relation to Abraham (Rom. 4:13-22). Yet sometimes the use of the word signals the illocutionary act, as it does in Hebrews and Jeremiah: "Now he has promised, 'Once again I will shake not only the earth, but the heavens also'" (Heb. 12:26); "I will fulfil the promise. . . . I will cause a righteous Branch to spring forth for David; and he shall execute justice" (Jer. 33:14-15).

This helps us to address a long-standing problem in speech-act theory that has persisted from Austin to the present. Austin rejected any criterion of vocabulary or grammar to isolate or identify illocutionary acts.[308] Yet he lists sixteen "behabitives," twenty-seven "verdictives," forty-six "exercitives," thirty-three "commissives," and more than fifty "expositives" in terms of English verbs.[309] Searle takes Austin to task for confusing "illocutionary verbs" with "illocutionary acts."[310] Yet his own revised "taxonomy of illocutionary acts" includes "such sentences as . . ." with a utilization of similar lists, if under modified headings.[311] In Tsohatzidis's 1994 volume, Daniel Vanderveken contributes a characterization of illocutionary acts in the form of a highly complex logical system in formally operational terms deemed to constitute nonbasic productions of the five basic forces of "assert," "commit," "direct," "declare," and "express." His work here is logical and rigorous, and draws heavily on formal symbolic logical operators.[312] Nevertheless, Vanderveken's volume of 1990 includes a massive and detailed list (no doubt the largest and most comprehensive available) of (i) 70 English *verbs* classified under "English assertives"; (ii) 32 English *verbs* under "English commissives"; (iii) 56 English *verbs* under "English directives"; (iv) 85 English *verbs* under "English declaratives"; and (v) 28 English *verbs* under "English expressives."[313] He lists nearly three hundred "performative" *verbs*. Yet Vanderveken recognizes the shape of the problem. He notes, "I will only be concerned here with the paradigmatic central illocutionary meanings of

308. Austin, *How to Do Things with Words*, 4-7, 58-78.

309. Austin, *How to Do Things with Words*, (i) 79, 83; (ii) 152; (iii) 154-55; (iv) 156-57; (v) 161-62.

310. Searle, *Expression and Meaning*, 9-11.

311. Searle, *Expression and Meaning*, 9-11.

312. Daniel Vanderveken, "A Complete Formulation of Simple Logic of Elementary Illocutionary Acts," in *Foundations of Speech Act Theory*, ed. Tsohatzidis, 99-131.

313. Daniel Vanderveken, *Principles of Language Use*, vol. 1 of *Meaning and Speech Acts* (Cambridge: Cambridge University Press, 1990), 169-217.

speech-act verbs, and I will have to idealize even these meanings somewhat in my semantic analysis."[314] "Many speech-act verbs have *several* uses" (his italics).[315] My work reflects the ambiguity found here. In *New Horizons in Hermeneutics,* I listed 27 "directives" or "exercitives" in the biblical texts; 14 biblical "commissives"; 14 biblical "declaratives"; and some 20 "expressives" drawn from biblical texts.[316] Yet I also recognized that more was at issue than specific uses of specific vocabulary.[317]

The paradigm case of acts of promise serves to show that while the use of concordances may alert us to passages in the biblical writings that *prima facie* invite attention for the study of speech acts, Hebrew or Greek verbs provide no more than *possible* indicators of illocutionary acts, which provide useful starting points but may also signal dead ends that fail to lead to illocutions. Literature on curses, vows, blessing, promise, and confession assists our inquiry but takes us only part of the way.[318]

(3) Acts of *promise* bring to light most clearly *the commitments and responsibilities of agents of promise within an intersubjective, public, extralinguistic world of ethical undertaking and address.* Steven Davis makes clear in the first place that Cartesian individualism has no place in the speech situation of promise. He writes, "The criterion of individuation of illocutionary acts like promising . . . is not individualistic."[319] "An act of promising depends on the linguistic practice of a speaker's linguistic community . . . an utterance of 'I promise to do A' will place him under an obligation to do A," as Searle also affirms.[320] This provides a second consideration. Searle makes clear the intersubjective aspects in his section subtitled "How to

314. Vanderveken, *Principles of Language Use,* 169.
315. Vanderveken, *Principles of Language Use,* 168.
316. Thiselton, *New Horizons in Hermeneutics,* 299.
317. Thiselton, *New Horizons in Hermeneutics,* 283-307.
318. Cf. Herbert C. Brichto, *The Problem of "Curse" in the Hebrew Bible* (Philadelphia: Society of Biblical Literature and Exegesis, 1963); Tony W. Cartledge, *Vows in the Hebrew Bible and the Ancient Near East* (Sheffield: JSOT Press, 1992); O. Cullmann, *The Earliest Christian Confessions* (London: Lutterworth, 1949); Vernon H. Neufeld, *The Earliest Christian Confessions* (Leiden: Brill, 1963); C. Rose, "Verheissung und Erfühlung . . . ," *Biblische Zeitschrift* 73 (1989): 178-91; D. R. Worley, "God's Faithfulness to Promise: The Hortatory Use of Commissive Language in Hebrews" (Ph.D. diss., Yale University, 1981).
319. Steven Davis, "Anti-Individualism and Speech Act Theory," in *Foundations of Speech Act Theory,* 215; cf. 208-19.
320. Davis, "Anti-Individualism and Speech Act Theory," 216; see also Searle, *Speech Acts,* 60.

Promise."[321] He observes, "'I promise' and 'I hereby promise' are among the strongest illocutionary force indicating devices for *commitment* in the English language" [his italics]. . . . The essential feature of a promise is that it is the undertaking of an obligation to perform a certain act. . . . This condition distinguishes promises . . . from other kinds of speech-acts."[322]

This has exceptional importance both for biblical theology and for the hermeneutical significance of illocutions that are also commissives. First, Walhout's emphasis on *action and agency* is further vindicated, as is Lundin's critique of *individualism and autonomy.* Responsibilities and commitments radically condition "autonomy." This also strengthens Walhout's concern with *ethics and teleology.* We have already noted Pannenberg's comment that *temporal duration and separation* enhance what is at stake in living out the disposition or character of *being faithful* as part of one's stable identity (*SysT,* 2:202). The biblical writings place an emphasis on the ethical demand for faithfulness and speech ethics that is difficult to exaggerate. "A lying tongue . . . a false witness" stand among what count as "abominations" to the Lord (Prov. 6:17, 19). Deceitful speech does not go unpunished (Ps. 120:3-4). Speakers will be held accountable for speech that is "empty," unfulfilled, or "inoperative" in life (Greek *argos;* Matt. 12:36). William Baker traces the biblical background to speech ethics in his work on speech ethics in James. Rash, unperformed promises are worse than no promises. Hence "set a guard over my mouth, O Lord" (Ps. 141:3; cf. Eccles. 6:11). "Controlled speech" is vital in the Old Testament, Apocrypha, and Pseudepigrapha, in Qumran, rabbinic literature, the Greco-Roman world, and the New Testament.[323] The Epistle of James calls for "personal integrity in speech. . . . Uncontrolled speech is detrimental to society. . . . One's words should be consistent with one's deeds."[324] Elsewhere I have argued this point with reference to the logical paradox about "Cretan liars" in Titus 1:12-13, where the coherence between first-person utterances and lifestyle is the unnoticed issue.[325]

---

321. John Searle, "How to Promise," in *Foundations of Speech Act Theory,* ed. Tsohatzidis, 60.

322. Searle, "How to Promise," 57-61.

323. Baker, *Personal Speech-Ethics in the Epistle of James,* 27-33, 43-46, 49-52, 55-58, 75-79.

324. Baker, *Personal Speech-Ethics in the Epistle of James,* 281, 284.

325. Anthony C. Thiselton, "The Logical Role of the Liar Paradox in Titus 1:12, 13: A Dissent from the Commentaries in the Light of Philosophical and Logical Analysis," *Biblical Interpretation* 2 (1994): 207-23.

This achieves its highest theological climax in the biblical understanding of God as one who chooses in sovereign freedom to constrain that freedom by graciously entering into the constraints imposed upon action by undertaking covenantal promise. On this basis, believers can know where they stand with God and receive assurance: his promissory illocutions are liberating. This also has implications for the status of prophets or apostles who proclaim promise on behalf of God or in his name. Wolterstorff has shown the factors that make such a notion philosophically intelligible. In terms of speech-act theory, it introduces a third point under the present consideration: in addition to the intersubjective world of the speaker and addressee, and the responsibilities and ethical obligations of the agent of promise, attention needs to be paid to the *status* of the speaker. Does the speaker speak in his or her own name, or in the name of another? Has the speaker the right and the power, as well as the moral integrity, to make and to perform the promise? In biblical studies, discussions of apostleship are extensive and often (but not always) helpful.[326]

(4) *Promising* constitutes a *very strong illocutionary act,* in contrast to much wider definitions or understandings of speech acts that at the other end of the spectrum taper into the *weak or trivial.* Wolterstorff seems to suggest that *any* utterance or "locution" can be used to *count as* an illocution *in* its utterance. In a "weak" sense this is true. Nevertheless, in 1973 Geoffrey Warnock proposed a very helpful distinction between *strong* and *weak* speech acts that lie at either end of the spectrum.[327] As we have observed, Bultmann's entire program of demythologizing depends on *counting* most "objective" descriptions in the New Testament *as* volitional, existential challenges. Here the problem derives not simply (as I argued above and elsewhere more extensively) from Bultmann's devaluing of description and his inability to explain how self-involving utterances relate to extralinguistic states of affairs, but also from the fact that far from all of his transpositions constitute "strong" or "serious" speech-acts that are grounded in "institutional" facts. I argued above that the precise nature of

326. One of the more suggestive studies that combines sociological and theological issues is John H. Schütz, *Paul and the Anatomy of Apostolic Authority* (London: Cambridge University Press, 1975), but most constructive in its emphasis on apostleship as pointing away from the self to the Christ-event is Jeffrey A. Crafton, *The Agency of the Apostle: A Dramatic Analysis of Paul's Response to Conflict in 2 Corinthians* (Sheffield: JSOT Press, 1991).

327. Geoffrey J. Warnock, "Some Types of Performative Utterance," in *Essays on J. L. Austin,* ed. Isaiah Berlin et al. (Oxford: Clarendon Press, 1973), 69-89.

"institutional facts" permits *"counts as"* to become *"constitutes,"* especially, I may add, if the status of the speakers or agents is also affirmed in multiple traditions and contexts.

An increasing number of writers are now viewing *all* texts, including all texts of the New Testament, as speech acts. This offers certain advantages. It ensures that agents "mean" what they wish or will purposively to declare, state, express, promise, convey, or whatever as a temporally conditioned eventful action. It directs attention to speech as a communicative act between a "sender" and a "receiver," or between agents and audiences, and it avoids two problems that Wittgenstein identified as generating confusion: the assumption that language always serves to "convey thoughts"; and the mistake of confusing the "physical properties" or *forms* of speech with speech *functions* or constitutive use.[328] Early in my work I took several linguistic forms — for example, "What about the points?" and "This is poison!" — to show these forms could perform utterly diverse functions (the latter, for example, could be a request to fetch a doctor, a warning not to drink from the same bottle, a cry for vengeance, or a rebuke about an over-strong beverage).[329]

All the same, this "weak" understanding of speech acts threatens to degenerate into the subjective (anything can "count as" anything); worse, speech-acts may become so diffused that those important illocutionary acts which (1) *entail serious obligations on the part of the speaker;* (2) *presuppose serious institutional facts* (which in the sense identified by Searle [1995] rest on extralinguistic "brute" facts); and (3) *achieve transformative effects not by causal perlocution but through institutional illocution,* come to *drop from view as paradigmatic or "strong" illocutions.* Thus Savas Tsohatzidis is right to commence his five-hundred-page volume entitled *Foundations of Speech Act Theory* (1994) with the declaration that "Illocutionary acts . . . constitute the primary subject matter of speech act theory."[330] All illocutions are speech acts. Whether or not all speech acts are also illocutions, they are not all illocutions in the "strong" or *serious* sense characteristic of *promise.*

328. Wittgenstein, *Philosophical Investigations* §304; here he states that we must make "a radical break with the idea that language always functions in one way . . . to convey thoughts."; In §108 he observes that linguistic understanding is analogous to "stating the rules of the game not describing their [chess pieces'] physical properties."

329. Thiselton, *Language, Liturgy, and Meaning* (Nottingham: Grove, 1975), 3, 10.

330. Tsohatzidis, "Ways of Doing Things with Words," in *Foundations of Speech Act Theory,* 1.

In our earlier book, *The Responsibility of Hermeneutics,* I conceded by way of analogy that in extreme, emergency circumstances a chisel *could* be used as (could count as) a screwdriver, or a priceless Beckstein *could* be counted as fuel for a fire. Newspapers *could* be used for wrapping up fish or garbage (some deservedly so). Nevertheless, in normal circumstances such "counting as" would be deemed *irresponsible,* even reckless.[331] When a tradition of the kind discussed by Gadamer and Jauss has become established, and Jauss's "public intersubjective world" lies open to view, the promissory speech-acts of, for example, the biblical covenants do not merely *count as* promises; they *constitute* promises. To "count" these "as" anything less is *ethically to violate* their textual action.

Here the importance of agency and action emerges once again. Indeed, let us return to Walhout's territory, namely the relation between ethics and teleology or eschatology. The author of the Epistle to the Hebrews would never accept that Christian faith is action based *subjectively alone* on what believers *count as* promise, for his detailed exposition of the *institutional facts* of the sacrificial system, priesthood, Christology, the blood of Christ, and above all the new covenant explains that all this *constitutes* guaranteed promise which is irrevocable. However, Walhout also explored the transformative effect of entering the "possible worlds" of fiction. In this context another of my doctoral candidates, Richard Briggs, is currently exploring the relation between imagination and "counting as" in speech-act theory. For without doubt, as we observed from reader-response approaches to the parables of Jesus, the first steps of faith may well begin with entry into a "*possible* world" where *counting as* begins to shape new understanding. The "weak" end of the spectrum may play an important role also.

(5) Finally, *promise* provides a paradigm case of *how language can transform the world of reality.* There is no need to recapitulate here ground already covered in *New Horizons in Hermeneutics.* There I endorsed Searle's contrast between (1) a "direction of fit" in which sometimes (e.g., in assertions) language can reflect the world (i.e., the world or reality remains the controlling test of the truth of speech); and (2) a "direction of fit" in which at other times (e.g., in effective promises) language can bring the world of reality into a closer match with what has been written or spoken (i.e., the words remain the controlling test of whether the promise has

---

331. Lundin, Thiselton, and Walhout, *The Responsibility of Hermeneutics,* 107-8.

been performed or fulfilled).[332] François Recanati similarly discusses the "direction of correspondence" between words and world.[333] *Directives,* it goes without saying, also seek to change extralinguistic states of affairs by the utterance of appropriate words in appropriate situations by duly appointed persons, or by speaking agents with appropriate status.

What has been said about the context of *serious* responsibilities and *serious* institutional states of affairs applies here. We are not considering simply or primarily the causal rhetoric of psychological persuasion, which results in perlocutions that are independent of illocutionary acts. In the context of biblical theology, the relation between illocutionary acts of *promise* and illocutionary *directives* sums up the heart of the gospel, including, more strictly, the Pauline contrast between gospel and law. The world order is characterized by failure, evil, suffering, and fallenness, which does not accord with God's will for its future. Hence *transformation* and *change* constitute the purposive goal of God's word: of the word as Christ, the word as scripture, and the word to which the church bears witness through its life and preaching. Two kinds of speech acts may bring the world into conformity with the purposes of God. *Directives* play a role, for faith entails obedience. A regime of *directives* corresponds to the dispensation of *law of change by human endeavor. Promise* provides the covenantal ground on which transformation by the gracious action of God ultimately depends. The covenant of *promise* is a dispensation of *grace: of change by divine agency, giving and given.* Only thus can the seer of the Apocalypse of John utter the declarative pronouncement "I saw a new heaven and a new earth," and add this promissory utterance: "and God himself will be with them; he will wipe every tear from their eyes, and death shall be no more... . It is *done*" (Rev. 21:1-6).

---

332. Thiselton, *New Horizons in Hermeneutics,* 31-35, 294-307; Searle, *Expression and Meaning,* 3-8.

333. François Recanati, *Meaning and Force: The Pragmatics of Performative Utterances* (Cambridge: Cambridge University Press, 1987), 150-63.

Selected Bibliography

Abrams, M. H. *The Mirror and the Lamp: Romantic Theory and the Critical Tradition.* New York: Oxford University Press, 1953.

——. *Natural Supernaturalism: Tradition and Revolution in Romantic Literature.* New York: Norton, 1971.

Allenback, J., A. Benoit, et al., eds. *Biblia Patristica: Index des citations et allusions Bibliques dans la litterature Patristique.* 5 vols. Paris: Éditions du Centre de la Recerche scientifique, 1975-.

Althaus, Paul. *The Theology of Martin Luther.* Trans. Robert C. Schultz. Philadelphia: Fortress, 1966.

Apel, Karl-Otto. *Towards a Transformation of Philosophy.* Trans. Glyn Adey and David Frisby. London: Routledge, 1980.

——. *Understanding and Explanation: A Transcendental-Pragmatic Perspective.* Trans. Georgia Warnke. Cambridge: MIT Press, 1984.

Auden, W. H. *Collected Poems.* Ed. Edward Mendelson. New York: Random House, 1976.

——. *Forewords and Afterwords.* Ed. Edward Mendelson. New York: Random House, 1973; reprint, Vintage, 1989.

Austin, J. L. *How to Do Things with Words.* Cambridge: Harvard University Press, 1962.

Bakhtin, Mikhail M. *The Dialogic Imagination: Four Essays.* Ed. Michael Holquist. Trans. Caryl Emerson and Michael Holquist. Austin: University of Texas Press, 1981.

——. *Problems of Dostoevsky's Poetics.* Trans. R. W. Rotsel. Ann Arbor: Ardis, 1973.

Barth, Karl. *Church Dogmatics.* Ed. G. W. Bromiley and T. F. Torrance. Trans. G. T. Thomson et al. Edinburgh: T. & T. Clark, 1957-75.

241

————. *The Theology of John Calvin.* Trans. Geoffrey W. Bromiley. Grand Rapids: William B. Eerdmans, 1995.

Bauman, Zygmunt. *Intimations of Postmodernity.* London: Routledge, 1992.

Belknap, Robert. *The Structure of the Brothers Karamazov.* Paris and The Hague: Mouton, 1967.

Bernstein, Richard J. *Beyond Objectivism and Relativism: Science, Hermeneutics, and Praxis.* Philadelphia: University of Pennsylvania Press, 1983.

Blake, William. *Jerusalem.* In *The Poetry and Prose of William Blake,* ed. David Erdman. Garden City, N.Y.: Doubleday, 1970.

Bleich, David. *The Double Perspective: Language, Literacy, and Social Relations.* New York: Oxford University Press, 1988.

Bloom, Harold, ed. *Romanticism and Consciousness: Essays in Criticism.* New York: Norton, 1970.

Booth, Wayne. *The Company We Keep: An Ethics of Fiction.* Berkeley and Los Angeles: University of California Press, 1988.

Boucher, M. *The Mysterious Parable: A Literary Study.* Washington, D.C.: Catholic Biblical Association of America, 1977.

Brooks, Cleanth. *William Faulkner: The Yoknapatawpha Country.* New Haven: Yale University Press, 1963.

Brown, Alexandra R. *The Cross and Human Transformation.* Minneapolis: Fortress, 1995.

Bruns, Gerald. *Hermeneutics Ancient and Modern.* New Haven: Yale University Press, 1992.

Bultmann, Rudolf. *Glauben und Verstehen: Gesammelte Aufsatze.* 4 vols. Tübingen: Mohr, 1964-65.

————. "New Testament and Mythology." In *Kerygma and Myth: A Theological Debate,* ed. Hans-Werner Bartsch, trans. Reginald H. Fuller. 2 vols. London: SPCK, 1953-62.

Carlisle, Janice. *The Sense of an Audience: Dickens, Thackeray, and George Eliot at Mid-Century.* Brighton, Eng.: Harvester, 1982.

Carpenter, Mary Wilson. *George Eliot and the Landscape of Time: Narrative Form and Protestant Apocalyptic History.* Chapel Hill: University of North Carolina Press, 1986.

Carr, David. *Time, Narrative, and History.* Bloomington: Indiana University Press, 1986.

Cartledge, Tony W. *Vows in the Hebrew Bible and the Ancient Near East.* Sheffield: JSOT Press, 1992.

Chatman, Seymour. *Story and Discourse: Narrative Structure in Fiction and Film.* Ithaca: Cornell University Press, 1978.

Clines, D. J. A. "Deconstructing the Book of Job." In *The Bible as Rhetoric: Studies in Biblical Persuasion and Credibility,* ed. M. Warner. London: Routledge, 1990.

————. *What Does Eve Do to Help?: And Other Readerly Questions to the Old Testament.* Sheffield: JSOT Press, 1990.

Crafton, A. *The Agency of the Apostle: A Dramatic Analysis of Paul's Response to Conflict in 2 Corinthians.* Sheffield: JSOT Press, 1991.

Crews, Frederick, et al. *The Memory Wars: Freud's Legacy in Dispute.* New York: New York Review of Books, 1995.

Crossan, John D. *The Dark Interval: Towards a Theology of Story.* Niles, Ill.: Argus, 1975.

Culler, Jonathan. *The Pursuit of Signs — Semiotics, Literature, Deconstruction.* London: Routledge; Ithaca: Cornell University Press, 1981.

————. *Structuralist Poetics: Structuralism, Linguistics, and the Study of Literature.* London: Routledge; Ithaca: Cornell University Press, 1975.

Cullmann, O. *The Earliest Christian Confessions.* London: Lutterworth, 1949.

Davies, Norman. *Europe: A History.* Oxford: Oxford University Press, 1996; reprint, New York: HarperCollins, 1998.

DeJean, Joan E. *Ancients against Moderns: Culture Wars and the Making of a Fin de Siècle.* Chicago: University of Chicago Press, 1997.

De Man, Paul. *Blindness and Insight: Essays in the Rhetoric of Contemporary Criticism.* 2nd ed., rev. Minneapolis: University of Minnesota Press, 1983.

Demson, David E. *Hans Frei and Karl Barth: Different Ways of Reading Scripture.* Grand Rapids: William B. Eerdmans, 1997.

Descartes, René. *Discourse on the Method and Meditations on First Philosophy.* Ed. David Weissman, trans. Elizabeth S. Haldane and G. R. T. Ross. New Haven: Yale University Press, 1996.

————. "Rules for the Direction of the Mind." In *The Philosophical Works of Descartes,* trans. Elizabeth S. Haldane and G. R. T. Ross. vol. 1. N.p.: Dover, 1955.

Dodd, C. H. *The Parables of the Kingdom.* London: Nisbet, 1948.

Dostoyevsky, Fyodor. *The Brothers Karamazov.* Trans. Richard Pevear and Larissa Volokhonsky. New York: Vintage, 1991.

Draisma, Sipke, ed. *Intertextuality in Biblical Writings: Essays in Honour of Bas van Iersel.* Kampen: J. H. Kok, 1989.

Dyck, Elmer, ed. *The Act of Bible Reading.* Downers Grove, Ill.: InterVarsity, 1996.

Eco, Umberto. *The Role of the Reader.* London: Hutchinson, 1981.

————. *Semiotics and the Philosophy of Language.* Bloomington: Indiana University Press, 1984.

————. *A Theory of Semiotics.* Bloomington: Indiana University Press, 1976.

Eliot, George. *Adam Bede.* Ed. Stephen Gill. Harmondsworth, Eng.; New York: Penguin, 1980.

Ellis, John M. *The Theory of Literary Criticism: A Logical Analysis.* Berkeley and Los Angeles: University of California Press, 1974.

Emerson, Ralph Waldo. *Emerson: Essays and Lectures.* Ed. Joel Porte. New York: Library of America, 1983.

Fairlamb, Horace L. *Critical Conditions: Postmodernity and the Question of Foundations.* Cambridge: Cambridge University Press, 1994.

Faulkner, William. *Absalom, Absalom!* New York: Vintage, 1990.

Ferrari, S. M. *Die Sprache des Leids in den paulinischen Peristasenkatalogen.* Stuttgart: Katholisches Bibelwerk, 1991.

Fiebig, Paul. *Altjüdische Gleichnisse und die Gleichnisse Jesu.* Tübingen: Mohr, 1904.

Fish, Stanley. *Is There a Text in This Class?: The Authority of Interpretive Communities.* Cambridge: Harvard University Press, 1980.

—————. "Why No One's Afraid of Iser." In *Doing What Comes Naturally: Change, Rhetoric, and the Practice of Theory in Literary and Legal Studies.* Durham, N.C.: Duke University Press, 1989.

Fliegelman, Jay. *Prodigals and Pilgrims: The American Revolution against Patriarchal Authority, 1750-1800.* Cambridge: Cambridge University Press, 1982.

Fowl, Stephen E. *Engaging Scripture: A Model for Theological Interpretation.* Malden, Mass.: Blackwell Pubs., 1998.

Frei, Hans. *The Eclipse of Biblical Narrative: A Study in Eighteenth- and Nineteenth-Century Hermeneutics.* New Haven: Yale University Press, 1974.

Froehlich, Karlfried. "Church History and the Bible." In *Biblical Hermeneutics in Historical Perspective: Studies in Honor of Karlfried Froehlich,* ed. Mark Burrows and Paul Rorem. Grand Rapids: William B. Eerdmans, 1991.

Funk, Robert Walter. *Language, Hermeneutic, and Word of God.* New York: Harper & Row, 1966.

—————. *Parables and Presence: Forms of the New Testament Tradition.* Philadelphia: Fortress, 1982.

Gadamer, Hans-Georg. "Gadamer on Gadamer." In *Gadamer and Hermeneutics,* ed. Hugh J. Silverman. New York: Routledge, 1991.

—————. *Hans-Georg Gadamer on Education, Poetry, and History: Applied Hermeneutics.* Ed. Dieter Misgeld and Graeme Nicholson. Albany: State University of New York Press, 1992.

—————. *Hegel's Dialectic: Five Hermeneutical Studies.* Trans. P. Christopher Smith. New Haven: Yale University Press, 1976.

—————. *Philosophical Hermeneutics.* Trans. and ed. David E. Linge. Berkeley and Los Angeles: University of California Press, 1976.

—————. "Reflections on My Philosophical Journey." In *The Philosophy of Hans-Georg Gadamer,* ed. Lewis E. Hahn. Chicago: Open Court, 1997.

—————. *Truth and Method.* Trans. Joel Weinsheimer and Donald Marshall. 2nd rev. ed. New York: Crossroad, 1989.

Gebauer, Gunter, and Christoph Wulf. *Mimesis: Culture, Art, Society.* Trans. Don Reneau. Berkeley and Los Angeles: University of California Press, 1995.

Gennette, Gerard. *Narrative Discourse: An Essay in Method*. Trans. Jane E. Lewin. Ithaca: Cornell University Press, 1980.

———. *Narrative Discourse Revisited*. Trans. Jane E. Lewin. Ithaca: Cornell University Press, 1988.

Gibson, A. B. *The Religion of Dostoevsky*. London: SCM, 1973.

Gibson, Walker. "Authors, Speakers, Readers, and Mock Readers." *College English* 11 (1950): 265-69.

Giddens, Anthony. *The Consequences of Modernity*. Cambridge: Polity; Oxford: Blackwell, 1990.

Gill, Stephen, ed. *William Wordsworth*. New York: Oxford University Press, 1984.

Gillespie, Michael Allen. *Nihilism before Nietzsche*. Chicago: University of Chicago Press, 1995.

Godsey, J. D. "The Interpretation of Romans in the History of the Christian Faith." *Interpretation* 34 (1980): 3-16.

Grant, P. *Reading the New Testament*. London: Macmillan, 1989.

Grilka, J. "Zur Interpretation der Bibel — Die Wirkungsgeschichte." In *Interpretation of the Bible, 1589-1601*, ed. J. Krasovec. Ljubljana: Slovenian Academy; Sheffield: Sheffield Academic Press, 1998.

Gunther, Klaus. *The Sense of Appropriateness: Application Discourses in Morality and Law*. Trans. John Farrell. Albany: State University of New York Press, 1993.

Habermas, Jürgen. *The Theory of Communicative Action*. Trans. Thomas McCarthy. 2 vols. Cambridge: Polity, 1987-91; Boston: Beacon, 1984-87.

Hacking, Ian. *The Emergence of Probability*. Cambridge: Cambridge University Press, 1975.

Hahn, Lewis E., ed. *The Philosophy of Hans-Georg Gadamer*. Chicago: Open Court, 1997.

Harrisville, Roy A., and Walter Sundberg. *The Bible in Modern Culture: Theology and Historical-Critical Method from Spinoza to Käsemann*. Grand Rapids: William B. Eerdmans, 1995.

Hatch, Nathan. *The Democratization of American Christianity*. New Haven: Yale University Press, 1989.

Hegel, G. W. F. *Introduction to the Lectures on the History of Philosophy*. Trans. T. M. Knox and A. V. Miller. Oxford: Clarendon Press, 1985.

———. *Phenomenology of Spirit*. Trans. A. V. Miller. Oxford: Oxford University Press, 1977.

Heidegger, Martin. *Being and Time*. Trans. Joan Stambaugh. Albany: State University of New York Press, 1996.

Hirsch, E. D. *Validity in Interpretation*. New Haven: Yale University Press, 1967.

Hobsbawm, Eric. *The Age of Extremes: A History of the World, 1914-1991*. New York: Vintage, 1996.

Holland, N. "Transactive Criticism: Re-creation through Identity." *Criticism* 18 (1976): 334-52.

Ingarden, Roman. *The Literary Work of Art: An Investigation of the Borderlines of Ontology, Logic, and Theory of Literature.* Trans. George G. Grabowicz. Evanston: Northwestern University Press, 1973.

Iser, Wolfgang. *The Act of Reading: A Theory of Aesthetic Response.* Baltimore: The Johns Hopkins University Press, 1978.

James, William. *A Pluralistic Universe.* In *William James: Writings, 1902-1910,* ed. Bruce Kuklick. New York: Library of America, 1987.

Jauss, Hans Robert. *Literaturgeschichte als Provokation.* Frankfurt: Suhrkamp, 1970.

———. "Paradigmawechsel in der Literaturwissenschaft." *Linguistische Berichte* 3 (1969): 44-56.

———. *Toward an Aesthetic of Reception.* Trans. Timothy Bahti. Minneapolis: University of Minnesota Press, 1982.

Jeremias, Joachim. *The Parables of Jesus.* Trans. S. H. Hooke. Rev. ed. New York: Scribner, 1972.

Jones, G. V. *The Art and Truth of the Parables: A Study in Their Literary Form and Modern Interpretation.* London: SPCK, 1964.

Jones, Malcolm V. *Dostoyevsky after Bakhtin.* Cambridge: Cambridge University Press, 1990.

Jones, Malcolm V., and Garth M. Terry, eds. *New Essays on Dostoyevsky.* Cambridge: Cambridge University Press, 1983.

Jüngel, Eberhard. *God as the Mystery of the World: On the Foundation of the Theology of the Crucified One in the Dispute between Theism and Atheism.* Trans. Darrell L. Guder. Grand Rapids: William B. Eerdmans, 1983.

Kaiser, Walter C. *Toward an Exegetical Theology: Biblical Exegesis for Preaching and Teaching.* Grand Rapids: Baker, 1981.

Kaiser, Walter C., and Moisés Silva. *An Introduction to Biblical Hermeneutics: The Search for Meaning.* Grand Rapids: Zondervan, 1994.

Kant, Immanuel. "An Answer to the Question: What Is Enlightenment?" In *What Is Enlightenment? Eighteenth-Century Answers and Twentieth-Century Questions,* ed. James Schmidt. Berkeley and Los Angeles: University of California Press, 1996.

Kazin, Alfred. *God and the American Writer.* New York: Knopf, 1997.

Keats, John. "On First Looking into Chapman's Homer." In *The Complete Poetry and Selected Prose of John Keats,* ed. Harold Edgar Briggs. New York: Modern Library, 1951.

Kermode, Frank. *The Sense of an Ending.* London: Oxford University Press, 1967.

Klauck, Hans-Josef. *Allegorie und Allegorese in synoptischen Gleichnistexten.* Münster: Aschendorff, 1978.

Kögler, Hans-Herbert. *The Power of Dialogue: Critical Hermeneutics after Gadamer and Foucault.* Cambridge: MIT Press, 1996.

Kort, Wesley A. *Narrative Elements and Religious Meanings.* Philadelphia: Fortress, 1975.

―――. *Story, Text, and Scripture: Literary Interests in Biblical Narrative.* University Park: Pennsylvania State University Press, 1988.

Lauer, Robert H. *Temporal Man: The Meaning and Uses of Social Time.* New York: Praeger, 1981.

Lentricchia, Frank. *After the New Criticism.* Chicago: University of Chicago Press, 1980.

Levinas, Emmanuel. *Time and the Other.* Trans. Richard A. Cohen. Pittsburgh: Duquesne University Press, 1987.

Liddell, Robert. *The Novels of George Eliot.* New York: St Martin's, 1977.

Litfin, Duane. *St. Paul's Theology of Proclamation: 1 Corinthians 1–4 and Greco-Roman Rhetoric.* Cambridge: Cambridge University Press, 1994.

Lotman, Juril. *The Structure of the Artistic Text.* Trans. Ronald Vroon. Ann Arbor: University of Michigan Press, 1977.

Lundin, Roger. *The Culture of Interpretation: Christian Faith and the Postmodern World.* Grand Rapids: William B. Eerdmans, 1993.

―――, ed. *Disciplining Hermeneutics: Interpretation in Christian Perspective.* Grand Rapids: William B. Eerdmans; Leicester: Apollos, 1997.

Luther, Martin. "Answer to the Hyperchristian, Hyperspiritual, and Hyperlearned Book by Goat Emser in Leipzig — Including Some Thoughts Regarding His Companion, the Fool Murner." In *Martin Luther's Basic Theological Writings*, ed. Timothy F. Lull. Minneapolis: Fortress, 1989.

―――. "The Blessed Sacrament of the Holy and True Body and Blood of Christ, and the Brotherhoods." In *Martin Luther's Basic Theological Writings*, ed. Timothy F. Lull. Minneapolis: Fortress, 1989.

―――. "The Freedom of a Christian." In *Martin Luther: Selections from His Writings*, ed. John Dillenberger. New York: Anchor, 1951.

MacIntyre, Alasdair. *After Virtue: A Study in Moral Theory.* 2nd ed. Notre Dame: University of Notre Dame Press, 1984.

―――. *Three Rival Versions of Moral Enquiry: Encyclopaedia, Genealogy, and Tradition.* Notre Dame: University of Notre Dame Press, 1990.

Mananzan, Mary John. *The Language Game of Confessing One's Belief: A Wittgensteinian-Augustinian Approach to the Linguistic Analysis of Creedal Statements.* Tübingen: M. Niemeyer, 1974.

Marsden, George. *Fundamentalism and American Culture: The Shaping of Twentieth-Century Evangelicalism, 1870-1925.* New York: Oxford University Press, 1980.

Melville, Herman. *Moby-Dick.* Ed. Harrison Hayford and Hershel Parker. New York: Norton, 1967.

Meyerhoff, Hans, ed. *The Philosophy of History in Our Time: An Anthology Selected.* Garden City, N.Y.: Doubleday, 1959.

Meyers, R. B., and K. Hopkins. "A Speech-Act Theory Bibliography." *Centrum* 5 (1977): 73-108.

Mills, Kevin. *Justifying Language: Paul and Contemporary Literary Theory.* New York: St. Martin's, 1995.

Milosz, Czeslaw. *The Collected Poems, 1931-1987.* New York: Ecco, 1988.

Moltmann, Jürgen, et al. *The Future of Hope: Theology as Eschatology.* Ed. Frederick Herzog. New York: Herder & Herder, 1970.

———. *The Spirit of Life: A Universal Affirmation.* Trans. Margaret Kohl. London: SCM, 1992.

———. *Theology of Hope: On the Ground and the Implications of a Christian Eschatology.* New York: Harper & Row, 1967.

———. *The Trinity and the Kingdom: The Doctrine of God.* Trans. Margaret Kohl. San Francisco: Harper & Row, 1981.

Morson, Gary Saul, and Caryl Emerson. *Mikhail Bakhtin: Creation of a Prosaics.* Stanford: Stanford University Press, 1990.

Murav, Harriet. *Holy Foolishness: Dostoevsky's Novels and the Poetics of Cultural Critique.* Stanford: Stanford University Press, 1992.

Murphy, Nancey. *Theology in the Age of Scientific Reasoning.* Ithaca: Cornell University Press, 1990.

Neufeld, Dietmar. *Reconceiving Texts as Speech Acts: An Analysis of 1 John.* Leiden: E. J. Brill, 1994.

Neufeld, Vernon H. *The Earliest Christian Confessions.* Leiden: E. J. Brill, 1963.

Nietzsche, Friedrich. "On the Uses and Disadvantages of History for Life." In *Untimely Meditations,* trans. R. J. Hollingdale. Cambridge: Cambridge University Press, 1983.

———. *The Portable Nietzsche.* Trans. and ed. Walter Kaufmann. New York: Penguin, 1976.

———. *Twilight of the Idols and the Anti-Christ.* Trans. R. J. Hollingdale. London: Penguin, 1990.

Oberman, Heiko. *Luther: Man between God and the Devil.* Trans. Eileen Walliser-Schwarzbart. New Haven: Yale University Press, 1989.

Ong, Walter J. *The Presence of the Word: Some Prolegomena for Cultural and Religious History.* Minneapolis: University of Minnesota Press, 1981.

Ozment, Steven. *The Age of Reform, 1250-1550: An Intellectual and Religious History of Late Medieval and Reformation Europe.* New Haven: Yale University Press, 1980.

Pannenberg, Wolfhart. *Systematic Theology.* Trans. Geoffrey W. Bromiley. 3 vols. Grand Rapids: William B. Eerdmans, 1991-98.

Plank, Karl A. *Paul and the Irony of Affliction.* Atlanta: Scholars Press, 1987.

Plantinga, Alvin. *Warrant and Proper Function.* New York: Oxford University Press, 1993.

———. *Warrant: The Current Debate.* New York: Oxford University Press, 1993.

Plantinga, Alvin, and Nicholas Wolterstorff, eds. *Faith and Rationality: Reason and Belief in God.* Notre Dame: University of Notre Dame Press, 1983.

Porter, S. E. "Reader-Response Criticism and New Testament Study: A Response to A. C. Thiselton's *New Horizons in Hermeneutics.*" *Journal of Literature and Theology* 8 (1994): 94-102.

———. "Why Hasn't Reader-Response Criticism Caught On in New Testament Studies?" *Journal of Literature and Theology* 4 (1990): 278-92.

Recanati, François. *Meaning and Force: The Pragmatics of Performative Utterances.* Cambridge: Cambridge University Press, 1987.

Reed, Walter L. *Dialogues of the Word: The Bible as Literature according to Bakhtin.* New York: Oxford University Press, 1993.

Richter, Jean Paul Friedrich. *Flower, Fruit, and Thorn Pieces; or, The Married Life, Death, and Wedding of the Advocate of the Poor, Firmian Stanislaus Siebenkäs.* Trans. Edward Henry Noel. Boston: James Munroe, 1845.

Ricoeur, Paul. *The Conflict of Interpretations: Essays in Hermeneutics.* Ed. Don Ihde. Evanston: Northwestern University Press, 1974.

———. *Figuring the Sacred: Religion, Narrative, and Imagination.* Ed. Mark I. Wallace, trans. David Pellauer. Minneapolis: Fortress, 1995.

———. *Freud and Philosophy: An Essay on Interpretation.* Trans. Denis Savage. New Haven: Yale University Press, 1970.

———. *Hermeneutics and the Human Sciences: Essays on Language, Action, and Interpretation.* Trans. and ed. John B. Thompson. Cambridge: Cambridge University Press, 1981.

———. *Interpretation Theory: Discourse and the Surplus of Meaning.* Fort Worth: Texas Christian University Press, 1976.

———. *Lectures on Ideology and Utopia.* Ed. George H. Taylor. New York: Columbia University Press, 1986.

———. *Oneself as Another.* Trans. Kathleen Blamey. Chicago: University of Chicago Press, 1992.

———. *The Symbolism of Evil.* Trans. Emerson Buchanan. Boston: Beacon, 1967.

———. *Time and Narrative.* Trans. Kathleen McLaughlin and David Pellauer. 3 vols. Chicago: University of Chicago Press, 1984-88.

———. "Toward a Hermeneutic of the Idea of Revelation." In *Essays on Biblical Interpretation,* ed. Lewis S. Mudge. Philadelphia: Fortress, 1980.

Riffaterre, Michael. *Semiotics of Poetry.* Bloomington: Indiana University Press, 1978.

Rorty, Richard. *Contingency, Irony, and Solidarity.* Cambridge: Cambridge University Press, 1989.

————. *Philosophy and the Mirror of Nature.* Princeton: Princeton University Press, 1979.

Savage, Timothy B. *Power through Weakness: Paul's Understanding of the Christian Ministry in 2 Corinthians.* New York: Cambridge University Press, 1996.

Sayers, Dorothy. *The Mind of the Maker.* San Francisco: Harper & Row, 1987.

Schama, Simon. *Citizens: A Chronicle of the French Revolution.* New York: Knopf, 1989.

Schleiermacher, Friedrich. *The Christian Faith.* Ed. H. R. Mackintosh and J. S. Stewart. Edinburgh: T. & T. Clark, n.d.

————. *Hermeneutics: The Handwritten Manuscripts.* In *Friedrich Schleiermacher: Pioneer of Modern Theology,* ed. Keith Clements. London: Collins, 1987.

Schmidt, James, ed. *What Is Enlightenment? Eighteenth-Century Answers and Twentieth-Century Questions.* Berkeley and Los Angeles: University of California Press, 1996.

Scruton, Roger. *From Descartes to Wittgenstein: A Short History of Modern Philosophy.* New York: Harper & Row, 1981.

Searle, John R. *The Construction of Social Reality.* London: Allen Lane, 1995.

————. *Expression and Meaning: Studies in the Theory of Speech Acts.* Cambridge: Cambridge University Press, 1979.

————. *Intentionality: An Essay in the Philosophy of Mind.* Cambridge: Cambridge University Press, 1983.

————. *Speech Acts: An Essay in the Philosophy of Language.* London: Cambridge University Press, 1969.

Silverman, Hugh J., ed. *Gadamer and Hermeneutics.* New York: Routledge, 1991.

Simpson, Eileen. *Orphans: Real and Imaginary.* New York: New American Library, 1987.

Stein, Robert H. *Playing by the Rules: A Basic Guide to Interpreting the Bible.* Grand Rapids: Baker, 1994.

Steiner, George. *After Babel: Aspects of Language and Translation.* New York: Oxford University Press, 1975.

————. *No Passion Spent: Essays, 1978-1995.* New Haven: Yale University Press, 1996.

————. *Real Presences.* Chicago: University of Chicago Press, 1989.

Stern, Fritz, ed. *The Varieties of History: From Voltaire to the Present.* New York: Vintage, 1972.

Stoeber, Michael. *Evil and the Mystics' God.* Toronto: University of Toronto Press, 1992.

Stout, Jeffrey. *Ethics after Babel: The Languages of Morals and Their Discontents.* Boston: Beacon, 1988.

————. *The Flight from Authority: Religion, Morality, and the Quest for Autonomy.* Notre Dame: University of Notre Dame Press, 1981.

Sullivan, Robert R. *Political Hermeneutics: The Early Thinking of Hans-Georg Gadamer.* University Park: Pennsylvania State University Press, 1989.

Sutherland, Stewart. *Atheism and the Rejection of God: Contemporary Philosophy and "The Brothers Karamazov."* Oxford: Blackwell, 1977.

Taylor, Charles. *Sources of the Self: The Making of the Modern Identity.* Cambridge: Harvard University Press, 1989.

Thielicke, Helmut. *The Doctrine of God and of Christ.* Vol. 2 of *The Evangelical Faith,* trans. and ed. Geoffrey W. Bromiley. Grand Rapids: William B. Eerdmans, 1977.

————. *Modern Faith and Thought.* Trans. Geoffrey W. Bromiley. Grand Rapids: William B. Eerdmans, 1990.

————. *Prolegomena: The Relation of Theology to Modern Thought Forms.* Vol. 1 of *The Evangelical Faith,* trans. and ed. Geoffrey W. Bromiley. Grand Rapids: William B. Eerdmans, 1974.

Thiselton, Anthony C. "Authority and Hermeneutics: Some Proposals for a New Agenda." In *A Pathway into the Holy Scripture,* ed. P. E. Satterthwaite and D. F. Wright. Grand Rapids: William B. Eerdmans, 1994.

————. "Christology in Luke, Speech-Act Theory, and the Problem of Dualism in Christology after Kant." In *Jesus of Nazareth: Lord and Christ: Essays on the Historical Jesus and New Testament Christology,* ed. Joel B. Green and Max Turner. Grand Rapids: William B. Eerdmans; Carlisle: Paternoster, 1994.

————. *Interpreting God and the Postmodern Self: On Meaning, Manipulation, and Promise.* Grand Rapids: William B. Eerdmans, 1995.

————. *Language, Liturgy, and Meaning.* Nottingham: Grove, 1975.

————. *New Horizons in Hermeneutics: The Theory and Practice of Transforming Biblical Reading.* London: HarperCollins; Grand Rapids: Zondervan; Carlisle: Paternoster, 1992.

————. "The Logical Role of the Liar Paradox in Titus 1:12, 13: A Dissent from the Commentaries in the Light of Philosophical and Logical Analysis." *Biblical Interpretation* 2 (1994): 207-23.

————. "New Testament Interpretation in Historical Perspective." In *Hearing the New Testament: Strategies for Interpretation,* ed. Joel B. Green. Grand Rapids: William B. Eerdmans; Carlisle: Paternoster, 1995.

————. "The Parables as Language-Event." *Scottish Journal of Theology* 23 (1970): 437-68.

————. "The Supposed Power of Words in the Biblical Writings." *Journal of Theological Studies* 25 (1974): 283-99.

————. "Thirty Years of Hermeneutics." In *Interpretation of the Bible,* ed. J. Krasovec, 1559-74. Ljubljana: Slovenian Academy; Sheffield: Sheffield Academic Press, 1998.

————. *The Two Horizons: New Testament Hermeneutics and Philosophical De-*

scription: With Special Reference to Heidegger, Bultmann, Gadamer, and Wittgenstein. Grand Rapids: William B. Eerdmans, 1980.

Thomas, Keith. *Religion and the Decline of Magic.* New York: Scribner, 1971.

Thoreau, Henry David. *Thoreau: A Week on the Concord and Merrimack Rivers, Walden, The Maine Woods, Cape Cod.* Ed. Robert F. Sayre. New York: Library of America, 1985.

Tilley, Terrence W. *The Evils of Theodicy.* Washington, D.C.: Georgetown University Press, 1991.

Todorov, Tzvetan. *The Poetics of Prose.* Trans. Richard Howard. Ithaca: Cornell University Press, 1977.

———. *Theories of the Symbol.* Trans. Catherine Porter. Ithaca: Cornell University Press, 1982.

Tolbert, Mary Ann. *Perspectives on the Parables: An Approach to Multiple Interpretations.* Philadelphia: Fortress Press, 1979.

Toulmin, Stephen. "Descartes in His Time." In *Discourse on Method and Meditations on First Philosophy,* ed. David Weissman. New Haven: Yale University Press, 1996.

Tracy, David. *The Analogical Imagination: Christian Theology and the Culture of Pluralism.* London: SCM; New York: Crossroad, 1981.

Vanderveken, Daniel. "A Complete Formulation of a Simple Logic of Elementary Illocutionary Acts." In *Foundations of Speech Act Theory: Philosophical and Linguistic Perspectives,* ed. Savas L. Tsohatzidis. London: Routledge, 1994.

———. *Principles of Language Use.* Vol. 1 of *Meaning and Speech Acts.* Cambridge: Cambridge University Press, 1990.

Vanhoozer, Kevin J. *Is There a Meaning in This Text?* Grand Rapids: Zondervan, 1998.

Via, Dan Otto. *The Parables: Their Literary and Existential Dimension.* Philadelphia: Fortress, 1967.

———. "The Prodigal Son: A Jungian Reading." *Semeia* 9 (1977): 21-43.

Warnock, G. J. "Some Types of Performative Utterance." In *Essays on J. L. Austin,* ed. Isaiah Berlin et al. Oxford: Clarendon Press, 1973.

Watson, Duane F., and Alan J. Hauser. *Rhetorical Criticism of the Bible: A Comprehensive Bibliography with Notes on History and Method.* Leiden: E. J. Brill, 1994.

Watson, Francis. *Text and Truth: Redefining Biblical Theology.* Edinburgh: T. & T. Clark, 1997.

Weber, Max. *The Protestant Ethic and the Spirit of Capitalism.* Trans. Talcott Parsons. New York: Scribner, 1958.

Weinsheimer, Joel. *Gadamer's Hermeneutics: A Reading of "Truth and Method."* New Haven: Yale University Press, 1985.

———. *Philosophical Hermeneutics and Literary Theory.* New Haven: Yale University Press, 1991.

Whitman, Walt. *Whitman: Poetry and Prose.* Ed. Justin Kaplan. New York: Library of America, 1982.

Wimsatt, William K. *Hateful Contraries: Studies in Literature and Criticism.* Lexington: University of Kentucky Press, 1965.

Witherington, Ben. *Conflict and Community in Corinth: A Socio-Rhetorical Commentary on 1 and 2 Corinthians.* Grand Rapids: William B. Eerdmans; Carlisle: Paternoster, 1995.

Wittgenstein, Ludwig. *Philosophical Investigations.* Trans. G. E. M. Anscombe. 2nd ed. Oxford: Blackwell, 1958.

Wittig, S. "A Theory of Multiple Meanings." *Semeia* 9 (1977): 75-103.

Wolterstorff, Nicholas. *Art in Action: Toward a Christian Aesthetic.* Grand Rapids: William B. Eerdmans, 1980.

———. *Divine Discourse: Philosophical Reflections on the Claim That God Speaks.* Cambridge: Cambridge University Press, 1995.

———. *John Locke and the Ethics of Belief.* Cambridge: Cambridge University Press, 1996.

———. *Works and Worlds of Art.* Oxford: Clarendon Press, 1980.

Wood, James. "The All of the If." *The New Republic,* 17 March 1997, 29-36.

Index

255

INDEX